EXPLORING GREEN LANES

and the stories they tell

NORTH & NORTH-WEST DEVON

FIFTY-ONE WALKS

Valerie Belsey

green books

First published in 2008
by Green Books Ltd
Foxhole, Dartington, Totnes, Devon TQ9 6EB
edit@greenbooks.co.uk www.greenbooks.co.uk

Text printed by TJ International, Padstow, Cornwall
on 100% recycled paper

To the best of our knowledge all details in
this book are correct at the time of going to print.
We welcome any feedback from users:
please email valeriebelsey@lycos.co.uk

ISBN 978 1 900322 21 8

Contents

There is no set way in which to explore these lanes, which range over 1,600 square miles. The list below begins in Devon's heartland, works north-westwards and then north-eastwards and back to mid-Devon. But whichever order you choose to explore the lanes, you will always find yourself wondering what lies just beyond the end of the lane you are in. Happy exploring!

Walks in the mid-Devon area leading northwards

Walks in the Tiverton area

Then walking south-east towards Tiverton for walks between the A361 and the B3221.

Moving north-westwards on the B3358 then joining the old A361 on the edge of Exmoor and on the A39 towards the coast.

Walks in the north–east coastal area

Walks in the Barnstaple area

Moving south between the A377 and the A386 for walks in the Great Torrington area.

Walks in the Great Torrington / Bideford area

Moving towards the far north-west and the Hartland area between the A388 and the A39.

Walks in the Hartland area

Moving south-eastwards on the A388 towards Holsworthy, then still further eastwards on the A3072.

Walks in the Holsworthy area

Walks in the Okehampton area

Then moving south-east towards North Tawton, north of the A3072.

Walks in Devon's heartland

WHAT IS A GREEN LANE?

"An unmetalled road bounded on either side which may or my not be a right of way and which once was used for a variety of purposes, but now is mainly used for recreation." – *The Dartington Institute Study on Green Lanes, 1985*

FOREWORD

Since she was seven Clare has walked the deep lanes of Devon – sometimes with a horse or dog for company – but more often alone.

Nearly 30 years later we inherited a stand of commercial woodland just outside the village. Clare had known the woods all her life, and she and our daughter used to canter along the rides, taking care not to let their ponies trip in the myriad holes made by rabbits, badgers and foxes.

Then the trees were about as tall as a man, but today they tower above us. Walking under the canopy reminds me of Thomas Hardy in *The Woodlanders*:

> "I knew the men who planted these trees and kept the rides clear of brambles and his words ring so true. 'They are old association . . . He must know all about these invisible ones of the days gone by, whose feet have traversed the fields which look so grey from his windows; recall whose creaking plough has turned those sods from time to time; whose hands planted the trees that form a crest to the opposite hill; whose horse and hounds have torn through that underwood; what birds affect that particular brake; what bygone domestic dramas of love, jealousy, revenge, or disappointment have been enacted in the cottages, the mansion, the street or on the green." – Thomas Hardy, *The Woodlanders*

And now thirty years later we still love walking the deep lanes.

Depending on how much time we have, we can set off in any direction and make a circular walk, never retracing our steps. The shortest walk takes us over farmland, down to the River Torridge where we often see a heron rise, and more rarely, a salmon leap. In a field we come to a stone cross marking the spot where a fisherman drowned in a pool over 100 years ago, not far from the confluence of the two rivers. Along the Okement there are egrets, otters and kingfishers, as well as hare, deer, badgers and foxes. At the top of the stony path leading up from the river another cross leans out to greet us from the bank – reminding us of the monks who used this lane for many centuries, on their way down to ford the river on their way to their monastery on the other side.

We pass a tiny iron door in the bank, almost hidden by grass and bracken – it opens on rusty hinges to reveal a beautifully crafted stone-lined well, full of water, now unused, but for generations of cottagers their only clean water supply. Beside the well is an ancient, deliciously scented rose, flowering profusely every summer despite a complete lack of attention.

As we walk down the gradual incline towards home I am always reminded of the men and women who have tramped this lane. Ahead of me is a gently sloping hill where bronze axe-heads have been found and beside me in the hedgerow, depending on the season, are the familiar faces of celandines, primroses, daffodils, violets, bluebells, foxgloves, orchids, honeysuckle, briar roses – and in the distance the purple hills of Dartmoor.

Michael and Clare Morpurgo

INTRODUCTION

If you have ever walked out into the commercial centre of a city at the dead of night, and wondered at the silence and about the people who throng there by day, then this is the book for you.

For when you step into the green lanes of mid-, west and north Devon, you enter into a network of ways which once thronged with travellers of all kinds, both by day and by night. Most of these lanes were formed when the majority of the population lived and worked in the countryside. Travellers came from the towns into the villages, not as is the reverse today. These routes have been dedicated to the people who once used them so much, and who told stories along them, and about them.

> "Every lane has its own history; it is not there by accident: and every twist it makes once had some historical meaning, which we can sometimes decipher today, but not often."
> – W. G. Hoskins, *The Devon Historian*

To find out why a given lane follows the particular route that it does, we need to look for clues to solve the mystery that it offers.

Is the lane named after the place where it leads to or is situated – such as 'Mill Lane', 'Mine Lane' or 'Well Lane', for example? Or did its physical appearance lead to its naming – such as 'Stoney Lane', 'Slippery Lane' or 'Mucky Lane'? Or is it about what happened there, such as 'Milkaway Lane', 'Gropy Lane' or the alarming 'Scratchyface Lane'?

How this selection was made

As long as people have used these lanes there have been stories, and the people who told them were the people who worked and walked the lanes and the land. They may have been talking about the hunting parson in the Rectory, the poacher caught by the bailiff, the flighty glove-makers of

Torrington, or the mighty stag which they had seen pass in front of them and which they could have shot if they had wanted to. Until the second half of the twentieth century they were probably just walking between work and home, church and home, the local market and home, with plenty of time for tales to be told.

Everyone walked everywhere, and journey times were not to be measured – just endured and tramped. These stories have been taken from all the centuries that the lanes have known and from the people who have trodden, driven or ridden along them. This was my main criteria in making this selection of walks.

Alongside their dramatic potential – and in reality, preceding it – comes the landscape itself. This selection of lanes covers all the different habitats of the area. North Devon has been formed by three main river systems: the Exe, the Taw and the Torridge, fed by the many smaller rivers which run through sunken valleys. But all of Devon is set in a highland zone, and the trees to be found here range from birch to cedar, mostly in small woodlands with some conifer plantations in the west.

Most of the area covered here comes within the culm grassland measures. You will find purple moor grass, sweet vernal grass, sedges and knapweeds here. For grazing purposes, the lanes were routes into reclamation from moorland into pasture land over the centuries. The abundance of wildlife to be found here owes much to the absence of humankind.

So when you are there, look out for anything from sea birds to barn owls, sedges to scabiouses, brimstone butterflies to emperor dragonflies and, of course, if you are very lucky, otters. Some of these walks run close to the more remote nature reserves of the Devon Wildlife Trust (see Andrew Cooper's book *The Secret Nature of Devon*), and are worth a detour. Devon's mineral wealth has been well excavated over the centuries, and even today you will come across a surprising number of working quarries on these walks, as well as the disused mines and quarries on the maps.

There are some green lanes which are so well known that I have not entered them here, such as Heddon's Mouth, Hatherleigh's green lane with a Crimean War hero's monument along its way, Marsland Mouth, and also around Lynton and Lynmouth. Some areas have kept all their lanes in use, and so they have all been tarmacked.

It has often been said that Exmoor and Dartmoor are the great wildernesses of Devon. How can that be so, when they both have such high visitor numbers on a daily basis? They have been written about extensively over the centuries, and have monthly magazines dedicated to them. When exploring the green lanes for this book throughout the long hot summer of 2006, I never met another walker – just very occasionally a farmer or a local resident. The summer temperatures broke many records, and I have occasionally made references to signs in nature which point towards climate change and to changes in farming practices. There have been many agricultural revolutions; this has led to the present absence of descendants of generations of field-based workers.

This walkers' wilderness has been created by the gradual de-industrialisation and agricultural mechanisation of Devon's countryside; yet it still guards the memories of those who once walked, and walked, and walked, and walked here every day. Look out for them on your way.

The chronological approach for the armchair reader

There are many ways of exploring highway history. The history of individuals and the nature of the topography through which they pass are just two. For the armchair walker in particular, there is the chronological approach. If you wish to follow the course of history through these lanes, then the following is one way to do so.

Starting with early man and leading into the Celtic pre-Christian era, there are the lanes with ancient ridgeway connections at Challacombe, Bampton, Bideford, Abbotsham, and Beaford. There are the sacred groves, the 'nymets' of the Dumnonii around the Taw – at King's Nympton for example. Moving on to the Romans, there are remnants of roads around North Tawton. Many lanes kept the local Roman connections throughout the period of the kingdom of the Dumnonii even though there are no records of this. There are many Saxon lanes, such as those still in use at Hartland, Romansleigh and Highampton. Nearly all the places in this book with Anglo-Saxon place name elements such as '-ton' and '-cot' indicate continuous farming: over 600 years of tramping between settlements and fields.

Early Christian sites are present in most of the villages covered here, most interestingly in Bishop's Tawton, Templeton, Hartland, Bridestowe and Lydford. Saints came over from Wales and Ireland, and monasteries were established – sometimes to tend the sick, for example at Taddiport. Medieval deer parks and mines were reached by highways and hidden forest lanes, in places such as Morebath and North Molton. Wherever there was a forest or a mine, there were roads along which to transport the deer, timber, stone and minerals. Farms, mills and woollen manufacturing were established and developed throughout the twelfth to fourteenth centuries, a period represented in the Umberleigh, Washfield and Great Torrington routes. There was much travelling between monasteries, Chantry chapels and newly founded parishes such as at Morebath and Sampford Courtenay, the latter being very much affected by the Prayer Book Rebellion of 1549. There were many displaced persons wandering about seeking work and seeking alms. Then there was the horror of the Black Death as witnessed at Templeton. As the roads deteriorated during this period we can only assume that the road patterns, now firmly established, were maintained, especially between market towns, as best they could be after the breakup of the Monasteries. There were always higglers, packmen and badgers (dealers in dairy products) carrying goods about the countryside by packhorse as well as carrier carts and the more primitive truckamucks and butts.

Moving into the Elizabethan era – the merchant-venturer period – there are the seafaring connections at Chambercombe, Ilfracombe, Bideford, Abbotsham, Hartland and Bridestowe, to name just a few. In the lead-up to the Civil War some attention was paid to the state of the roads, which we can see at Holsworthy and Great Torrington.

However bad the roads were, they were always good enough for the militia to move around, as we see at North Wyke in the sixteenth century. Communications were vital during the Civil War period, and we visit places near Crediton, Okehampton and the Cornish borders which saw action (and where people no doubt used many lanes as escape routes). Between 1750 and 1850 the population of England rose from 5½ million to 16½ million: more mouths to feed and souls to be saved. In the early 1800s, in the north-west of the county, there was an upsurge of itinerant preachers coming from Cornwall and filling the gaps where absentee and inactive Church of England rectors should have been. The Bible Christians, often led by farm labourers, had record congregations in places such as Northlew, Bratton Clovelly and Ashbury, and all the other villages and crossroads where Bible Christian Chapels stand out on the horizon. The late eighteenth century saw the flourishing of big estates such as at Knightshayes, Bishop's Tawton and Swimbridge. And although the landowners would have liked to have had complete dominion over the land and rivers of their estates, poachers still persisted, as we see at Monkleigh, for example.

Many green lanes which are actually called 'Green Lane' are associated with cattle droving close to the moors or leading to market towns and ports. And always there was farming: whatever happened in the mining industries, the potteries, the clay pits, to the church congregations, the changes in the Poor Law, the creation of turnpike roads – there was always farming. (See Rose Ash and Winkleigh for examples of the yeoman farmer just carrying on.)

After the First World War, when the big estates finally began to fall apart and servants and hired hands were not available, we see struggles for continuity and survival such as at Winkleigh, Crediton and Georgeham.

The age of leisure begins in the inter-war period, when market gardens flourished, such as those found at Bishop's Tawton on the Taw, and at Combe Martin and Ilfracombe on the coast, all with lanes leading to the railway lines built at the turn of the twentieth century. The railways heralded a boom for cattle farmers too, with branch lines in places such as Bampton and Holsworthy.

Then, of course, there is the coming of the age of the motor car and the creation of the new main roads into north Devon such as the Atlantic Highway and the North Devon Link Road. The majority of the lanes in this book remain as lanes because of these larger developments.

Finally, since the 1980s, there are those lanes which have become incorporated into the many new trails created for explorers in north Devon. There are those which are associated with the tales of modern-day literary heroes, such as Ted Hughes at North Tawton, and Henry Williamson, whose writings relate to almost everywhere in this area. There are those which are associated with present-day political agitations, such as the fascists at Buckland Brewer in the 1940s. The list of lane users is endless, and you will be adding to it as you tramp along.

"As long as the length of the green lane are the stories it will tell."

The maps

In 1983 a government scheme called the Green Lanes Project set out to survey, research and restore green lanes in the county of Devon. It was a scheme which wanted to see the results of its survey available to the public in the form of maps, written walks and educational material. At the time of its closure, when I was no longer participating in the project, I heard that over forty Ordnance Survey maps to the scale of 1:2500 covering the whole of the county and covering the walls of the project's headquarters had been put in a waste bin. I recovered the binful, and spent two days prising them apart and labelling them up. Most, but not all, showed where green lanes were to be found. The South Hams have used information from these maps to produce maintenance programmes, guided walks and cycle routes. In the South Hams there is also the 'On the Right Tracks' scheme, and my book *Exploring Green Lanes in the South Hams* – but what about the rest of the county?

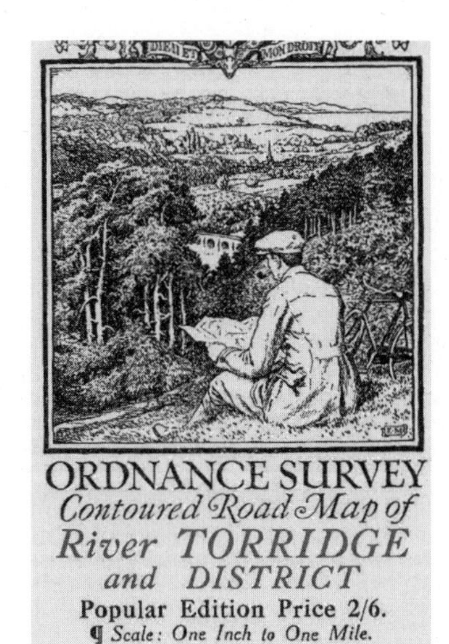

ORDNANCE SURVEY
Contoured Road Map of
River TORRIDGE
and DISTRICT
Popular Edition Price 2/6.
¶ Scale: One Inch to One Mile.

Not until the making of the Definitive Map, and the publication of the new OS Explorer series of maps in 2005 did I begin to find out what had been happening over the years.

When writing this book and using the old maps I had rescued, I did not look at the new ones until the final stages. It then became obvious that the green lanes project information had been used to expand the Rights of Way system throughout the county. This collection includes many of those lanes which once appeared as white roads on the old maps, and which now appear overlaid with a line of broken green dots or green crosses, sometimes complete with local names. I have tried to incorporate and refer to as many as these as possible. I have also tried to include in the walks some of the new areas of moor and woodland that can be explored as a result of the new Right to Roam Act. Many walks link to established trails such as the Tarka Trail or the Two Moors Way.

The base maps here use the 1890 one inch to a mile OS series of maps, and also the Popular and the New Popular editions. Many features such as smithies, corn mills, railway lines, rifle ranges, orchards, woodlands, chapels etc., have gone, but most of the basic road patterns remain unchanged, and this includes above all green lanes. By using these older maps you will feel more in touch with the landscape through which you pass, and be given one more piece of the highway history jigsaw to fit in.

This is not a gazetteer of all the green lanes in the area, or an in-depth consideration of their status and uses. Many of the circuits include long sections of made-up roads with surfaces upon which walkers have as much of a right to tread as tyres. These minor roads thread through the countryside and settlements which parcel up the Devon landscape into many different habitats.

I have indicated when there is more than one green lane which seems to cover the same route, and have marked these with crosses, along with footpaths or minor roads, to add variety to the route.

Although arriving was not always thought better than travelling (as Robert Louis Stephenson once suggested), in the uncomfortable past, 'tramping' was always to be kept to a minimum. I mention this as an apology to those original lane users, who would not have seen the point of walking around in circles! However, these walks are for the most part circular, or linked to a bus or railway route for you to catch on the return stretch (for example Route 4, King's Nympton). Some walks are town-based and very short (e.g. Route 31, Bideford); others are rambling, and focused in the countryside and its history through which they pass (see Route 34, Parkham; Route 51, Tedburn St Mary; and Route 47, North Tawton).

The area

Devon is a large county to explore, and so this book has restricted itself to the green lanes to be found in mid-Devon from Crediton and Tiverton northwards to the Exmoor border, over to the north to Hartland, down to Welcombe, keeping west, and north-east again up to Lydford.

It is a landscape of medieval market towns situated near the main rivers of the area. From these, minor roads thread out across the valleys, ridgeways and moors to villages, small settlements or single farms. Sometimes the green lanes you find here may not lead to any of these, but just to the sea, the river's edge, round a moor, through a wood, along a copse edge, or to the site of an old chapel or church or a disused mine.

Inland Devon has not been greatly sought out by holidaymakers or developers as yet, and retains a remoteness and wildness born from the early difficulties of communications. Even with the coming of the railways and improved roads the sheer length, steepness, narrowness, twistiness, depth and dampness of the lanes still deter many visitors.

As this volume deals with north and north-west Devon, it does not include Tavistock. It also does not include the well-documented and discussed ways on Dartmoor and Exmoor; only on the periphery of these moors will you find true green lanes.

As you work your way through these walks you will see the value of them as wildlife corridors linking the many habitats through which you will pass. Green lanes can do this; roads can not.

How to walk your way through this selection

Preferably using the public transport links from Exeter and Plymouth, you can work your way round circuits as and when they arise along the route you are travelling. They are arranged here starting in mid-Devon, travelling to the north-east, then to the north-west and down back to mid-Devon again. All circuits appear on the following OS Explorer and Outdoor Leisure (OL) Series of Maps:

111 *Bude, Boscastle and Tintagel* (Route 39, corner only)
112 *Launceston and Holsworthy*
113 *Okehampton, Hatherleigh, North Tawton and Lapford*
114 *Exeter and the Exe Valley*
139 *Bideford, Ilfracombe and Barnstaple*
126 *Clovelly and Hartland*
127 *South Molton and Chulmleigh*
OL 9 *Exmoor*
OL 28 *Dartmoor*

If you are an armchair walker (and don't actually want to do any walking at all, but would like to read about the history, the people, their stories and the varied landscapes in this part of Devon), then read away in any order you wish!

Questions

These are placed at the end of each walk, and relate to something you see or read about whilst walking. Some are very straightforward, and others require a little detective work. Answers can be found on page 247.

Links to public transport

In the government budget for spring 2006 there was a clause which encouraged those over 60 to rush out and stand by a bus stop for their free rides throughout the county – and indeed now throughout the country (although the buses are not free before 9.30 a.m. on weekdays). The yellow bus pass has opened up the huge county of Devon for those with the time to explore it. It is also the best way to do so in pursuit of green lanes. You do not have to worry about trying to park against some hedgerow in a narrow lane and hoping that tractors can squeeze by and lorries won't smash off your wing mirrors. You do not have to come back to the place from where you started, but are free to catch the bus further along its route or on its return. In some places, buses also link up with local trains.

This book has been researched and walked by travelling out from Totnes in south Devon using public transport on a daily basis. So, if you already live in mid-, north or north-west Devon it is going to be easy for you to explore all of these circuits by studying the regional timetables. Some of these walking circuits set out from towns such as Great Torrington or Holsworthy but most just drop you off in the middle of nowhere. As the bus trundles away and the silence of the countryside surrounds you, your exploration begins.

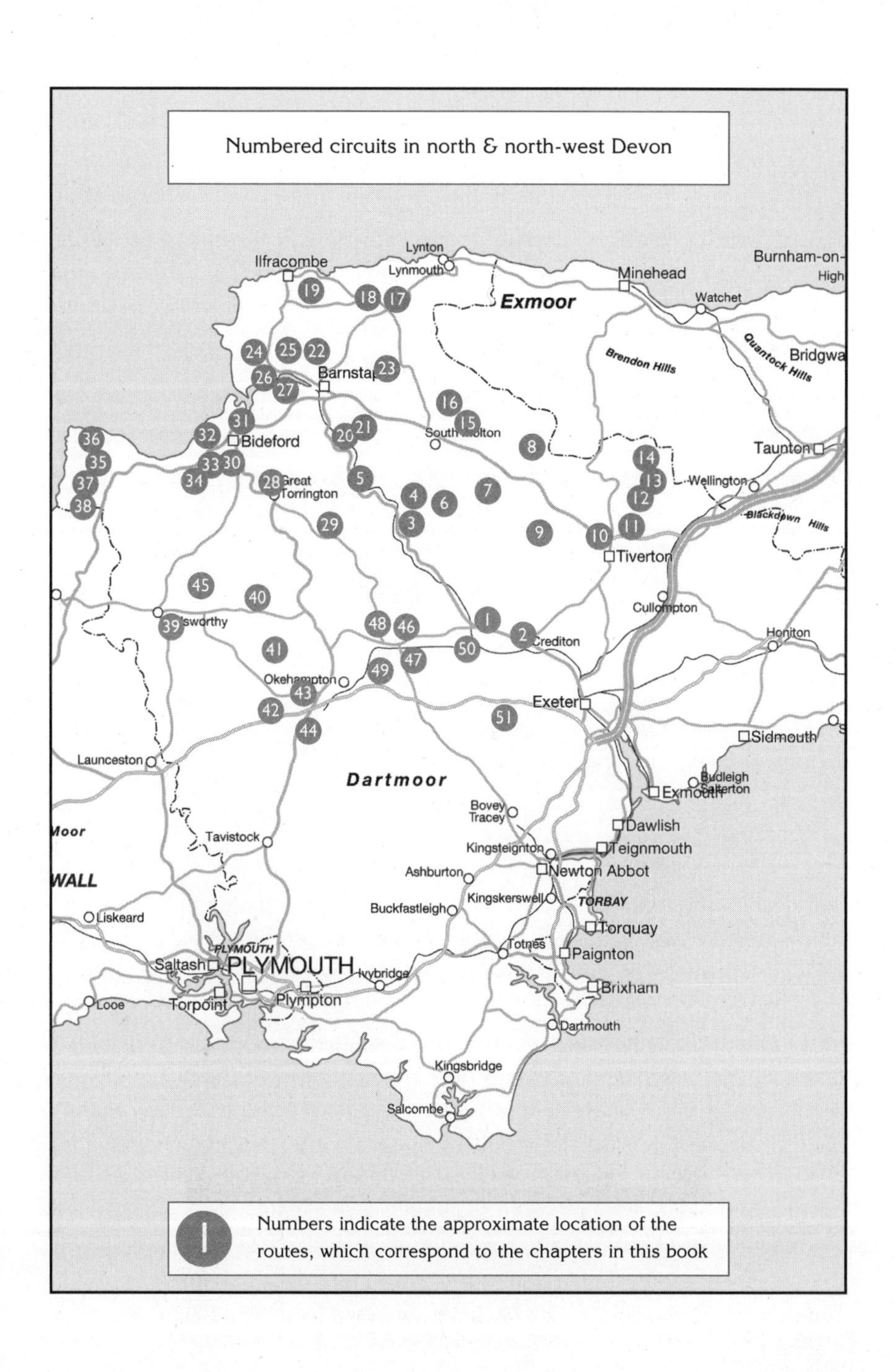

Numbered circuits in north & north-west Devon
Lynton
Lynmouth
Ilfracombe
Minehead
Burnham-on-
Watchet
Exmoor
Brendon Hills
Quantock Hills
Bridgwa
Barnstaple
South Molton
Taunton
Wellington
Blackdown Hills
Bideford
Great Torrington
Tiverton
Cullompton
Holsworthy
Crediton
Honiton
Okehampton
Exeter
Sidmouth
Launceston
Dartmoor
Budleigh Salterton
Exmouth
Bovey Tracey
Dawlish
Tavistock
Kingsteignton
Teignmouth
Newton Abbot
Ashburton
Kingskerswell
TORBAY
Buckfastleigh
Torquay
Liskeard
Totnes
Paignton
PLYMOUTH
Saltash
Ivybridge
Brixham
Looe
Torpoint
Plympton
Dartmouth
Kingsbridge
Salcombe
Moor
WALL
Numbers indicate the approximate location of the routes, which correspond to the chapters in this book

Route 1

COPPLESTONE

From farm labourer to foreign secretary: the Ernest Bevin Way

OS Explorer Map 113

This walk is dedicated to Ernest Bevin, who strove all his life to bring back all the respect due to those who worked the land. As Robin Stanes says in his *History of Devon*: "Devon has a landscape made by peasants." This long walk through Anglo-Saxon settled lands begins to reveal this truth, which becomes more and more apparent as you walk your way through history, and through this book.

Conditions: Some standing water.

Distance: 5-6 miles.

Starting point: Copplestone Railway Station, SS767032.

At the station entrance turn left towards Copplestone and admire the new housing estate, which has been put up to reflect the style of the other farm buildings in the area and has been named Bassetts, the original address recorded in the Census for Ernest Bevin.

(1) Take a complete turn to the right along the road until you come to a labourer's cottage called originally 'Lee Mount', and note the plaque before returning towards Copplestone. On your right you pass a tollhouse next to an 'Ebenezer' Bible Christian Chapel 1888, once attended by Ernest Bevin. Like many social reformers of this period, he owes a lot of his skill in speech-making to the style of nonconformist preachers he would have heard here.

(2) Opposite the Post Office turn left up Bewsley Hill, stopping to read the information board put up by the Parish Paths Partnership, which tells you that the fields around date back in shape to the thirteenth century. Once

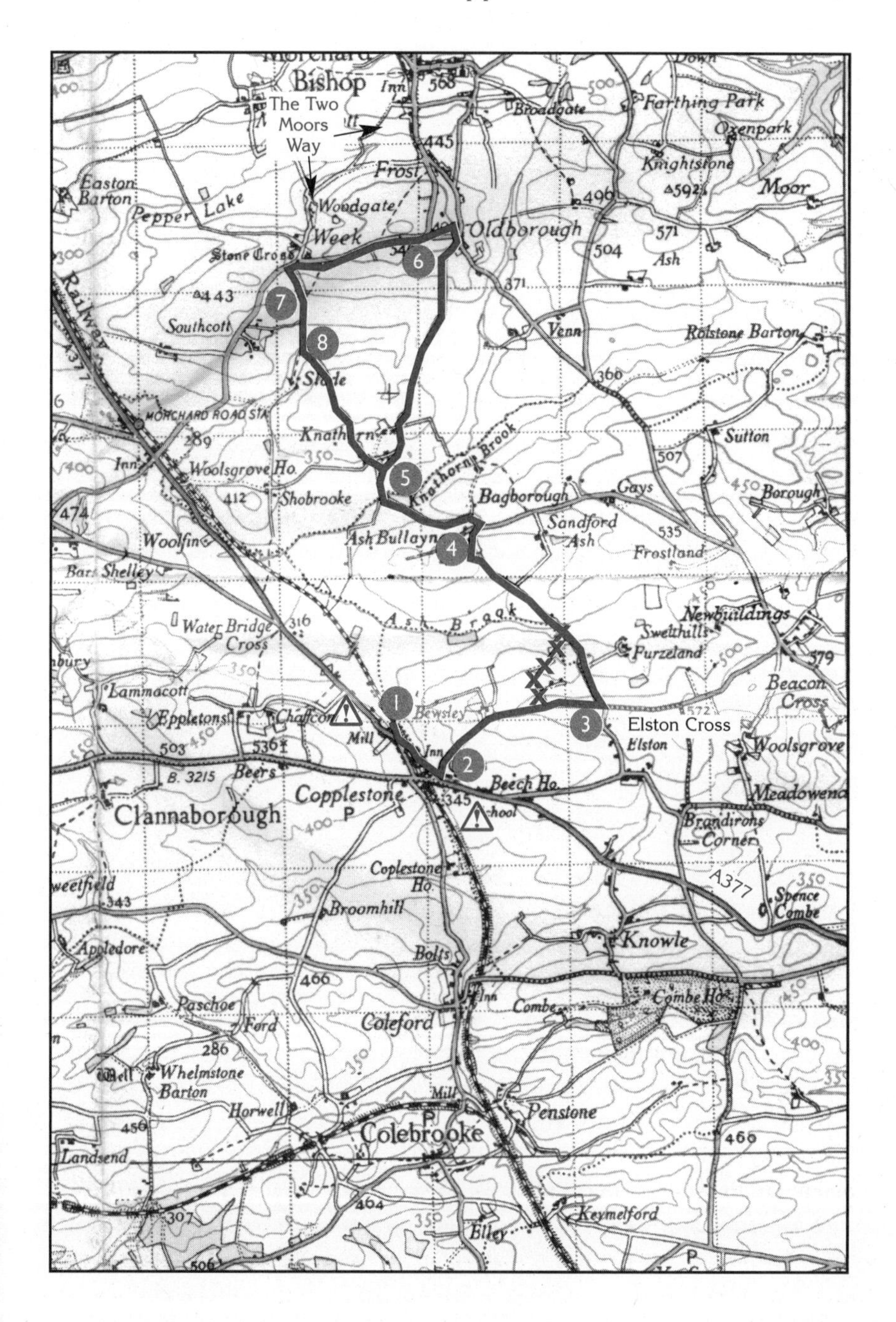
Bishop
The Two
Moors
Way
Farthing Park
Ozenpark
Knightstone
Moor
Easton
Barton
Pepper Lake
Woodgate
Week
Oldborough
Stone Cross
Ash
Southcott
Venn
Rolstone Barton
Slade
MORCHARD ROAD STA
Knathorn
Sutton
Knathorne Brook
Woolsgrove Ho.
Shobrooke
Bagborough
Gays
Borough
Sandford
Ash
Ash Bullayne
Frostland
Woolfin
Shelley
Newbuildings
Water Bridge
Cross
Swelthills
Furzeland
Lammacott
Beacon
Cross
Eppletons
Bewsley
Mill
Elston Cross
Elston
Woolsgrove
Inn
B. 3215
Beers
Beech Ho.
Copplestone
Clannaborough
Meadowend
Brandirons
Corner
Coplestone
Ho.
A377
Spence
Combe
Broomhill
Appledore
Knowle
Bolts
Combe Ho.
Paschoe
Combe
Ford
Coleford
Whelmstone
Barton
Horwell
Penstone
Colebrooke
Landsend
Keymelford
Elley

at the top you get great views of Dartmoor and the Blackmoor Hills.

(3) At Elston Cross turn left to enter one of the longest green lanes I have encountered in Devon. This is fertile country, heavily farmed throughout by smallholders, whose picturesque cottages such as 'Brendon' appear throughout this walk – picturesque now, cold and damp then. The hedgerows have a great amount of holly and hazel in them, and you are often walking on grass.

The initial section forms a parish boundary and it is worth counting the number of hardwood species in one thirty-yard stretch on one side only to ascertain the date of the lane. There are great pollarded oaks and some beeches along its length.

(4) At Ash Bullayne turn left into a very minor road down to Knathorne Brook and up to a green lanes crossroads.

(5) Here take the high road marked 'Bridleway 47' to your right. This is another very long stretch of lane, leading up to Oldborough. This name implies an early Iron Age settlement, and so predates the importance of the Copple Stone itself below, and the much later turnpike road, and the railway in 1855. Between these dates we have this well-marked lane being used for transporting timber, arable produce, wheat, barley and corn, for driving cattle along, and for transporting the sandstone from the nearby quarry. It has an open, drover's feel to it mainly – look out for the crab-apple trees which appear in the hedgerows.

Towards the end it drops down into a dark way, then goes up to its once defended hilltop.

(6) Turn left here and rest a while at Jane Way's Grave. (Way was a very common name here – one James Way was a Bible Christian.)

You are walking a ridgeway now, until you drop down again into a sunken lane at **(7)** on the left opposite the cows of Weeke farm.

When you reach Slade **(8)** take the footpath to your left, which becomes a green lane, and keep to your left over fields, which takes you back to **(5)**. This is a walk through once densely populated and heavily laboured arable and pasture country. It is tranquil now, but for the distant rumblings of roads radiating from the Copple Stone, the occasional rattle of the railway in the Yeo valley and the drones of passing planes. If you listen carefully, you might hear the sighs of a farm boy trudging along beside you, or the scampering feet of one of the North Devon Savages from Nymet Rowland, come to relieve an idle traveller of a few pence. But that is the beginning of another story, another lane.

By the way

The plaque on the cottage called 'The Mount' (formerly 'Tiddly Winks'), opposite an old mill marked 'Davey's Mills 1906', reads as follows:

Ernest Bevin 1881-1951
Farm Labourer, Founder – Transport and General Workers Union 1922
M.P. 1940
Minister of Labour 1940
Foreign Secretary 1945
Lived here 1889-1894

Here are the beginnings of a very interesting story. Ernie, originally from Winsford in Somerset, attended Hayward Boy's School in Crediton until he was eleven, and left being able to read and write. Taking his labour certificate with him, he went to work on a nearby farm at Chaffcombe, working a ten-hour day, six days a week, for sixpence a week.

He moved to Bristol and worked as a carter for over fifteen years. It was appropriate that from this he went on to become the founder of the Transport and General Workers Union. He went on to become the Foreign Secretary who led the world into peace after the second world war.

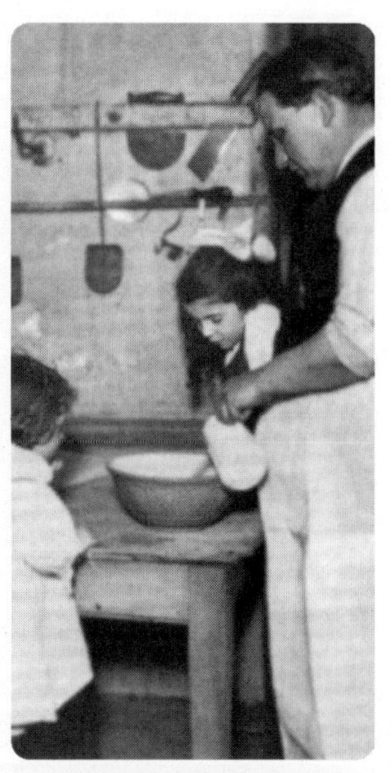

Man of the people: Bevin prepares a meal to show how little could be had from a weekly wage of £3 12s 6d for a docker's family.

The Copple Stone of the village, mentioned in a charter of 974, is unfortunately placed in a position where you can't study it, but it represents the beginnings of land divisions for the Church, Lords and peasants alike. It marks the meeting of three parishes, and is in memory of the Bishop of Exeter (Bishop Putta) who was murdered in the tenth century by those still believing in Celtic values. Copplestone has been blighted by being an important meeting place for traffic travelling both north to south and east to west. The Copple Stone still stands at a site associated with murderous activities.

Other green lanes in the area

From Knowle Cross (where some common land is still held) to Coleford.
At Lapford from Court Barton to Bury Barton. (Built on the north-west corner of a Norman fort, a consecrated chapel was built here in 1434.)

Links

With the Two Moors Way at **(7)**.
Reachable on the Tarka Line Railway, which runs between Exeter and Barnstaple, and on two or three bus routes from Exeter to Barnstaple and other local runs out from Crediton.
Route 50 for further connections with Bishop Putta of Exeter.

Question

What colour is the sandstone here?

The village bird-scarer.

Route 2

CREDITON

Within a stone's throw from two worlds

OS Explorer Map 114

Not only does this walk join two very important roads which belong to both the north and south of the county (the A377 and the A30), but it also takes you straight into the area to be explored.

Conditions: Steep in places and slippery.

Distance: 3 to 4 miles, 6 to 8 miles for the Posbury circuit, and 4 to 6 if you begin in Tedburn.

Starting point: Down from Station Cross, passing Fordton Terrace, take the bridleway to your right at SX838994.

(1) This bridleway runs between the River Yeo and the railway track, and must have been used by the early Christians making their way to St Boniface's Anglo-Saxon Cathedral in the town. Turn left over Yeoton Bridge and into Uton. In the twelfth century there was a chantry chapel for the Bishop of Crediton here. If you go straight on, then down a rough track to the right you will find the site of the Lady Well whose waters had curative powers for the eyes.

(2) Return from following the lane straight ahead here, retracing your steps to Culvery Cross. From here climb up the minor road to your right to Uton Steep, passing the old stump of a cross at Court Barton in Venny Tedburn. After the footpath and bridleway sign on the right there is an unmade road to your left.

(3) This is one of the many unclassified roads (status to be decided) that you will come across on these walks. This is a steep lane, a ridgeway: these follow dry areas above valley bottoms. See Grundy's Ridgeway map on page 180.

This lane merits an attempt at hedge-dating by counting the number of hardwood species on one side for a 30-yard length. My count came to eight, taking the date of the lane back to the twelfth century.

(4) There is a well-cobbled camber at the top. Turn off to the right here. Just before the crossroads, veer right to see the beautiful Chapel at Oldridge. Although it only dates from 1835, its blue and yellow glass windows with a floral motif and the gas lamps inside give it a much more ancient feel.

(5) At the next crossroads (Tomhead Cross) turn right into an unmade lane which will take you at its end through into woodlands.

(6) Turn right into a minor road by Blackalder Wood and continue down passing the entry point to the unclassified lane at **(3)**. To your left at

(7) Chestnut Cottage, you enter a bridleway lined with marker oaks each at least 150 years old. Passing along the edge of Meetford Wood you sense the power and overwhelming presence of the woodlands which once completely covered this area.

(8) At this T-junction you stand within view of Posbury Fort. Here you can turn left and get closer to the tree-girt slope where Saxons and the green-man-worshipping Devon Celts once fought; or turn right and make your way back to the sanctuary of **(9)** the Proprietary Chapel of St Luke at Posbury along the minor road. In the 1830s, one of the first training colleges for teachers of deaf and dumb children was set up here. The school became a model for St Luke's teacher training college in Exeter. It is a beautiful place, and there has been a sanctuary here for many years; retreats are still held at Posbury St Francis. There is yet another precious site here at

(10) Posbury Clump, perfectly placed on the curve of the road overlooking the Blackdown Hills amidst acres of rolling grain fields. It is a Site of Special Scientific Interest.

(11) Here you find yourself back in Uton, and can return into Crediton. There are many green lanes this side of the town, one of which is known as Cromwell's Cut, which is where the Parliamentarians rallied after the Civil War. But unlike Lord's Meadow, which is where the Royalists rallied during the Civil War, it does not appear on any signposts.

By the way

Crediton is significant for its links with the early church in Devon, as you will see on the town signs which greet you: St Boniface 909-1050. This makes

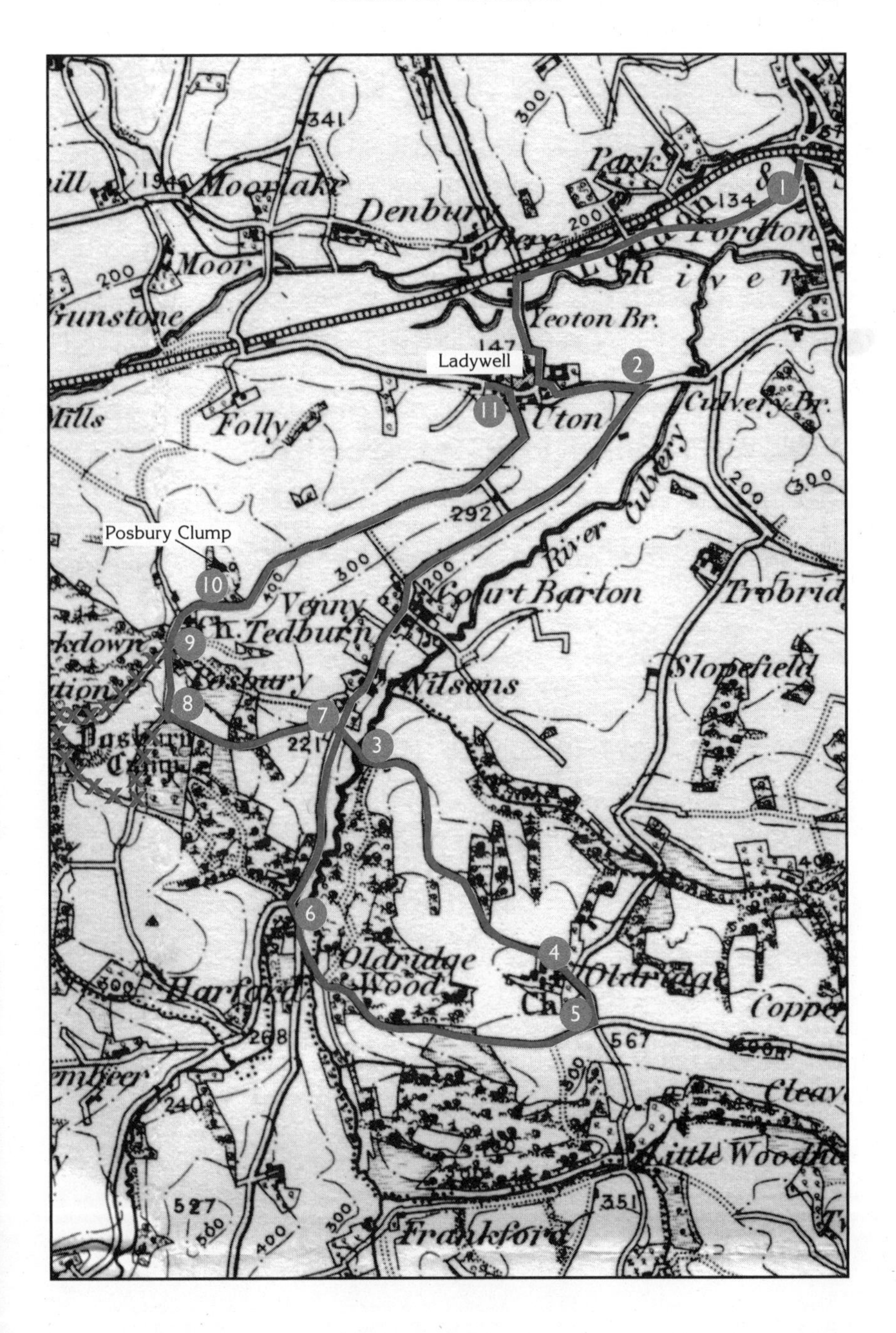
Ladywell
Posbury Clump
1
2
3
4
5
6
7
8
9
10
11
Moorlake
Denbury
Moor
Park
Yeoton Br.
Folly
Uton
Culvery Br.
River Culvery
Venny
Ch. Tedburn
Court Barton
Trobrid
Slopefield
Nilsons
Posbury
Oldridge Wood
Oldridge
Hartford
Little Woodh
Frankford
341
194
200
134
147
300
292
400
221
268
567
240
527
500
351

mid-Devon important as a stronghold against the Viking threat from the north. But at the same time it also welcomed the Celtic saints coming down from Wales and Ireland.

Other green lanes in the area

This is another example of a collection of green lanes running parallel to each other. They are making their ways to Tedburn St Mary or to Crediton, mostly keeping to the hilltops; but there is one which runs along the Lilly Brook and overlooks the River Ted.

Links

Route 51, Tedburn St Mary
Buses run through Crediton from Exeter to Barnstaple.
The Tarka Railway Line from Exeter to Barnstaple.

Question

Why didn't St Boniface like oak trees?

Route 3

CHULMLEIGH

Travellers' tales from the Little Dart

OS Explorer Map 127

The green lanes that you explore on this walk take you out along high, ancient ridgeways and down into secret valley depths. You will find many clues which point to the fact that Chulmleigh was once a communications crossroads for packhorses, carriers, coaches and drovers, but is now a quiet Devon town; fewer wheels roll its way, but it is still the hub of a thriving farming community. My thanks to Taw Valley Ventures Walking Group, who helped me explore this circuit.

Conditions: Very steep and rocky in places.

Distance: 4-5 miles

Starting point: SS687143. The town square or the church are both good places to start on this exploration, where you can see all the old coaching entrances, kicking stones and mounting blocks, along with local names in the churchyard, many of whom were once involved with the transport industry.

(1) Take the road to the right out of the lychgate and at Glebe Cottage turn left into what is signposted as an ancient trackway leading down to the Little Dart. This is Rocky Hill, which falls steeply and runs along a ridge as it descends. Any lane which dives down to and climbs up from a river is likely to be part of the ancient ridgeway system, along which humans first travelled as they gave greater safety, ease and visibility. But although high ground was easier to traverse than valley bottoms, obviously the latter were much more fertile areas, flatter to plough – and important for industry too, as we shall see.

This lane sinks to more than five feet below the field edges and has some fine vertical stonewalling on either side. The bench (more useful when ascending) was made by Middle Foundry, Sandacre. There are holly, oak, beech and alder in the hedge. There is a distinct path to the right through woodlands, which may have led to a quarry or been the site of a charcoal-burning platform. As we are bordering upon what was once Henry III's deer park in the thirteenth century at King's Nympton, it is not surprising to find that there are patches of laurel in the hedge here that would have been planted by gamekeepers for cover.

(2) Here we are at the Ford, which is now a bridge across the Little Dart. In the middle we pass from Chulmleigh to Chawleigh and from mid- to north Devon. There are kingfishers here, hoping to spear some fish or a frog before the otters take them. To the right at the far side of the bridge a passage – the width of a waggon or cart – has been cut so that those descending with hot wheel rims could plunge them into the water. This was also a useful technique to swell the dry felloes of a wheel in the summer. The lane now follows a fairly steep climb and a twisty one, built to break the speed of descending traffic.

(3) You come out of the green lane with Chawleigh Week Farm to your left. Keep left until you come to Chawleigh Week Cross. Take a while to admire the Mitchell Post, just one of a few now remaining which were hand-crafted from sturdy oak centre-posts and given the distinctive wavy board addition to the place name fingers. They were named after a carpenter from Landkey. Pause at the gate here to look out over towards Wembury, its hill-forts, and Dartmoor beyond.

(4) Take the road to your left towards Chulmleigh and Chawleigh. You are on a hilltop ridgeway in Darky Lane. Keep to the left at Ridgemont Cross and carry straight on to **(5)** Moortown Cross where you turn right towards Chawleigh. Here you pass Turnpike Cottage on the left. (See *By the way*, p.34). Take care at the junction with the Eggesford Station road at **(6)** Hollow Tree Cross. Which hollow tree is referred to it is impossible to say, but it is known that well into the nineteenth century families of labourers, whether in industry or farming, used to live in trees of great girth (see the Cookbury Route, p.213). You are now on your way to Chawleigh: notice the line of pines to your left, distinctive 18th-century additions to a landscape to make the course of a road more visible from afar. Large trees such as beeches were planted specifically for this purpose.

(7) Return to Hollow Tree Cross and take the footpath to your right back down into the valley again. This green lane begins as an open path, then drops down through ancient deciduous woodland, forming a wide lane as it

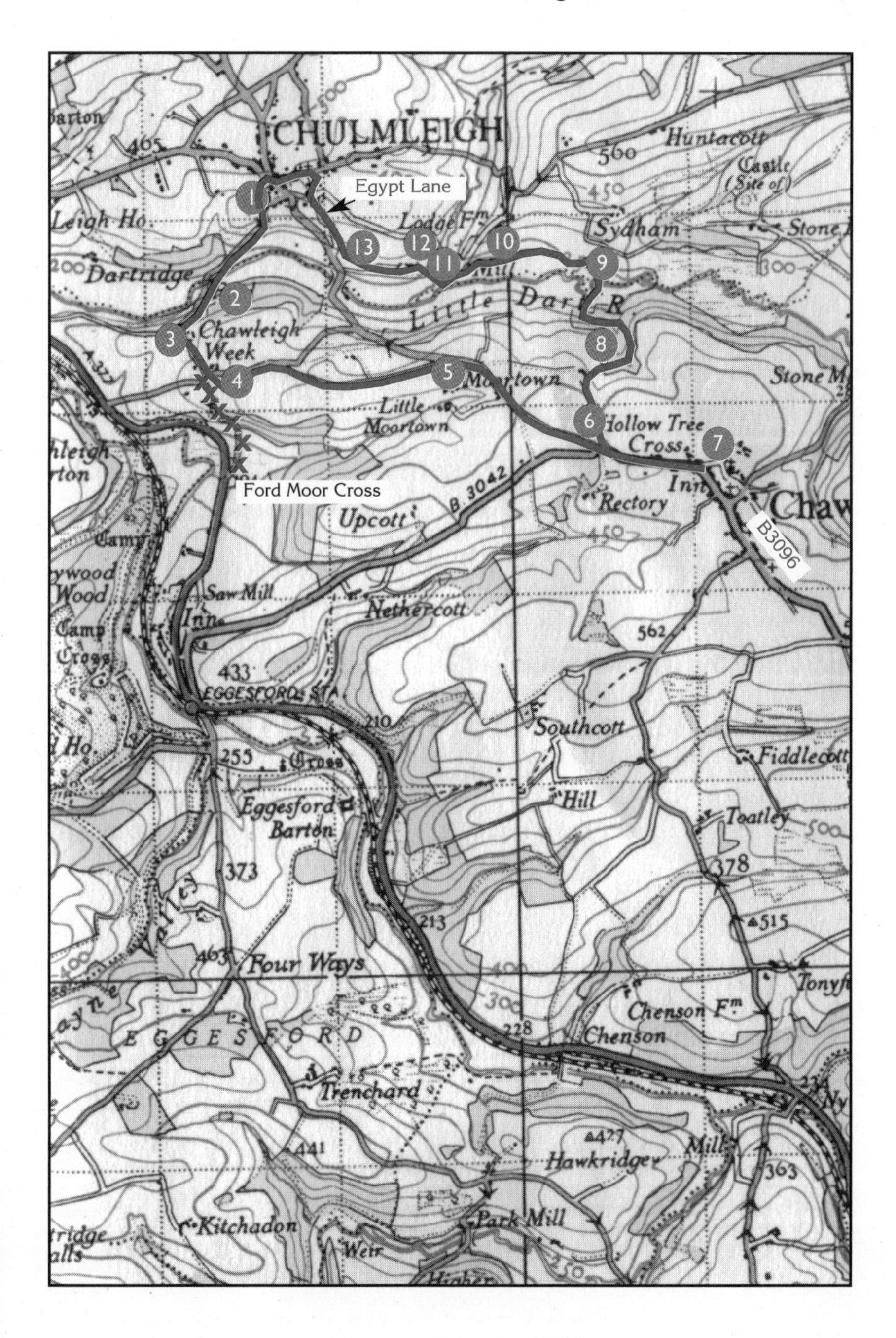
CHULMLEIGH
Egypt Lane
Huntacott
Castle (Site of)
Sydham
Lodge Fm
Dartridge
Leigh Ho.
Chawleigh Week
Little Dart R
Moortown
Little Moortown
Hollow Tree Cross
Inn
Chaw
B3096
Ford Moor Cross
B. 3042
Upcott
Rectory
Stone M
Camp
Wood
Saw Mill
Inn
Nethercott
Camp Cross
EGGESFORD STA.
Southcott
Cross
Eggesford Barton
Hill
Fiddlecott
Toatley
Four Ways
EGGESFORD
Chenson Fm
Chenson
Tonyf
Trenchard
Hawkridge
Mill
Kitchadon
Park Mill
Weir
Higher

goes. Follow the footpath arrows at **(8)** sharply to the right through a dark pine tunnel where a fine footbridge fords the Little Dart again. The river flows shallower here, and is home to dippers and wagtails.

(9) Turn left now and enter a broad river meadow with plenty of evidence of fox and badger activity. As we approach Park Mill, remember that the water used in the fulling process here would have added to the fertility of waterside meadows such as these. You pass from one meadow to the next and make for the right-hand corner.

(10) Cross over Park Mill leat by a series of ingenious footbridges and once in the meadow turn left towards the corner of the field where you exit into **(11)** Park Mill Lane. Keep to the left and cross over a stream, then take the footpath to the left which brings you out into a road. Keep right and take the minor road which is at the foot of **(13)** Egyptian Hill. Turn right up this steep path, once the haunt of gypsies perhaps. Within living memory this is where a tall nettle grew through a fallen roof to win first prize in Chulmleigh's tallest nettle competition!

By the way

Chulmleigh has always been at the centre of many routes for trade, migration and the myriad reasons generations have had for moving through the county, or just from settlement to settlement. Trains of packhorses carried goods into the town, including wool from Spain which had been landed at Barnstaple and was distributed to the spinsters and weavers here in the fifteenth and sixteenth centuries.

Later on, Chulmleigh had its own mill at Park, and the packhorses and carriers with waggons brought goods in and out. There were the Richards, Atts, Rowes, Westerns, Tuckers, Hannafords, Jurys and Joints all involved in this trade. Sarah Joint was one of quite a few females in the profession. She ran coal up to the depot from Eggesford Station to the East Street Depot.

Then there are the Turners, still in operation in the coach and bus business. From the 1780s onwards, no less than five turnpike trusts from towns in the north and south had interests here. Down in the valley, the coming of the railway in the 1840s must have been both a blow and a blessing for Chulmleigh.

The town weathered this change in communication patterns, and today the legacy of its importance remains, as services and goods still come and go. As its residents say, this is the place where you can live a sustainable, happy life in a working landscape.

Other green lanes in the area

Many are to be found over the valley up towards Burrington.

Links

Eggesford Station on the Tarka Railway Line. You have to walk up from the station to Chulmleigh. Turner's coaches and buses are based in and run between Barnstaple and Exeter. With King's Nympton and the Ridge and Valley Walk.

Question

Where can you see a decorated kicking-stone?

Route 4

KING'S NYMPTON

Tarka's Junction Pool in the valley of the sacred groves

OS Explorer Map 127

This walk passes through the once-wooded lands of the sacred groves or 'nymets' in this area. Groves are very distinct from plantations, and it is ironic that the first Forestry Commission Plantation was planted in nearby Eggesford in 1919. You will find it by road off the A377.

Conditions: Very muddy in places and with running water and standing water.

Distance: 3-4 miles.

Starting point: **(1)** From King's Nympton Station at SS663169.

(2) On leaving the station turn to your left and take the South Molton fork on the B3226. This is now known as the Fortescue Cross – previously the Fortescue Arms Inn stood here. You will pass by the The Posting House on your left, a reminder of the turnpike roads of the area. As you walk along you may just catch a glimpse to the left and in the distance of the King's Nympton Park house, which was built in the eighteenth century.

(3) Pass by the Newnham buildings and take a steep minor road to the right, passing Mount Pleasant on your left as you ascend. The lane is watery. Looking back you can see Junction Pool, where the River Mole joins the Taw. It was in such a place that Tarka the otter disturbed and ate the dace, an eel and a salt-water intruder, a plaice which had been ingested and then regurgitated by a heron after the heron had been shot by the water bailiff. Behind you is another part of the turnpike snaking up the hill to Burrington. The first eighteenth-century turnpikes from Exeter towards north Devon did not follow the Taw valley but snaked up and down between valleys and ridgeways.

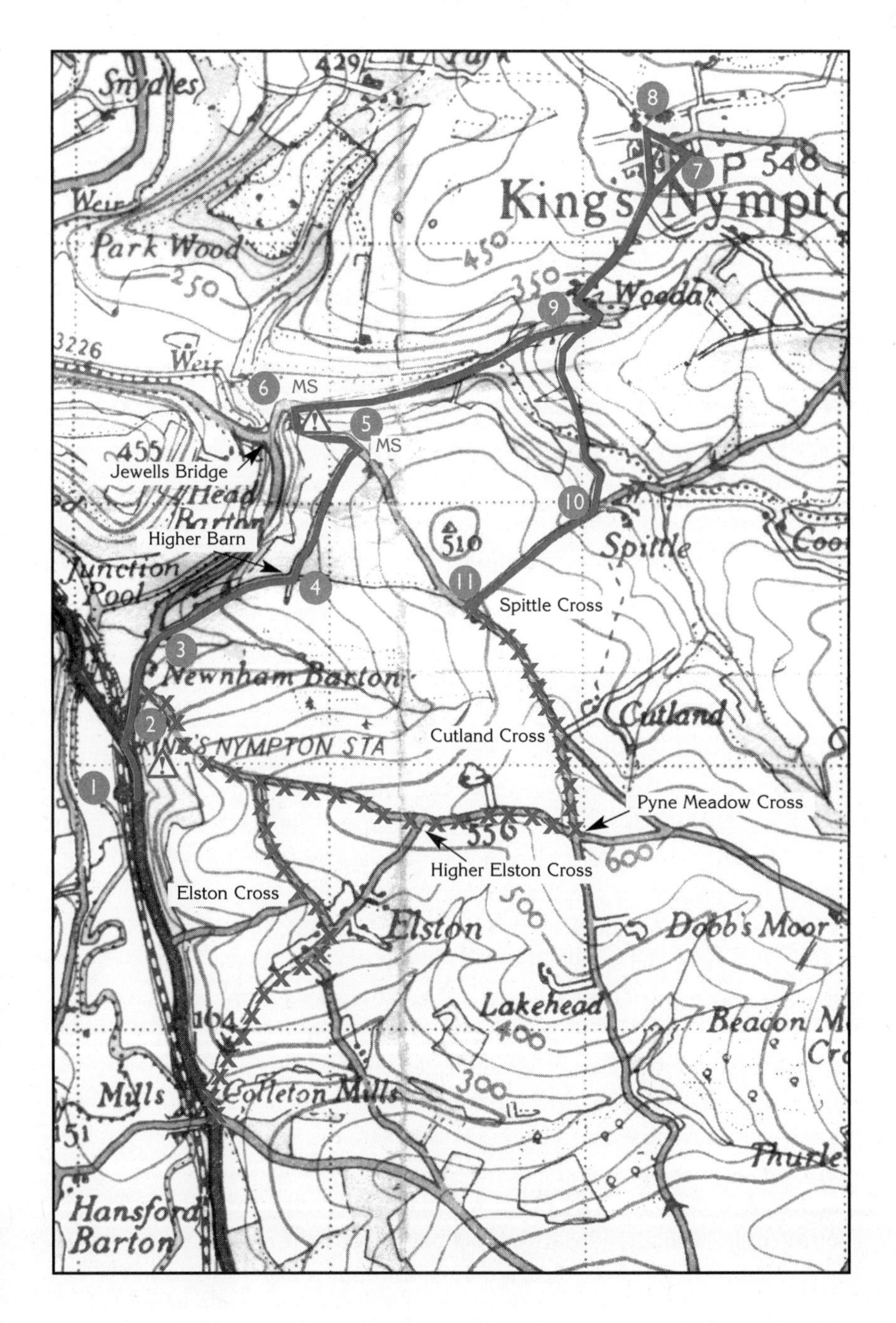
Snydles
429
Weir
Park Wood
250
450
350
King's Nympton
P 548
Wooda
3226
Weir
MS
MS
455
Jewells Bridge
Head Barton
Higher Barn
510
Junction Pool
Spittle
Spittle Cross
Newnham Barton
KING'S NYMPTON STA
Cutland
Cutland Cross
Pyne Meadow Cross
556
600
Higher Elston Cross
Elston Cross
Elston
500
Dobb's Moor
Lakehead
164
400
Mills
Colleton Mills
300
151
Hansford Barton

(4) As you reach the top, the lane ahead disappears into a field. Veer left and follow the green lane to the top. There is some standing water here. At the end there are two large trees – both pollarded, one an oak, one a beech.

(5) Take the pebbledash road to the left and descend a steep windy road to Hillhead Cross. On the corner here there is a large milestone reading 14 Barum, meaning 14 miles to Barnstaple. The river Taw runs right in front of you, volumes having been added not only from the Mole but also only a few miles downstream from the Little Dart.

(6) Take a sharp right here towards King's Nympton and follow the road through beautiful beech woods on your right, where straight oaks seem to have sprouted tutus against the ravages of browsing deer. The river Tongue chases away to your left.

Notice at Wooda Bridge the sign to the bridleway which you will take later. This village was declared to be Devon's Village of the Year in 1999 by the Council for the Preservation of Rural England. All is neat and clean, with whitewashed thatched cottages. The population of 642 that was recorded in 1878 would undoubtedly not all have lived in such neat houses.

Although we now stand in tranquil, well-managed countryside, just over a hundred years ago there were riots here directed against the introduction of threshing machines. Wooda is an Anglo-Saxon place-name element, here referring to the woods or groves as belonging to Saxon kings. Before them there were the Celts, who lived in these sacred 'nymets' along the Taw.

The deer park was a gift from Henry III in the thirteenth century to the Zulch family. It was Sir Lewis Pollard, father of 22 children, who first emparked the estate in the sixteenth century – then just forty acres – so that only the king's men could hunt there. It is worth exploring how the side lanes filter out into the fields from here.

(7) At the head of the road stands The Grove Inn, a memory of the sacred 'nymets' again. If you can get into the church, there are some roof bosses which depict the Green Man, the Celtic woodland god. **(8)** Turn back from the church with its striking copper spire, and descend once again with views of Dartmoor ahead.

Take the Bridleway at **(9)**. This passes down a well-used lane with a rocky and muddy surface. At Catham Lake there is a footbridge, and a short stretch of lane takes you up towards the ridgeways again.

(10) Turn right up to Spittle Cross where at **(11)** you can turn right towards King's Nympton Station. This is a fine ridgeway, and it will take you back to Hillhead and down to the Station. There are more green lane alternatives as indicated.

By the way

This walk runs above the valley where the Taw and Mole rivers meet. Although we think of this old way to Barnstaple as running along the valley, by road and rail, there were other ways up and onto the ridges which are visible on this walk. This is still hunting and shooting and, of course, if permitted, fishing country. The turnpike roads run clearly up out of the Taw valley here, and there is even a red post to discover in the area. These were often associated with the routes by which labourers were taken away for transportation to Australia.

Other green lanes in the area

There is a group to the south which lead to and from Colleton Mills.
They lead out of King's Nympton in an easterly direction and form a circular walk to Cadbury Barton and down over the Beacon to Chulmleigh.

Links

The Tarka Trail. The Umberleigh-Newton Route. The Tarka railway line.

Question

We are not on Exmoor country yet, so what kind of deer might you see?

Route 5

UMBERLEIGH & NEWTON TRACEY

Mills and market gardens

OS Explorer Map 127

This walk is dedicated to those noble providers of flour for all throughout the centuries – the millers. It takes you high up above the Taw, and gives commanding views over Exmoor and Dartmoor. This is a linear walk beginning at the railway station, and you can return there by bus. It runs up and over from agricultural lands towards the industrial kilns of the Fremington Pottery.

Conditions: Very muddy and steep in places – some fighting through required!

Distance: 3-4 or 4-6 miles.

Starting point: SS609237 Umberleigh Station. For a full day's walk and a round trip this is a good place to start.

(1) Leave the station, turning left and crossing over the wide-flowing Taw and over the A377 to **(2)** a very steep lane which runs to the right of The Rising Sun inn. It is lined with slate walling, and has always been a short cut up onto the Atherington road, the B3227.

Turn left at **(3)** as you turn at the top here there are views of Codden Beacon and Exmoor. This is a fairly busy road but gives a straightforward climb to the top at Atherington.

(4) Opposite the church here is a house where the most delicious pure Devon honey is for sale. On the wall is a plaque which reads 'J 1917 M. Verdun' – a memorial to just one of the 20,000 who fell on this first world war battlefield, mainly in the first hour. Mrs Woolacott, the bee-keeper and honey-vendor who now lives here, says that the initials stand for James Murch, and that there are still many Murches living below at Umberleigh. In

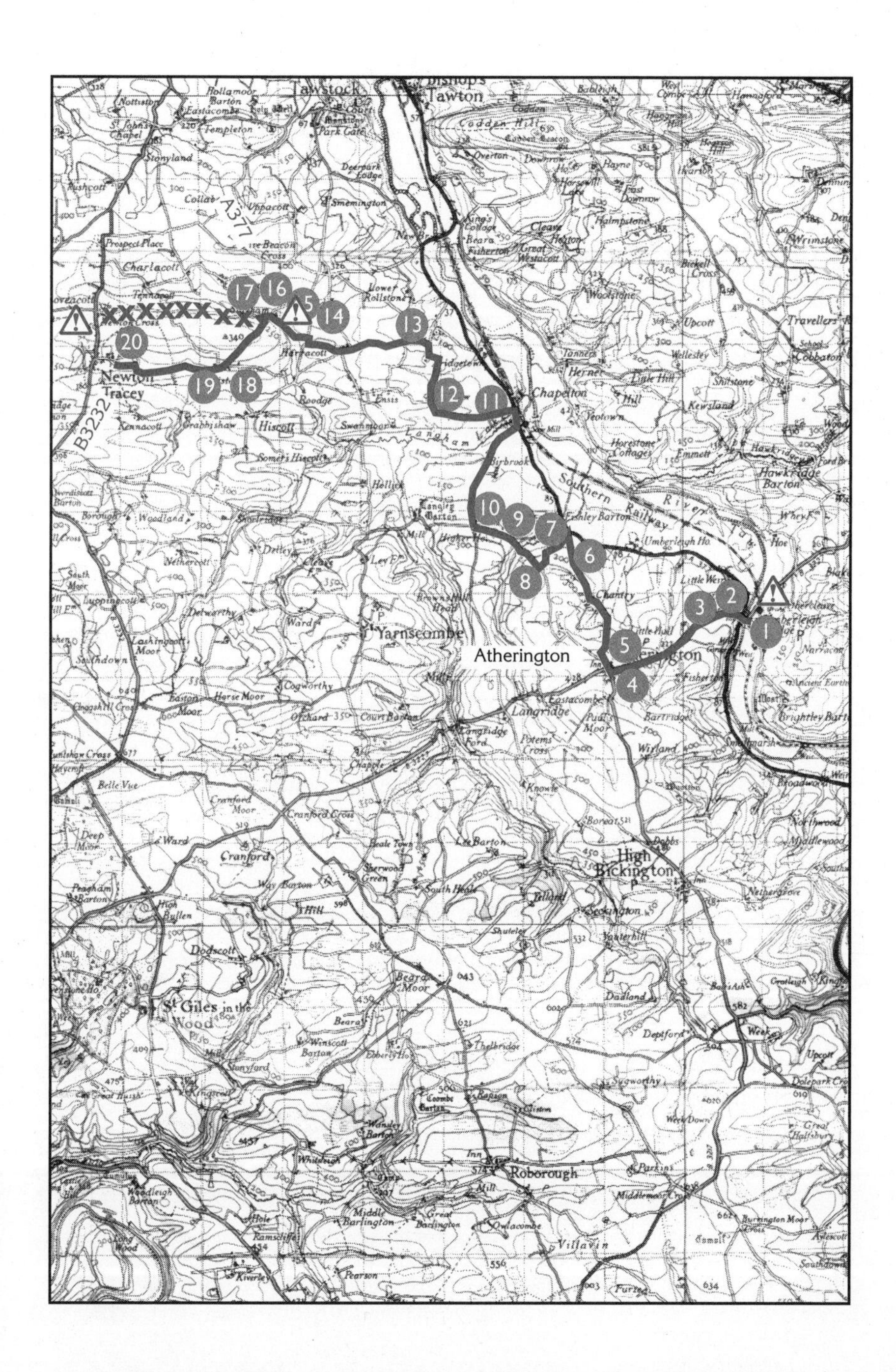
Atherington
Newton Tracey
Umberleigh
Chapelton
Yarnscombe
High Bickington
Roborough
St Giles in the Wood
Langridge
Cranford
A377
B3232
1
2
3
4
5
6
7
8
9
10
11
12
13
14
15
16
17
18
19
20

the nineteenth century there were market gardens in this area, specialising in plums and cherries – good news for the bees. Arthur Mee recorded in his parish-by-parish guide to Devon that the deaths of 11,796 Devon men are recorded on monuments throughout the county; he included this house plaque at Atherington and other individual memorials. (The male population of Devon in 1901 was 312,109.)

(5) Turn sharp right past the lychgate, which still has a lychstone upon which the coffins can rest, passing the School Room (1864). As you descend once again, Barnstaple Municipal Offices, Baggy Point and the white block of Saunton Hotel are in front of you. You descend almost to the A377 again, but at **(6)** take the footpath to the left over the field and into a minor road.

(7) Left again here, passing Rock View and up to where the green lane is on the bend at **(8)**. This is a very narrow lane, with brambles hanging overhead, but at least it is not muddy. You have to fight your way through this lane – watch out for fleeing deer. You come out and then cross a Ford where there is a small group of houses. Climb up to the left here and into a minor road at **(9)**.

Turn left towards Langley Cross and **(10)** turn right and follow the minor road down to the A377. Chapelton Mill is just to your right here, and there is a crossing which will take you up towards Bishop's Tawton (Route 21). To reach Newton Tracey, turn left and walk a short stretch of main road to Chapelton Cross where the old United Methodist 1914 Chapel stands.

(11) This short stretch of minor road brings you up high towards another challenging green lane **(12)** to your right at Hildrew. As you pass the farm, notice the orchard to your right. Although this lane is very 'stuggy' (local dialect for muddy), there are cobbles underfoot so you won't sink down completely.

(13) At the crossroads take the road to your left towards Harracott, and left again at Harracott Cross. Once more you are high up, with gorse appearing in the hedgerows. Go through this settlement and turn right by Signpost Cottage.

(14) Here on the bend is a short green lane to your left, which might be useful if you are on a circular route. Thankfully it is wide, and easy going.

(15) Take the next bend on the left into another minor road – they are getting more minor as you descend. You are now walking along in a valley, and Sideham farmhouse appears on your left at the junction below it.

(16) Turn left into another lane which is lined by very broad hedge-banks and is very wide. It descends to Sideham Bridge.

(17) You will have to decide here whether to take the lane to Sideham ('-ham' meaning the low lying watery lane, to your right), or take the lane on the higher ground of the '-cotts' to your left. Here I have suggested proceeding to Priestacott up the slope on the left. This lane is wide, surfaced with slate striations, and has a cobbled camber in places. It takes you high up for views over the Moors, and Newton Tracey Church soon comes into view. From here you can take the steep minor road at **(19)** or carry straight on.

The Bourchier Knot

(20) Having visited the church of St Thomas à Becket with its obvious Tracey connections, look outside for the Bourchier knot on the outside of the church. Some of the graves in this churchyard are covered in bricks. The direct route to Barnstaple passes close to Fremington where there were large brick factories and potteries.

You could carry on back to Chapelton Station (double check train times), or take the bus to Barnstaple which goes through Lovacott and Fremington. You get some good views of the Burrows on this bus. If you return to Umberleigh, there might be time to take a turn around the not-too-strenuous group of green lanes by the river.

By the way

In 1859 the Barnstaple Trust agreed on a special exemption from the tolls to persons going to and from Umberleigh Mill for the purposes of grinding corn for their own use, and not for sale; the miller's cart also went toll-free. The predominance of -cot as a place name element here is very noticeable: Tennacott, Linscott, Harracott, Kennacott etc. These farmers would have brought their corn along lanes often known as trussways. In the 1880s there were over 400 millers in Devon, but by 1935 this had dropped to 100.

There is another record of how things were at home in Atherington during the First World War. Marjorie Riddaway records:

> "We children used to be sent out from school two or three times a week to a place called High Bickington. There's a certain moss there that was very

absorbent, and they used it to make the cotton wool. We used to pick basketfuls, basketfuls in school time. It wasn't hard because moss isn't heavy."

Other green lanes in the area

You can cross the railway and river at **(11)** and go up to Bishop's Tawton.

Links

The Tarka railway line at Umberleigh and Chapelton.
Nearby Uppacott Wood at SS556282 is managed by Devon Wildlife Trust and is a fine mixed deciduous woodland with easy access.

Question

Umberleigh is a poetic-sounding name, but has nothing to do with umber, meaning a shade of brown. What is this place named after?

18th-century brick-making.

Route 6

ROMANSLEIGH AND MARIANSLEIGH

By ridge and valley, guided by a holy well, towards the north

OS Explorer Map 127

This walk will take you from one Celtic saint in the valley (St Ruman at Romansleigh) along ridgeroads and up and down valleys to another, a maritime one (St Marina of Mariansleigh).

This is another Celtic connection on the way to the north, Wales and Ireland. It is an area over which many pilgrims would have passed. These ways would also have seen migrants from these areas coming into north Devon looking for work.

Conditions: Very steep in places, with uneven cobbled ways.

Distance: 4-5 miles.

Starting point: Start at the church of Romansleigh SX727205 or at Kempstown on the A373 at SX728216.

Setting out from **(1)** Kempstown at Alswear, this first green lane is a steep climb out of the beautifully named Little Silver river valley. Many early fords and crossing places are described as "shining out like silver for the traveller to see". This stream is shaded over, perfect for spotting dippers. The lane is sharply cobbled and up to fifteen feet wide in places. The hedgerows contain some gorse, a reminder of the moors to come.

Go through the farmyard at Tidlake, with its imposing façade of local, blackish stone and cob-built outbuildings, and a stream emptying out into what appears to be a large, cast-iron bucket from a local quarry.

(2) The lane comes out onto a top ridge road to Mariansleigh, with sweeping views towards the sea beyond.

(3) From here St Marina brought her Celtic faith in 1245. Woodlands were dominant here for centuries, as were the woodland managers and a strong squirearchy hand-in-glove with the clergy. In the porch there is a reminder of those times, which sought to encourage church-going, and something else which was not always in evidence: fairness. It reads: "*All Seats in this Church are Free.*" This gave no excuse for non-attendance, however steep the way or bad the weather.

(4) At Town Livings crossroads, turn right to descend, making sure that you have the church on your right as you go down.

(5) There is now a perilous crossing of the A373 to be made on a sweeping steep bend.

(6) The green lane opposite begins in the bend of the river, so follow the signs over the stile to your right into a meadow behind the Church Hall, then through a gate to your left and into Oxham Lane. There is a stand of feathery larch to your right, and as you climb on your way to St Ruman's Well at Romansleigh, skylarks sing and buzzards gyre. Another indicator of the age of these woodland remnants persists in the presence of the delicate bright white umbellifer, *Pimpinella major*. The presence of Oxham Copse and Northam Copse down by the A373 again confirms that the woodland here was grown for commercial use, for coppice wood products such as tools and hurdling. (There is still a woodman's workshop opposite Rowcliffe.)

(7) St Ruman's Well is hidden behind the church through a gate into a short section of holloway which must have been visited by countless pilgrims. It is well hidden, for worshipping at a Celtic shrine in the early days of Anglo-Saxon Christianity was popular but risky. The well stands on an ancient track which runs round the church. The many green lanes in this woody area date back to times when communities wanted to stay away from major routes after the Romans had left. As the lanes here show, people communicated from settlement to settlement and, although ridgeways and trackways brought tools and goods, they also brought invading armies. The closed, lane-linked communities of Mariansleigh and Romansleigh survived.

(8) You can now return along the A373 to Alswear to your left, but it is safer and there is more to see if you take the footpath along the river bank.

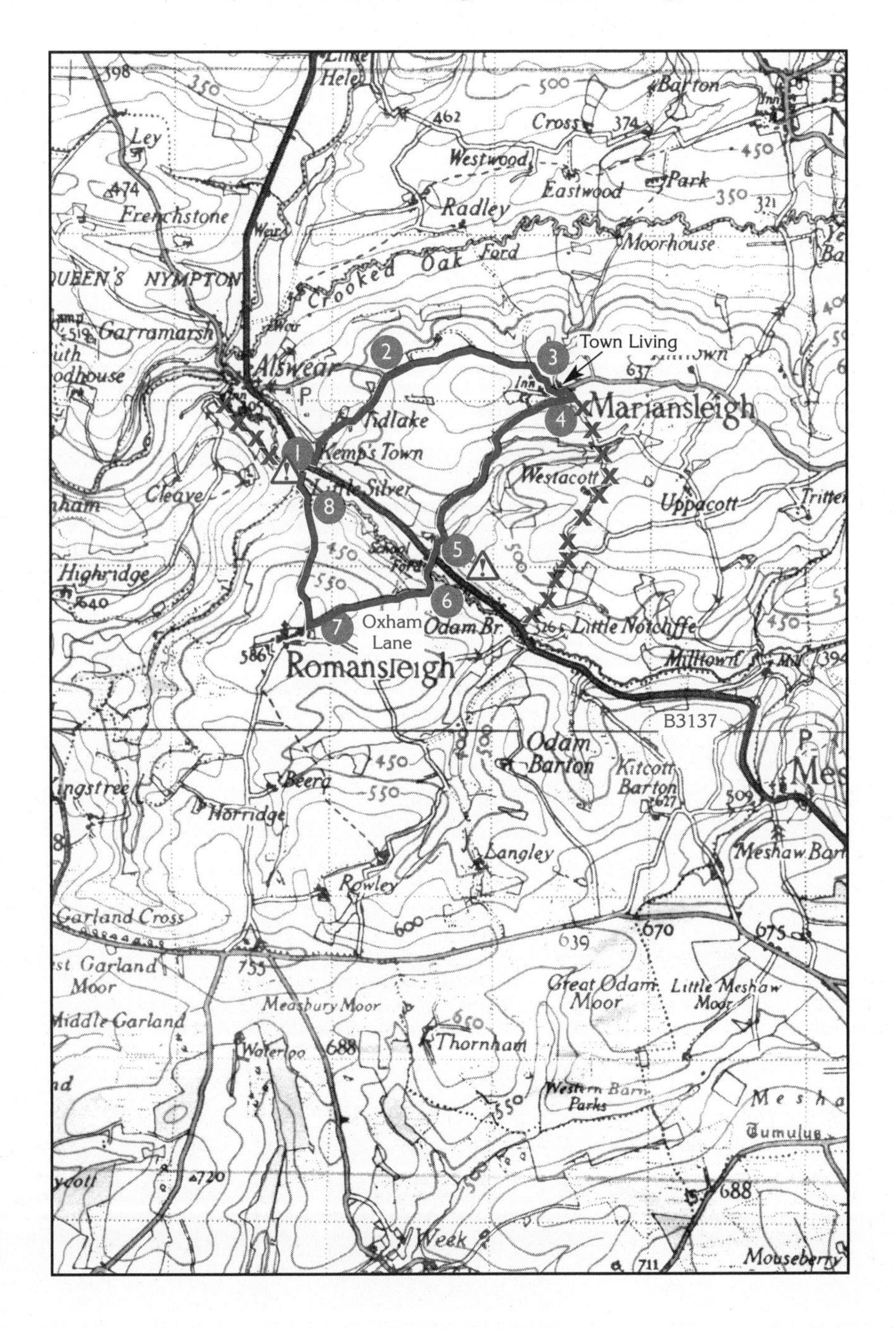
Town Living
Oxham
Lane
B3137
Romansleigh
Mariansleigh
Alswear
Tidlake
Kemp's Town
Westacott
Uppacott
Odam Br.
Little Notcliffe
Crooked Oak Ford
QUEEN'S NYMPTON
Garramarsh
Frenchstone
Westwood
Eastwood
Radley
Moorhouse
Cleave
Highridge
Odam Barton
Kitcott Barton
Beera
Horridge
Langley
Rowley
Garland Cross
Great Odam Moor
Little Meshaw Moor
Middle Garland
Measbury Moor
Thornham
Waterloo
Western Barn Parks
Tumulus
Week
Mouseberry
Milltown

By the way

One place name here reveals a tie with the woollen industry from the past: Odham relates to the growing of woad.

Just under twenty miles north of Tiverton in a north-easterly direction you will find yourself in a country full of moors: Odham, Radley, Oxen, Owl, Webbery and many more. In your transition from mid- to north Devon, these take you from once heavily wooded areas to the hard-won agricultural lands of the north where moorland still persists. Another important difference between north and south begins around here in the Little Silver Valley, and that is the presence of Celtic saints from Wales and Ireland. Travellers in the past along these ways would have been following a circuit of devotion.

Other green lanes in the area

Descending from Mariansleigh via Westacott Farm and Tongue Gate Hill. The presence of gate in a name often implies that the road was important enough to be gated (i.e. closed) and traffic controlled at some times.

There are some to the south-west which lead to Meshaw Moor, a County Wildlife Site belonging to Devon Wildlife Trust. This is a flower-rich meadow dominated by sweet vernal grass and containing rarities such as black knapweed.

Links

On the bus route from Tiverton to Barnstaple.

Question

You have found the well at **(7)**, and there is more evidence of the Celts nearby.

Oxham Lane

Route 7

ROSE ASH

A rose by another name

OS Explorer Map 127

The name Rose Ash conjures up bright red sunsets set against the hanging uptipped ash buds of winter. However, it actually refers to a landowner, one Ralph Esse. Remembering the difficulties that Sir Walter Raleigh's thick Devonian accent posed to the Court in London, maybe this mutation is easier to understand. This walk explores not only the valleys and ridgeways you traverse but also the distant moors which lie on the horizon. My thanks to the Reverend Dr Andrew Jones for a series of talks on the history of the area which I was fortunate to attend during the writing of this book.

Conditions: Muddy and slippery in places, but plenty of wide minor road walking.

Distance: 3-4 miles.

Starting point: SS788218. The village green.

(1) Here is a rarity in all of Devon: a church green. This one looks out over Dartmoor from the safe distance of deep farming country, created slowly over the centuries. It is red soil – not clay – which will cling to your boots from this area. The church is beautiful both inside and out, but this was not always the case, as in its long history this parish has weathered many an agricultural and social depression. Take the road to the right southwards passing Higher Ash Town on your left.

Follow this minor but once direct road down towards Witheridge until you reach **(2)** take the Bridleway on your left to East Catkill **(3)**. At this point, if you wish to explore further south then there is a bridleway which passes near to where there are remains of a cross and ends up at Ash Moor, where there was a Bible Christian Chapel known as Hope in 1858. If not, take the footpath over the ford or the green lane to **(4)** Nethercott Manor, **(5)** then over the field to the green lane known as Overcott Lane. Where you enter the lane from the field over a rickety gate, notice at Willow a very big monkey puzzle tree to your right. These trees were very much a must-have in the eighteenth century, when they were first introduced from Chile. The famous avenue at Bicton was supplied by Veitch's Nursery in Exeter.

(6) At the top of Overcott Lane take time to turn right and go to Five Crossways where there is an old branch of a cast-iron finger post still standing – but alas armless. This is also one of the Enclosure Roads created in the parish between 1869 and 1870 to claim Great and Little Ash Moors for more farming land; it is wide with drainage channels alongside and has a different feel from the other lanes so far walked in this parish. Returning to **(6)**, turn right down Gropy Lane – no prizes for guessing its derivation. I would like to think that pride came before a fall here, as a beautiful Bronze Age mirror was found in this parish, but I am not sure where. As you descend you may catch a glimpse of the very large rectory in the fields to your left.

(7) Turn left at Poadmarsh Cross towards Ash Mill.

(8) As you come into the hamlet, notice the little triangle of land to your right, which was once the parson's. He had a right to take produce from here. Before making for the bridleway on your left and your return, go down to a row of cottages on your right, one of which was the Old Post Office, the other the Old Store. You will see behind them a red-bricked building with ecclesiastical windows, with some stained glass at the top. This was the Sunday School.

(9) Take the bridleway at Rodesworthy Farm, which is tarmacked at its start and takes off over the steep fields towards Pearchay Farm and joins a minor road at **(11)**, where you turn right on your way back to the church and the village green.

By the way

From 1675–1948, eight generations of Southcombs served as vicars in this parish. Their time was not always spent in residence, but their influence over the mass of agricultural labourers in their care would have been considerable. They would have been on the board of the guardians of the poor, distributing help in money and kind, and they would have been magistrates dealing with local crimes. With the coming of enclosure in this area at the end of the 1860s and the subsequent loss of common land, many families would have

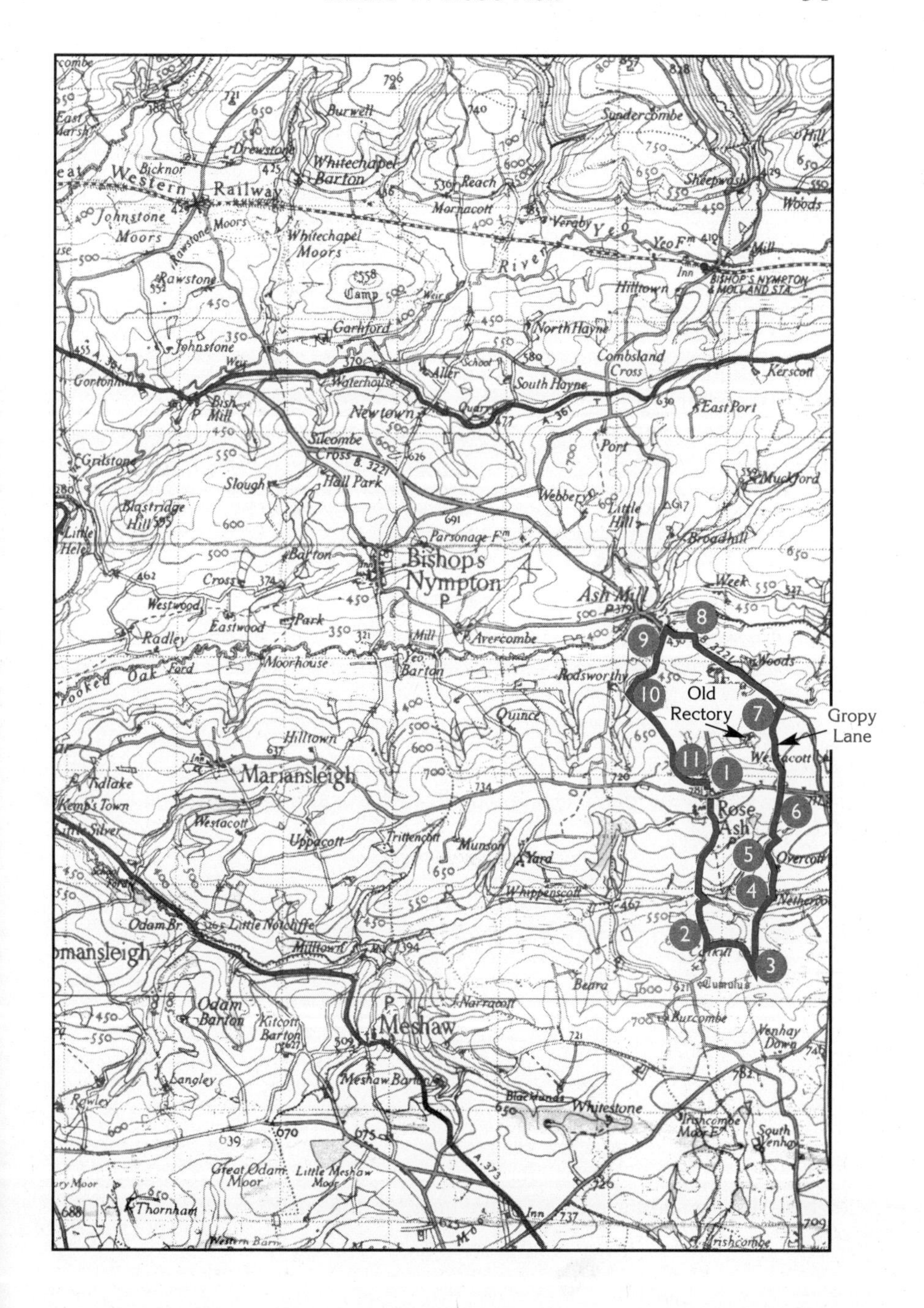
Old
Rectory
Gropy
Lane
1
2
3
4
5
6
7
8
9
10
11
Rose
Ash
Ash Mill
Bishops
Nympton
Mariansleigh
Meshaw
Western Railway
River Yeo
Burwell
Sundercombe
Whitechapel Barton
Whitechapel Moors
Johnstone Moors
Rawstone
Garliford
North Hayne
South Hayne
Combsland Cross
Kerscott
East Port
Bish Mill
Newtown
Silcombe Cross
Hall Park
Slough
Blastridge Hill
Webbery
Little Hill
Broadhill
Muckford
Parsonage Fm
Westwood
Eastwood
Radley
Moorhouse
Avercombe
Rodsworthy
Quince
Hilltown
Westacott
Overcott
Uppacott
Trittencott
Munson
Yard
Whippenscott
Little Notcliffe
Odam Br
Odam Barton
Kitcott Barton
Narracott
Burcombe
Beara
Cumulus
Venhay Down
Meshaw Barton
Whitestone
Blacklands
South Venhay
Great Odam Moor
Little Meshaw Moor
Thornham
Langley
Rowley
Irishcombe

suffered hardship.

> "The fault is great in man or
> woman who steals the goose
> from off the common;
> But what can plead that man's
> excuse who steals a common
> from the goose?"

There are records to show that sand was brought from the coast to fertilise these fields, and that horses were taken from here to East Knowstone to be shoed.

The quotation used on the title page of this book is nowhere more strongly felt than here.

> "A landscape is defined by those who have walked it."

Other green lanes found in the area

There are other green lanes in this area at Verhay, and eastwards towards Witheridge.

Links

Walks at Romansleigh, Route 6 and Knowstone, Route 8.
There is a bus route from Exeter to Barnstaple along the A373.

Question

As you look towards Exmoor, what is the name of the group of trees isolated towards the north-west?

Route 8

KNOWSTONE

A northern exile

OS Explorer Map 114

Poor old Knowstone – so cruelly cut off by modern road developments from its natural neighbours, expecially Rose Ash. The road-walking sections of this route tell us a lot about the green lanes which remain here and the highway history of the area.

Conditions: Very muddy in places.

Distance: 3-4 or 4-6 miles.

Starting point: SS829219. The parking area with public toilets and refreshments at Moor Town Cross on the North Devon Link Road, the Knowstone turn.

(1) Pass over the cattle grid on your way towards Knowstone, and you will soon find yourself on the edge of Knowstone and Rackenford Moor. This area contains half of all the culm grasslands in Devon. The purple moor grass dominates, and plants such as devil's-bit scabious break up the grassland savannah appearance in the summer. If you measure out a metre square in a damp patch you could count up to ten species of sedge here. It is an area to return to after this green lane walk.

(2) Follow the Two Moors Way sign and the sign to The Mason's Arms, Knowstone. This is a salt-and-peppered surface ridge road, once part of a toll road from Molland to Exeter. There is beech and holly here; the valley towards South Molton is on your left, and the foothills of Exmoor are ahead.

Unless the weather in which you are walking offers no break in the clouds, sooner or later a spotlight will appear on a field on these moorside slopes:

> "I have seen the sun break through
> to illuminate a small field
> for a while, and gone my way
> and forgotten it. But that was the pearl
> of great price, the one field that had
> the treasure in it. . . ."
>
> From *The Bright Field* by R. S. Thomas.

So watch out for glimpses of the church tower on your right.

(3) Go down and right into the village, taking time to visit this church with its unusual plastered tower. To return to the Henry Williamson influence in this area, his great-great-grandmother belonged to the Leaver family of Knowstone.

Knowstone is a northern village which once belonged to Hartland Abbey. Notice the era to which the village church, next to the school, belonged.

(4) Enter the longest green lane on this walk, which is a byway by passing in front of The Pound and Rosemary Chapel. This is a beautiful downward winding lane, reminding us of the Anglo-Saxon ploughed field pattern of lanes which is not often found in the area (see Rose Ash, Route 7).

Verna Rapley's little publication on farms and cottages here, which you will find in the church, tells us that Jack Boundy recalled in the 1980s that his grandfather from Luckett could remember oxen drawing the plough.

They started them early in the morning, and tried to avoid the mid-day sun. There is no danger of too much heat as you walk along this lane bounded by moss-covered hedgerows. As you enter the wood you pass over a ford where the water runs bright blue and milky-white, from clay soil runoff.

Once through Beaple's Wood (predominantly oak and ash), you ascend slowly to **(5)** Harpson Farm. Could the place-name element of hare, meaning

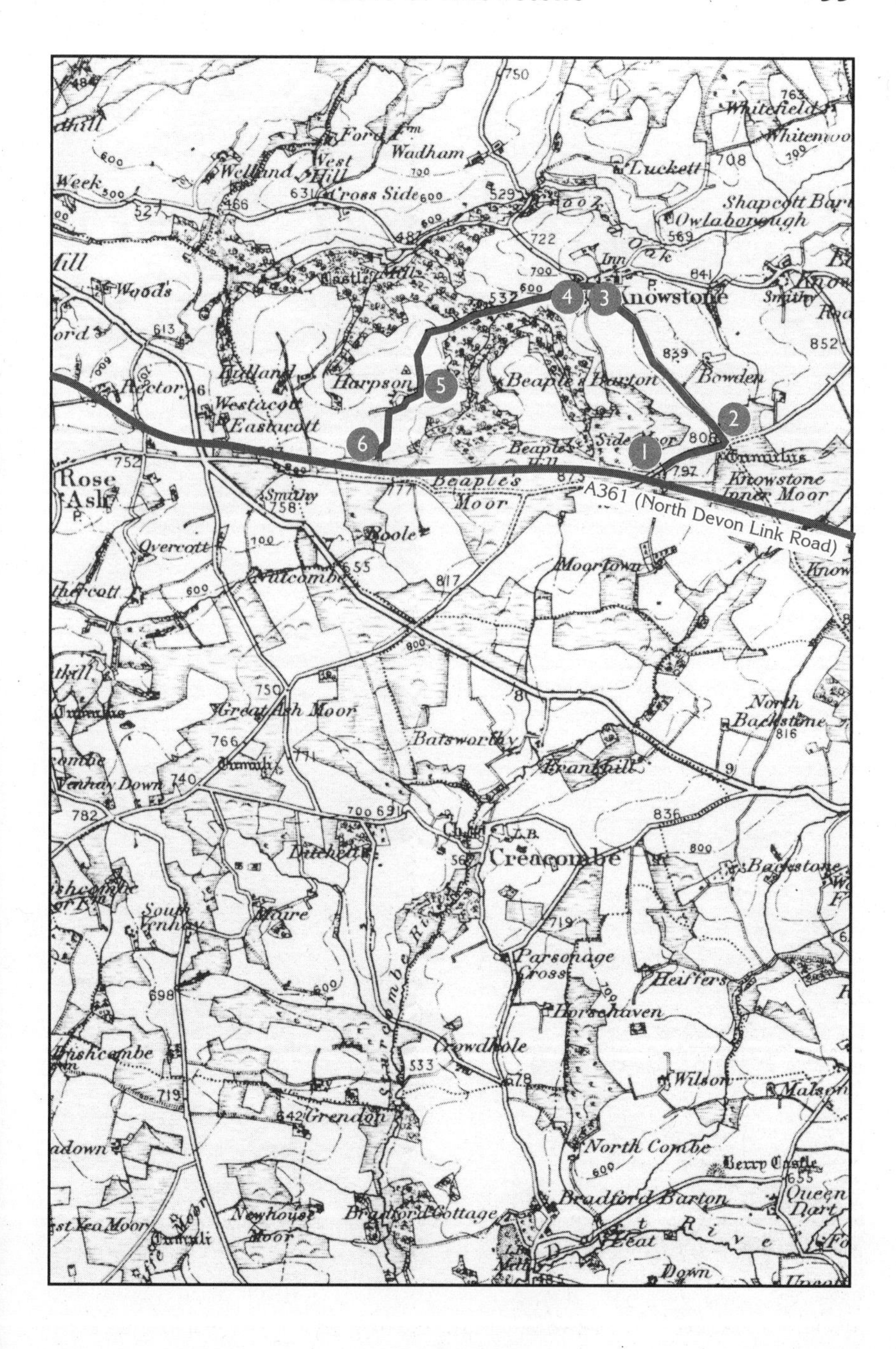
A361 (North Devon Link Road)
1
2
3
4
5
6
Knowstone
Wadham
West Hill
Cross Side
Luckett
Owlaborough
Shapcott Barton
Whitefield
Bowden
Beaples Barton
Harpson
Westacott
Eastacott
Rose Ash
Beaple's Moor
Knowstone Inner Moor
Moortown
Natcombe
Overcott
Great Ash Moor
Batsworthy
Creacombe
Ditchett
Parsonage Cross
Heifers
Horsehaven
Crowdhole
Wilson
Grendon
North Combe
Bradford Barton
Bradford Cottage
Newhouse Moor
Berry Castle
Yeat
Down
North Backstone
Backstone
South Venhay
Venhay Down
Moore
Woods
Smithy
Inn
Boole
Frankhill
Malson

path of the army, have been the origin of its name? There is a prehistoric enclosure in the woods of Harpson. There are some muddy sections to be negotiated here, and the sound of the Northern Link Road is with you again by the time you come to the end of this byway at **(6)**.

From here you will have to retrace your steps. However, when you reach Knowstone you could continue up to Wiston Cross and take the bridleway to Shapcott Barton.

You then join a minor road again at Eastacott Farm and follow the twisting road down to Rock Bridge and into Knowstone once more.

By the way

For this and the previous walk I am indebted to the Rev. Dr Andrew Jones who, during the Autumn of 2006, gave a series of very enjoyable informal and informative talks at his house concerning the church and this area. One area of interest he had concerned the positioning of signposts before distances were marked out by railways and major roads. Their erection seems to point towards the increasing importance and popularity of the south and the far west as opposed to the northern coast. However, Knowstone feels – and is – firmly placed close by Exmoor in north Devon.

Other green lanes found in the area

Only those listed in the links.

Links

The Two Moors Way.

Question

There is a lot of this fern, which has an alliterative sounding name, growing on the trees.

Route 9

TEMPLETON

The Knights of St John of the Cross come home to the Black Death

OS Explorer Map 114

This group of walks is in the heart of the county. You are always aware of the two moors of Dartmoor and Exmoor framing the minor, more delicate ones through which you pass. The subtle greens, yellows, browns and purples change under the big open skies and the big heavy rains of all the seasons. It is a landscape which is open but closes down in the miniature valleys of the Crooked Oak, Sturtcombe and Little Dart rivers. Many have passed this way, and a few chose to stay and steadily farm its calm acres. Nomansland, indeed; thankful are the few who live there now.

Conditions: Muddy conditions in the green lanes.

Distance: 3-4 miles.

Starting point: SS862125. You leave Tiverton by Long Drag Hill on the road towards Witheridge, the B3137.

(1) From Page's Cross take the road signed as a dead end. This leads north and drops down towards Ford Barton.

At **(2)** turn right before Ford Barton, and continue on through to the yard of Wood Farm.

(3) Go through this, keeping to your left along a steeply descending, slippery green lane which ends in a man-made glade where you might come across horses being exercised.

(4) Walk straight through here and take the second footbridge to the left, which leads up into a minor road with Partridge Farm at the top.

(5) Turn left here and go straight up towards Templeton. What will first come into view here is a squat, square tower just like those single tower Moorish castles you find dotted throughout Andalucia in Spain. This is the church founded by the Knights Templars. Inside you will see shields bearing red crosses and also the gold cross of the Knights Hospitallers. It was from here, St Margaret's, a chapel church built in 1335, that parishioners were taken during the Black Death in the 1350s to the mother church of St John's in Witheridge, for burial.

(6) Follow this route which the death carts took by turning right out of the church and up towards Temple Cross **(7)**. Then turn left again towards Templeton Bridge, another road signposted as being 'Unsuitable for Motor Vehicles'.

Furze peeps out of the beech hedges here, as you have climbed up onto a moorland plateau. Below are the mainly Saxon-founded farms with 'coombe' in their names, resting like chess pieces never to be moved. Just before the bridge, look out for Coombe Farm on the left, the original Knights of St John of the Cross settlement.

(8) This bridge over the Dart only dates back to 1835, and was built with some well-crafted spate holes at its side. The mill, however, standing to your right, and the crossing here in this once completely wooded valley, are much older.

(9) As you climb up, notice on the right set into the wall an oval granite tapering stone with a 'C' carved towards the top; these stones were put by important bridges post-1531 to denote that they had to be maintained (along with the 100 feet either side of the bridge) by any authority willing to do so. This dates from when the responsibility for bridges was taken away from the Church, along with their monasteries. There is also an Ordnance Survey trig point carved into this stone. You pass Rose Cottage to your right in Templeton Lane, as it is now called. A double hedge-bank of beech with linked roots at their base and tall uncoppiced poles at the top filters through images of Witheridge Moor to your right.

(10) Go straight over here at Witheridge Cross towards Rackenford, passing Palm Springs to your right. You are now on Witheridge Moor proper. A stark column of concrete rises up to your right: this is the OS trig point, for

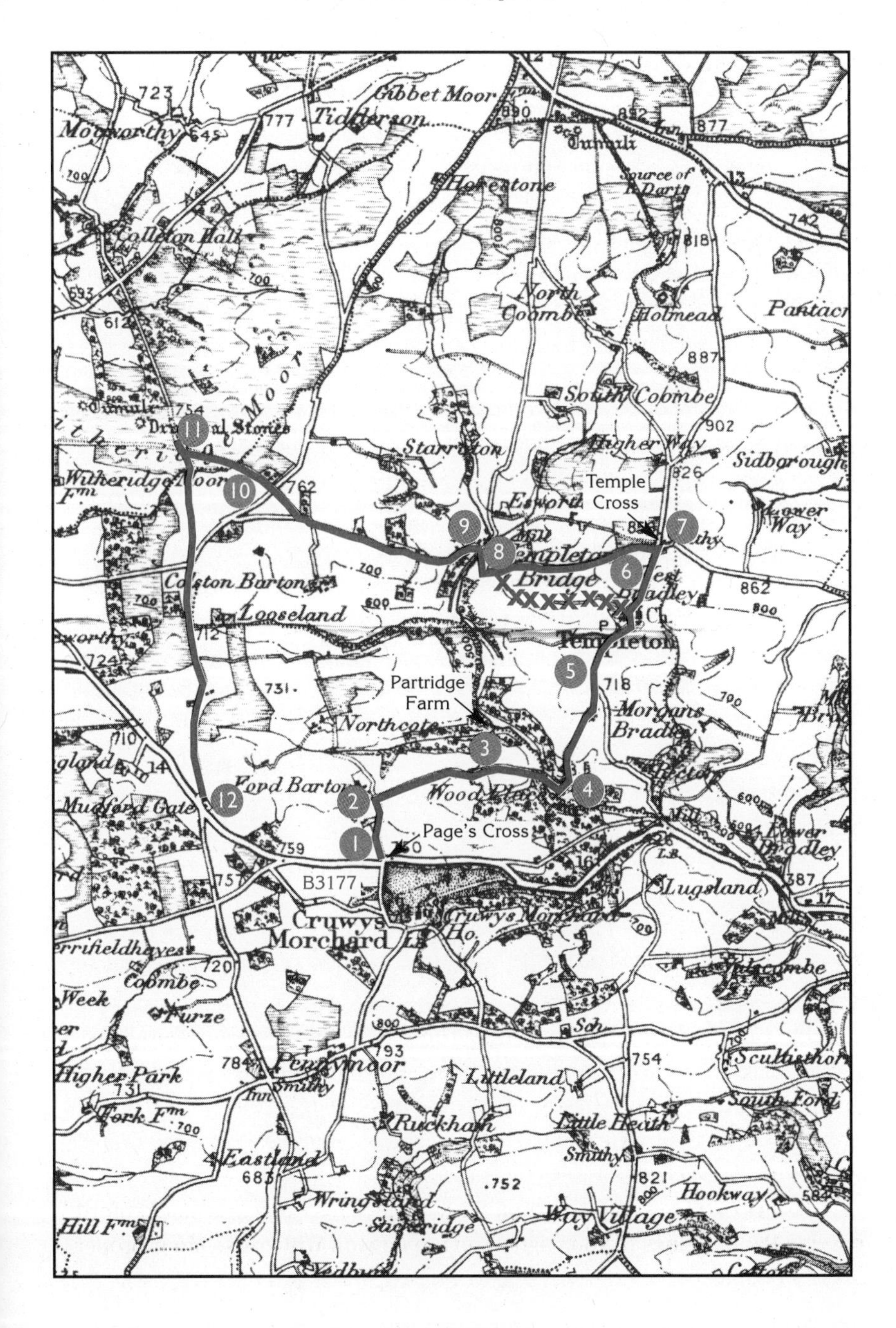
Gibbet Moor
Tidderson
Moorworthy
723
777
645
890
892
877
Tumuli
Horestone
Source of R. Dart
742
818
Colleton Hall
700
593
612
North Coombe
Holmead
887
South Coombe
902
Higher Way
826
Sidborough
754
Temple Cross
Lower Way
Witheridge Moor Fm
762
Templeton Bridge
Colston Barton
Looseland
862
800
712
724
731
Partridge Farm
Templeton
718
Morgans Bradley
Northcote
710
14
Ford Barton
Wood Place
Mudford Gate
Page's Cross
759
757
B3177
Lugsland
Lower Bradley
387
17
Cruwys Morchard
Cruwys Morchard Ho.
720
Coombe
Week
Furze
Sch
793
784
Pennymoor
754
Higher Park
731
Inn
Smithy
Littleland
South Ford
Ruckham
Little Heath
York Fm
Eastland
683
Smithy
821
Hookway
.752
Way Village
Hill Fm
1
2
3
4
5
6
7
8
9
10
11
12

you are 231 feet above sea level here.

(11) There is a path over towards the tumulus of the moor here, but look carefully for the low-lying groups of Druid Stones (shown on a 1930s map as being quite substantial standing stones), by your feet. Remembering the path of those Black Death tumbrils, W. G. Hoskins said that some victims fell off the carts in transit and never made it to St John's in Witheridge – perhaps they were left in the Nomansland area close by, or appropriately abandoned by the tumuli of the moor, which date back to the Bronze Age. To complete the circuit, walk back to **(12)** Mudford Gate with Dartmoor to your right as you go.

By the way

Templeton is named after the Knights Templars and the Knights Hospitallers of the twelfth century, who settled in this then woody area. There are two settlements with 'coombe' in their names here. Perhaps they did not do so well in the second phase of the Crusades, when landowners were taxed through the Saladin Tithe to raise money for these holy wars – not just on their property, but on their moveable goods too. The Church is St Margaret's, built in 1335 as a chapel to Witheridge.

Other green lanes in the area

Continue to walk Routes 7 and 8. There are some fine, more wooded bridleways to the east in the parishes of Washfield and Oakford.

Links

On the bus route from Tiverton to Barnstaple.

Question

What saint is represented by the Red Cross on the shields in the church?

Route 10

WASHFIELD

Home to fox and cubs

OS Explorer Map 114

This route follows in the footsteps of those involved in Tiverton's once-thriving woollen industry. Running close to the Exe in parts, you will get the feel of how many once worked here 'rasping' a living from the woollen trade at nearby Bolham.

Conditions: Minor roads and some muddy green lanes.

Distance: 3-4 miles.

Starting point: Why not walk out from Tiverton for this one, starting from the main bridge? SS954125.

(1) Take the road from the traffic-free shopping centre down towards the bridge, and cross over and out towards Heathcotes, following the All Routes signs.

Soon you will come to **(2)** the Washfield Stoodleigh turn. **(3)** Take the first right as indicated and the minor road to Washfield which passes Worth Hill and a fine row of standard beech, oak and ash on the right. Cross over the A361 and climb up to **(4)** the onion-finialed fingerpost on the rise which points towards Loxbeare as being 'Unsuitable for Heavy Traffic', but keep straight on. You will get views of the Tiverton area (Route 11) on the other side of the valley. You will come to Cotleigh, a fine collection of cob and red-brick buildings, one of which is known as The Coach House.

(5) Keep to the left here, and continue climbing to **(6)** the village green. Here is a touching memorial shelter to the 22 men from this area who died in the Great War. The churchyard of St Mary's is fenced off with horizontal wire and bar fencing put up by some who returned from that conflict and were desperate for work. The raised triangle has the autumn-flowering orange hawkweed growing in the grass.

(7) Now take the green lane opposite the church, signed as a footpath, with St Wynefrede's well on the right. Look above on the wall of what looks like a fortified manor house (Brook Farm) and you will see lettering which reads 'WYNEFRED R E MARBERD J.P. MS 1564'. When the Rev. Sabine Baring-Gould visited here, he commented on the small cell-like chamber over which these letters are written, saying that it faced exactly east, "but little is known about the significance of the lettering." Continue over the stile and into the meadow. Keep to the top hedgerow to your right, and the lane (although very low where it runs alongside the stream) will bring you to a footbridge. Here look out for a pollarded alder with a trunk indicating an age of at least 150 years. You will come up over the field and into the lane.

(8) Turn right into the minor road here. The house opposite, known as the Pound, has an interesting curve on its exterior indicating an oven by the chimney. Look back at the hedge pattern opposite to your right and you will see the small animal pound once used to round up stray cattle. Follow the roaring of the Link Road to your left until you come to **(9)** a sign on your right to Lower Pitt Farm. This willowy-wide lane will take you down over a ford where you turn back onto yourself **(10)** along the field edge which leads into a high green lane **(11)**. Turn right and pass the church again and continue to a house called Beeches (formerly Weeches).

(12) On your right take the green lane where hops grow and which leads down to the Exe over a steep field. The lane here leads along towards Bolham and some interesting sluice gates along the river bank here.

The grinding mills were used here for making brightly-coloured cloth dyes from exotic south and central American woods. But it does not sound like an easy process, as those who performed it were known as 'raspers' – so much for the tranquillity of the countryside in the past. This is an ancient site: there was a Roman fort here by the weir at Keeper's Cross. Retrace your steps, but this time keep to the lane by the river's edge down to **(13)** by Worth House and Swinesbridge. Follow the Exe Valley signs, and take the footpath over the field at the back of the allotments and by the river to come

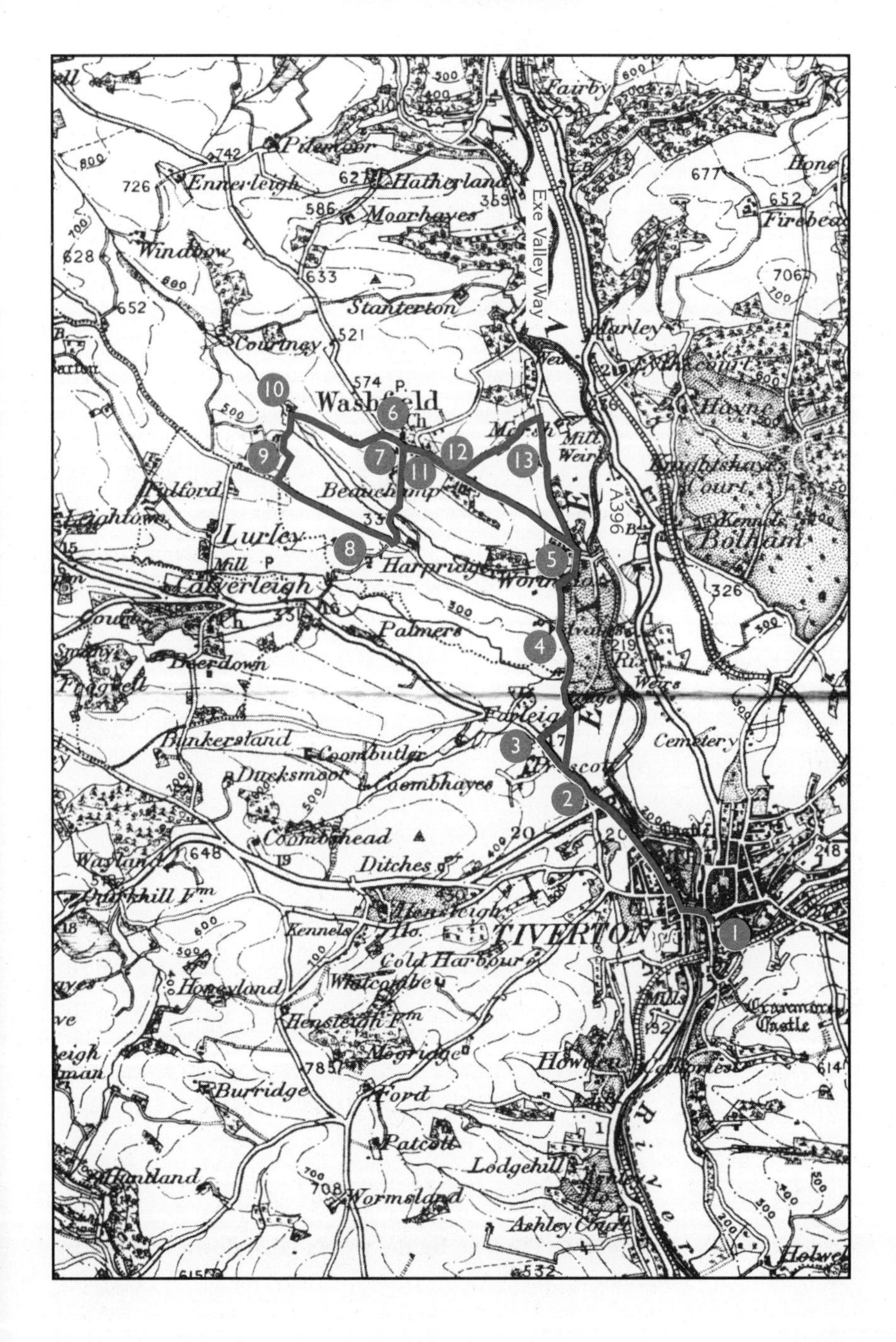
Washfield
Exe Valley Way
A396
TIVERTON
Stanterton
Moorhayes
Hatherland
Ennerleigh
Windbow
Courtney
Beauchamp
Lurley
Harpridge
Calverleigh
Palmers
Bolham
Knightshayes Court
Cemetery
Coombhead
Ditches
Cold Harbour
Honeyland
Burridge
Ford
Patcott
Lodgehill
Wormsland
Ashley Court
Duckmoor
Bunkersland
Coombhayes
1
2
3
4
5
6
7
8
9
10
11
12
13

out at Loughborough next to the Red Cross Headquarters. And so back to Tiverton, passing Heathcoats textile factory.

By the way

Tiverton's textile outworkers were involved in many processes at a distance from the town. They were just part of the multiplicity of trades taking place in the countryside alongside farming. There were the rural crafts of thatching, blacksmithing, flour-milling, charcoal-burning and bodging, to name just a few. As you see on many of these walks, there were working mines and quarries nearby too. Diversification for farmers is not a new thing: they have always been able to turn their hand to anything. But sometimes an industry needs help from above. In 1668 a law was passed, which was not repealed until 1814. It stated that:

> "No corpse of any person shall be buried in any shirt, shrift, sheet, or shroud, or anything whatsoever made of or mingled with flax, hemp, silk, hair, gold or silver."

The fine for not complying was £5 for the non-wool shroud provider, and £5 for any one involved in the funeral.

Other green lanes in the area

At Loxbeare and Calverleigh.

Links

The Exe Valley Way.
There are regular bus services to Tiverton from Exeter, and others go to Barnstaple and Taunton passing through Tiverton.

Question

The plant on the green, the orange hawkweed, has another name. There's still plenty of this modified activity in the area.

Route 11

TIVERTON

By parkland, orchard and pasture. Beware of hairy arms!

OS Explorer Map 114

When I first tried to follow existing rights of way northwards out of Tiverton I often came across remnants of ancient orchards. This walk through this fertile valley shows many different farming fortunes through the ages. It also follows some of the old pre-turnpike ways up the Exe Valley to the Moor.

Conditions: Steep in many parts, muddy and overgrown in some.

Distance: 3-4 or 5-6.

Starting point: SS959143.

Beginning on the north side of the North Devon Link Road, the A361. Buses for Cowley will take you in this direction, or from the centre you can follow the cycle path signs past the church and down towards the big roundabout on the link road.

(1) Follow the signs to the left towards Knightshayes, Bolham and the A386, and pass the house entrance at **(2)**.

Go under the railway bridge as you near Bolham. This railway linked Tiverton with Bampton from 1885, which was too late to help the textile industry established in the area since the fourteenth century. However, the big coaching inn opposite on the A396 still gives a feeling of the importance of this northerly exit from Tiverton. It was a coaching stop on the 1818 turnpike road.

(3) Retrace your steps from the road and turn sharp left up the footpath, which is also one of the Knightshayes Estate's private roads and is tarmacked most of the way to Marley Farm. Part of the lane to here has a concrete surface too.

(4) With Marley Farm on your left, framed by views of Dartmoor, turn right into a wide green lane with a raised, cobbled camber. There are eight or nine species of hardwood tree in the hedges here, taking the date of the lane back to at least 1100. It passes through field edges, occasionally losing one of its hedges on one side, as it works its way to Firebeacon.

(5) Go through the farm and pass the giant oaks, then exit into the road where a giant beech stands.

(6) You now follow the National Cycle Route 3 to the right down through Knightshayes. This is a beautiful lane, lined with ashes, oaks, beeches and firs. You go down through deciduous woodland by Beckers Down, and then through a gate by the huge walled garden of Knightshayes.

(7) Follow the wall to your left. There is a Douglas Walk signposted here, but continue down and under another barrier **(8)**. You come out into a minor ridgeway which leads from Bampton to Tiverton. You will hear the North Devon Link humming once again, and pass by a group of red-tiled farm buildings complete with pond.

(9) Turn left and follow the lane towards Chettiscombe. To your left lies part of the old mailcoach route from Bampton down to Tiverton. It was in Chettiscombe in 1860 that a hold-up attempt was made by a woman stepping in front of the coach and holding out her hand for money and mail. The driver noticed that the proffered hand was on the end of a very hairy arm. A crack of the whip in the would-be robber's direction saw the coach safely on its way.

(10) Take the footpath through this busy farm, which once had an extensive orchard surround it. The lane is called Leverlake Lane, and the open watercourse to your right confirms this.

(11) At the end of the lane, follow the signs along the road and back to Tiverton across the A361.

By the way

The minor roads used on this walk, although not green, are old ways which have crossed and joined settlements and habitats throughout the centuries and have remained constantly in use. They give us a feel for the changes in land appearance and land use between mid- and north Devon. It is important to remember that although Tiverton still has cotton-mill buildings, the peak of this industry, both in the town and outlying districts, was almost over by 1720.

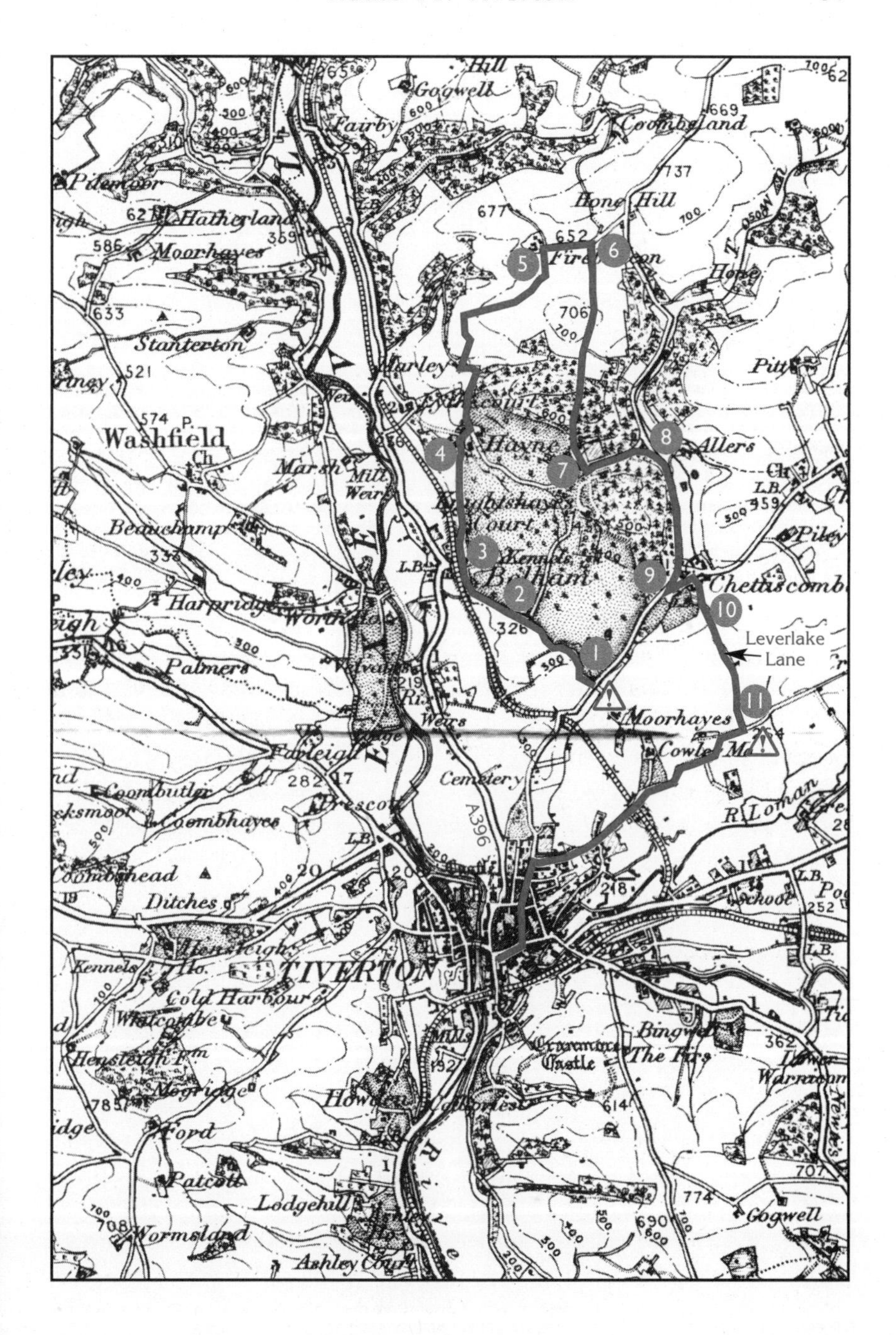
Gogwell
Fairby
Coombeland
669
737
Hone Hill
677
652
Firehouse
706
Hone
Pitt
Hatherland
Moorhayes
586
633
Stanterton
521
574
Washfield
Ch.
Harley
Hayne
Allers
Marsh
Mill
Weir
Knightshayes
Court
Kennels
Bolham
Chettiscombe
Leverlake
Lane
Beauchamp
Harpridge
Palmers
326
219
Weirs
Moorhayes
Cowley
Farleigh
282
Coombutler
Coombhayes
Cemetery
A396
R. Loman
Coombhead
Ditches
Kennels
TIVERTON
Cold Harbour
Whitcombe
Collipriest
Castle
Bingwell
The Firs
362
252
218
614
774
690
707
Ford
Patcott
Lodgehill
Wormsland
708
Ashley Court
Gogwell
1
2
3
4
5
6
7
8
9
10
11

Links

National Cycle Route 3. Washfield and Rackenford, Route 10.
There are regular bus services to Tiverton from Exeter, and others go to Barnstaple and Taunton passing through Tiverton.

Question

What is the name of the big coaching inn which stands at the northerly approach to Tiverton?

Route 12

BAMPTON

Bampton's bootmakers came too late for Bronze Age travellers

OS Explorer Map 114

This circuit is full of colour below, around and above your feet. This is because you are in an area of multicoloured limestone, of tumultuous upheavals of rocks now covered in almost emerald-green grass, all set against an ever-changing sky which draws in the rains from Exmoor's edge and the sea beyond.

Conditions: Muddy and slippery in places, pools of standing water.

Distance: 4-5 miles with the possible addition of 10-11.

Starting point: SS962222. The Toll House standing on the 1819-26 turnpike along the Exe Valley.

(1) Take the road which runs between the Toll House and the Quarryman's Rest pub. It is recorded that the Strong family, all seven of them, lived in the Toll House in 1851. Mr Strong, as well as being the toll keeper, was one of the 26 shoemakers and cordwainers living in Bampton. His wife was a shoe-binder. A cordwainer worked in specially dressed goatskin from Cordova in Spain, brought in from Bideford by packhorse trains along nearby Stoney Lane; there had been a tanning industry here since the 14th century. As the Strong family were so close to the point of entry into Bampton, maybe they had the pick of the fells (hides) carried by the mongers (traders).

(2) Turn left and follow the **NCR3** signs. You are now walking in the valley, with views of a half-wooded ridgeway to your left.

(3) Passing Giffords on your right, there is an option to make a loop of two green lane holloways which lead out towards a long bridleway at Bampton Down.

(4) Turn right at Gifford Cross, and take the road along towards Clayhanger. A steep climb brings you to Downhills Farm. **(5)** Turn left past the milk-churn stand, and after another steep climb, by turning left at **(6)** you will come into your green lane reward.

(7) From the start, the straightness of this lane compels you forward into its unsunken surface flanked by lines of magnificent pollarded beeches. You are in the east to west Bronze Age (1400-600 BC) track which led from Dorset to the north Devon coast. It is a bridleway for two miles, running at first high and wide along the ridgeway. The winds are strong up here, and many of the pollards, once humanly trimmed, show multiple arms reaching up to the clouds – the result of limbs lost too quickly over the centuries. It is an example of a lane which is ancient, but not sunken.

Hedge-dating here will not give a large number of species, but holly is in abundance. All the woodland around here was cleared by the 1250s, but watch out for the Anglo-Saxon acknowledgement of woodlands here in place names ending in '-hayne', meaning hedge. As it descends, narrows and twists down into a holloway, the surface reveals the many colours of Bampton limestone – red, yellow and purplish. Where it meets the schists, blacks and greys striate across the lane's surface, mixed with some rust-coloured ironstone banding. The washed-down red soil serves as a back-wash for all these colours. But be careful how you go.

(8) At Ford Mill crossroads, go straight over towards the mill and Bampton, where there is a sign reading 'Unsuitable for Long Vehicles'. You are still on the Bronze Age track, which will bring you back to the Toll House at **(1)**. As you approach the Toll House again, look out for a lime kiln in Ford Road to your left. Lime for fertiliser was burnt here until 1966. (For a short cut back to **(2)**, just past the mill on the left you can take the green lane to your left at **(9)** by a deserted-looking house. You pass through woodlands. At Pipshayne take the Bridleway to your left and over the fields, or stay on the lane which will bring you back to the cycle route at **(2)**.)

For added interest **(10)**, take the road to the right of the Toll House and look out for the Public Footpath sign leading up the hill behind. This is part of an ancient Celtic trackway which led to Seaton in the south and Molland and the north coast beyond. It is known both as Stony Lane and Crockford Lane. Despite the modern housing development through which it passes (followed by a very stony section) it has been well preserved up to where the Crockford Inn once stood. Here there is a field dedicated to the public

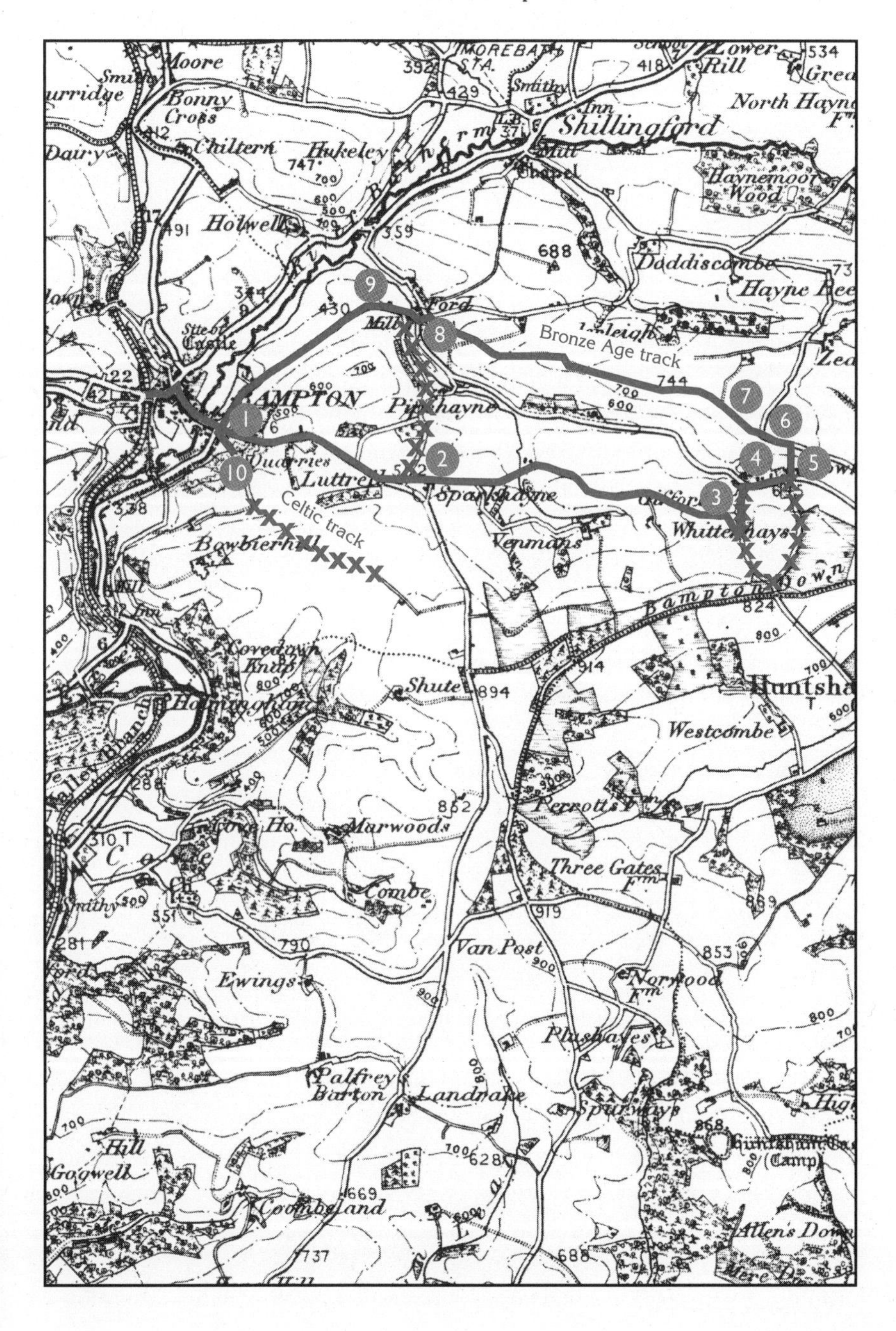
Bronze Age track
Celtic track
BAMPTON
Shillingford
Bonny Cross
Chiltern
Hukeley
Holwell
Doddiscombe
Haynemoor Wood
North Hayne
Luttrell
Sparkhayne
Venmans
Whitterhays
Quarries
Bowbierhill
Shute
Westcombe
Perrotts
Three Gates
Marwoods
Combe
Van Post
Ewings
Norwood
Plushayes
Palfrey Barton
Landrake
Spurways
Gogwell
Coombeland
Allen's Down

through the Countryside Stewardship scheme. From here there are good views over the town, and at your back there is the presence of the quarries which once made the town so prosperous.

By the way

Up until the first world war, footwear – or the lack of it – greatly affected your educational and employment opportunities. Shoemakers, mostly involved in repair work, were to be found from the 1800s in most villages. If there wasn't a blacksmith, then there were nearly always one or two shoe- and bootmakers, involved in more mending than making.

From the point of view of highway history, Bampton stands at a very ancient crossroads dating back to Bronze Age times. From south to north and east to west, traffic has worked its way along the Exe valley and up from the south to the north coasts, all using Bampton as a trading point. Being so close to Exmoor it has become famous as a trading point for cattle, and in the 1800s held the largest sheep fair in the Westcountry. The beginnings of the pony fair go back only to the 1850s and although the fair in October now continues without them, plans are ahoof to bring them back.

Other green lanes in the area

The loop at **(3)** to **(5)** above, leading to others on Bampton Down.
From Ford **(8)**, the loop leading towards Diptford and Shillingford.

Links

The Exe Valley Way. National Cycle Route 3. Route 10, Washfield, Route 11, Tiverton, and Routes 13 & 14, Morebath. Buses run along the Exe Valley and up to Taunton and Minehead.

Question

What is the lane at (10) called? A bridleway, and look to your left for another of its names.

Route 13

MOREBATH (A)

For the price of an Indulgence

OS Explorer Map 114

This is one of two walks based around the small hamlet of Morebath, and is made doubly enjoyable by being able to refer to Christopher Trickey, the churchwarden of Morebath between 1520 and 1574, who left us meticulous records of these times in his accounts.

Conditions: Steep and rocky in places.

Distance: 3-4 miles.

Starting point: **(1)** You can choose to begin at SS958225 by climbing up onto the Anglo-Saxon castle in Bampton (dating back to William the Conqueror's days) and taking the footpath to the west; alternatively, take the B3227 out towards Holwell Farm towards Hukeley Bridge.

(2) Holwell green lane starts just before here, and is to the left through the farmyard gate or to the side of it up the tractor path which leads into the lane. Because Christopher Trickey has documented a turbulent time in the history of the church, when Henry VIII was throwing his weight about, such abiding references to holy wells ('Holwell') seem to become more significant. Nearby Hukeley Bridge, named after Joan Hucley, was originally built in 1531.

Holwell Lane is a fairly steep lane with some deep exposed rock face gulleys – some of which are bright red – underfoot. There is a lot of sphagnum moss in the area, and there are oak trees towering above you on the banks, a common feature of the lanes in this area.

(3) You emerge at Chiltern Cross through a grassed-over flat area. Turn right here and follow the B3198 round, passing Lower Lodfin. There could be a familial connection here with Bicknor Bridge on Route 15, as a poor outcast known as William Bicner was living here at Lodfin and "delving stone".

It is recorded that the parish helped him out by giving him second-hand clothing. Perhaps this led him on to become a mason involved in the building of a bridge named after him.

(4) Keep to the left by Bonny Cross, thinking of the "walking women" written about by Trickey, who must have passed through here, were later "brought to bed of base born children", and sometimes received help from the parish. Others who are recorded as having bought passes to go through the parish of Morebath unharmed include slaves from Barbary, maimed soldiers, released prisoners-of-war, and families in distress. Watch out for an enamel sign, heralding a telephone box, which appears at the top of the hill by the road; you are now in Morebath.

(5) Follow the main road up, and on a bend at the top on the left you will see an old unusual lychgate-style bench built with wooden pegs. There is a byway sign here, which will take you into the next green lane to be climbed. It has a cobbled surface similar to that found on Route 12 at Bampton near the town centre. It begins narrowly, and widens out at the top with a double hedge-bank on the right as you descend. There is a well-placed seat here.

(6) Veer right into the road and up the hill towards the Timewells. Trickey records that in 1527 there was a harper called Timewell playing at the 'parish ale', the forerunner of fundraising coffee mornings.

(7) Turn right into the road (not the drive entrance) for Timewell House, which was rebuilt in Victorian times by Charles Harrod, founder of the shop where reputedly you can buy anything – even harps! This lane turns into a footpath after you have battled through the old green lane for a while on the bend. You walk out across a clear meadow with the lane to your left and come out at **(8)** with the entrance to Morebath Manor on your far left. However you turn right, and follow the road back to Morebath again, and return by the same route or by following the National Cycle Route signs down to Keens and across the old Taunton to Barnstaple railway line.

It is also safer to do this as the other lanes around Combe here are home to paintball skirmishes, which you might (or might not) want to indulge in. If you are staying in Morebath, now is the time to visit the church.

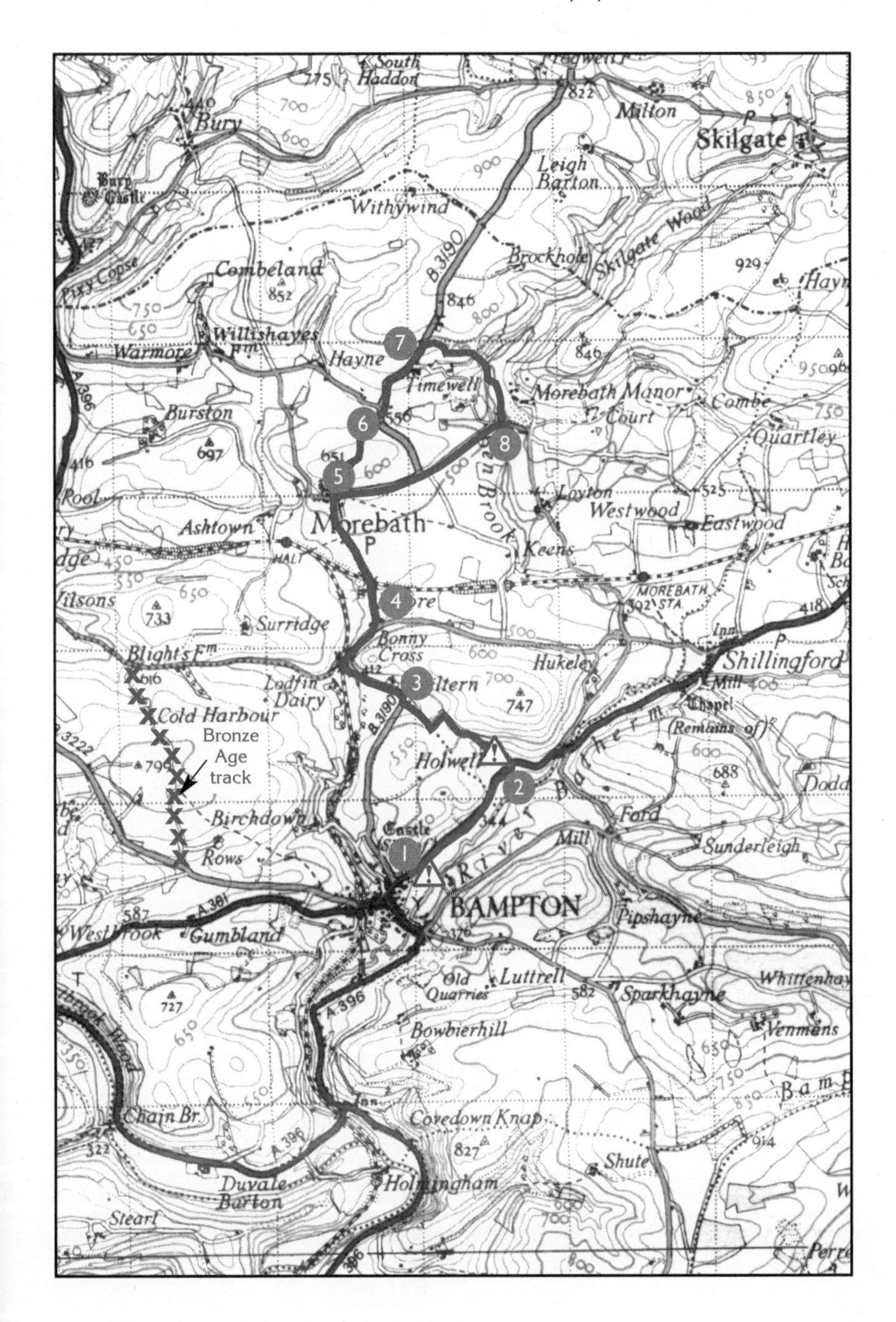
South Haddon
Bury
Bury Castle
Milton
Skilgate
Leigh Barton
Withywind
Brockhole
Skilgate Wood
Pixy Copse
Combeland
Willishayes
Warmore
Hayne
Timewell
Morebath Manor
Combe
Court
Quartley
Burston
Loyton
Westwood
Eastwood
Morebath
Ashtown
Keens
HALT
MOREBATH STA.
Wilsons
Surridge
Bonny Cross
Hukeley
Shillingford
Blight's Fm
Ludfin Dairy
Cold Harbour
Bronze Age track
Holwell
Birchdown
Rows
Ford
Sunderleigh
BAMPTON
Pipshayne
Gumbland
Old Quarries
Luttrell
Sparkhayne
Venmans
Bowbierhill
Chain Br.
Covedown Knap
Shute
Duvale Barton
Stearl
A 396
A 361
B 3190
B 3222

By the way

Before Henry VIII ordered otherwise, roads and bridges were maintained by the religious houses nearby; in this case, the Augustinian Priory over the border in Somerset at Barlynch. If you had committed some terrible crime, you could buy an 'Indulgence' or forgiveness for it by working on the construction of a bridge for a set number of days. However, in the case of Hukeley Bridge, Joan Hucley had not committed a crime, and therefore did not need to work at bridge-building in order to have the bridge named after her. In return for paying for the railings on the bridge, she was given the privilege of providing the church with a candlestick big enough for five lights.

The railings must have been so prominent that they were always associated with her. Her soul after death was provided for by the lighting of the five candles forever. This is what medieval believers needed to know, as the afterlife – and remembrance, often in the form of building chantry chapels in your house and employing a priest to pray for your soul after death – were believed to be more important than your time on earth.

Walk up through the town, passing the church and then the war memorial and up the lane to your right towards High Cross. Here on the right is a bridleway, beginning as a wide holloway, and another part of the Bronze Age trackway encountered near Bampton. It is wide and steep, and shaded over with ancient beech and oak coppice; and so ancient that in parts the roots make up the surface of the lane, binding the sole to the foot of the lane just as Mrs Strong bound her shoes. There are double hedge-banks here, covered in moss. If you follow this lane up to where it joins the Exe Valley Way it will lead you to Morebath and another circuit. But this is a great expenditure of leather; best return to the Strongs (see previous Route), to the shoemakers in the Toll House for some new shoes, or have a rest at the inn.

Other green lanes in the area

Those which feature in the next walk, plus remnants of lanes, now footpaths or bridleways, at Whitestone Down, Ashdown Farm and Coldharbour Farm.

Links

National Cycle Route Number 3. The Exe Valley Way at Coldharbour. Buses run along the Exe Valley and up to Taunton and Minehead. Buses run from Bampton to Minehead with limited stops at Morebath.

Question

Whose cow cake is suitable for all stock?

Route 14

MOREBATH (B)

Deep, deep 'Reformers' routes

OS Explorer Map 114

This is a very long route, taking you to the edge of Exmoor and back with quite a lot of road-walking. You will need it after Hawkridge Lane. You nudge into Somerset, and come close to the site of what once was Taunton's Priory at Barlynch.

Conditions: Very steep, muddy and slippery in places.

Distance: 5-6 miles.

Starting point: The church at Morebath SS954251, where you will find the answer to the question for this walk.

(1) Take the lane which leads north. If you take the main gate out of the churchyard, it is to your right; it was recorded in the 1530s as Gilbert's Lane. It is lined with oaks, spread equidistantly along its banks. The oaks on top of the banks are not as old as those which grow to form part of the bank, as these were originally part of the oak forests which covered all of this area. (Oakford is nearby).

(2) Hayne Cross is where Hawkridge Lane begins. When the monasteries were made illegal in 1536, a Dr Heynes was sent from Exeter with 12 recorders, and seemed to have spent a couple of years in the parish making sure that no relics were left in the church, that all statues and shrines to the saints including St John and Thomas à Becket were removed, and that St George's Day was no longer celebrated (see the church guide for further details).

Was this crossroads a point where people were checked for moving relics secretly about the parish? Was 'Hawk' a nickname for Dr Heynes? Hawkridge Lane is one of the most sunken – fifteen feet in places – and

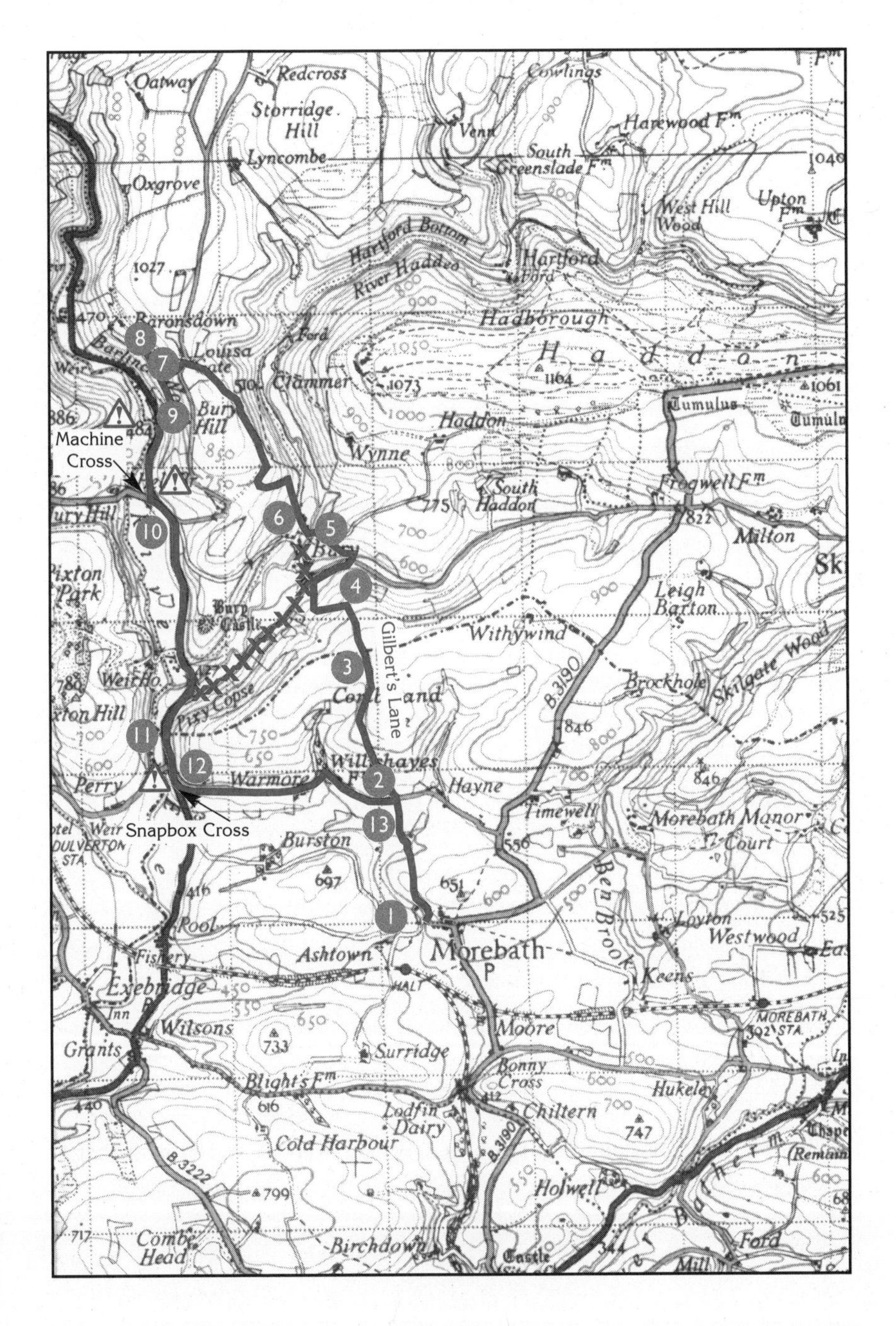
Machine Cross
Snapbox Cross
Gilbert's Lane
Morebath
Haddon
Hadborough
Storridge Hill
Redcross
Oatway
Lyncombe
Oxgrove
Baronsdown
Louisa Gate
Bury Hill
Clammer
Wynne
South Haddon
Frogwell Fm
Milton
Leigh Barton
Withywind
Brockhole
Skilgate Wood
Pixton Park
Pixy Copse
Weir Ho.
Warmore
Hayne
Timewell
Morebath Manor
Court
Burston
Ashtown
Exebridge
Wilsons
Grants
Surridge
Moore
Bonny Cross
Blight's Fm
Chiltern
Hukeley
Lodfin Dairy
Cold Harbour
Holwell
Combe Head
Birchdown
Westwood
Keens
Layton
Ben Brook
Hartford
Hartford Bottom
River Haddeo
Harewood Fm
South Greenslade Fm
West Hill Wood
Upton Fm
Venn
Cowlings

longest of the lanes you will meet on your explorations. Give yourself plenty of time to climb up through it, and notice its changing character as you go. There are lines of oaks, holly and beech on the double banks. The bent-over branches of the once-layered hedges can be up to three feet in girth, the wind whistling through the gaps now. There are cobbles, bare rock and grooves carved out of the sides of the lane in places.

(3) Here we come to the Hawkridge and the boundary with Somerset. A green lane runs to the right along the boundary here, and as you come out onto a plateau you can follow the boundary running over the fields in both directions. Plunge down again, or take the top path between the double hedge-bank, and just before reaching its end look over to the right and see Bury before you below. The enclosure on the map is visible from here as a dish with curved banks on either side. From here on to the end you are walking at least fifteen feet below the field line.

(4) You come out at Dyehouse Corner, where a sign tells you that you have just emerged from a Restricted Byway – no more wains from the disbanded Priory loaded with stained glass to block your way here. Now you have made it onto an even surface, consider and wonder how a load of stained glass, on five wains, was brought from the Priory up this path to Morebath. The stained glass is not in evidence in the church today.

Twenty-five households are recorded as having taken part in the dismantling of a chapel dedicated to St Mary, which stood at Bury and was used for the rebuilding of the Church House at Morebath. Trickey says that this was all performed by voluntary labour:

> "But if they should have done this for money, they would not have done it, and given such attendance, not for an angel and a nobel apiece for them, if it had not been to the church."

The parish sheep were probably driven up and down here on their way to Haddon Hill. With the Reformation well underway, there was a great sadness for the poorest parishioners in Morebath when the money which had been made from these parish sheep could no longer be used to keep a candle burning day and night in the church for the souls of those too poor to pay for such votives themselves. Carry straight on, passing the beautifully restored Gilclose, a 17th-century house and farm buildings to your left. Notice also the Bible Christian Chapel built in 1896.

(5) Go down towards the Ford and the askew-placed medieval bridge at Ford with its cobbled trackway. The pointed arches tell us that this was probably built by the monks of Barlynch. (At this point you may not want to carry further on into Somerset, and so can return via the lane to your left through Bury Cleeve and onto the A396.)

(6) If you continue, then cross the bridge and take another Restricted Byway to Louisa Gate.

(7) At the top, cross over beside a nature reserve set up by The League Against Cruel Sports. You will probably have seen some deer on your walk already.

(8) There is path to the left to link with the A396, signposted as a Road Used as a Public Path (RUPP). This is an interesting path with rhododendrons lining it in some parts and felled oaks showing the outline of some ridge and furrow ploughing in the fields to your right.

From **(9)** to **(12)** you are on the main road, but it is not too perilous – even joggers use it as part of their circuit. Once past Machine Cross, so named after the different kinds of machine which controlled the waters of half a dozen mills along the Exe here, you pass on your right a motte and bailey castle mound, heavily wooded. Turn off the road at Snapbox Cross and follow the minor road round to Hayne Cross **(13)** again. If you've no reliquaries to declare, then you can proceed safely down to Morebath once again!

By the way

These were turbulent times. First Henry VIII's Reformation changed the nature of worship and shifted centres of communication. The parishioners were no longer controlled by the monks who lived there. Yet this route directly up to the Moor continued for many years afterwards, for agricultural reasons.

Other green lanes in the area

Bampton, Route 12, plus previous Morebath Route.

Links

National Cycle Route 3. Buses run from Bampton to Minehead with limited stops at Morebath.

Question

Part of the church hedge to the left of the main entrance was maintained by Richard Rumbelow in 1531. This is what Trickey's records tell us, but how can we tell that this was so today?

Route 15

NORTH MOLTON

Towards the industrial north

OS Explorer Map 127

This walk takes you from the outskirts of South Molton to North Molton, climbing away from the many mills in the area up towards the beech and bracken of the lower slopes of Exmoor.

Conditions: Damp and steep.

Distance: 3-4 miles.

Starting point: SS722272.

(1) This is on the north side of the North Devon Link Road. Pass by the back of the small caravan site by the River Mole and you will begin to leave the roar of the Devon link road behind you. There are plenty of water-loving plants growing here, including cyprus sedge.

(2) At East Marsh carry along further up to a green lane junction at **(3)**. You may want to go and visit Bicknor Bridge down the lane to the right; if not, then follow a kerbed swoop to the right then over a stile into the bottom slope of a hilly meadow. There is a section of green lane here formed from five-foot-high sculptured furze bushes, which will take you into the predominantly conifer forest. On the river side of the path there is a row of pollarded alders, and many oaks here seem to have been layered.

(3) Turn left into Holdridge Lane and start climbing. There are well-worn grooves in the slate surface here. It is really only at this point that the winds of Exmoor in the trees begin to replace the sound of the cars on the North Devon Link Road. Through the hedges you can see acres and acres of willow, which is perhaps being grown as an alternative source of fuel.

(4) At the top, Bampfylde Clump comes into view as you turn right and walk into North Molton. There is much to enjoy in this village. The highway interest here centres around the highwayman Tom Faggus who, it is said, was a blacksmith here. Along with his horse Winnie he was famous for daring feats of escapology when confronted by constables. Retrace your steps to **(5)**; this minor road will take you down to your starting point by the River Mole, and gives good views over the valley and beyond.

(6) This will bring you out at the bottom of Burcombe Hill. You can walk back into South Molton from here, as there is a pavement all the way (put down by the railway company in 1871). This line ran from Barnstaple to Taunton and has, in part, been replaced by the North Devon Link Road.

By the way

North Molton is quite a large village, and gained its initial prosperity from the iron mines in the area. There were as many as 17 mines on both sides of the Mole Valley, producing iron, copper and occasionally gold, with stirring Victorian names reflecting the times of their greatest productivity: Prince Albert, Britannia, and Bamfylde – a local owner. His mine employed 100 men working at a depth of 700 feet. They earned a pound a week, and their assistants ('chaps') fifteen shillings. The ore was taken by packhorse trains running between North Molton, Combe Martin and Barnstaple. The one running between Charles and Goodleigh was a much-used route.

Other green lanes in the area

Return via Upcott and Burwell, or continue northwards to Heasley Mill.

Links

Buses run between Barnstaple, Exeter and Taunton into South Molton. There is a limited service from South Molton to North Molton.

Question

What is energy produced from plants called?

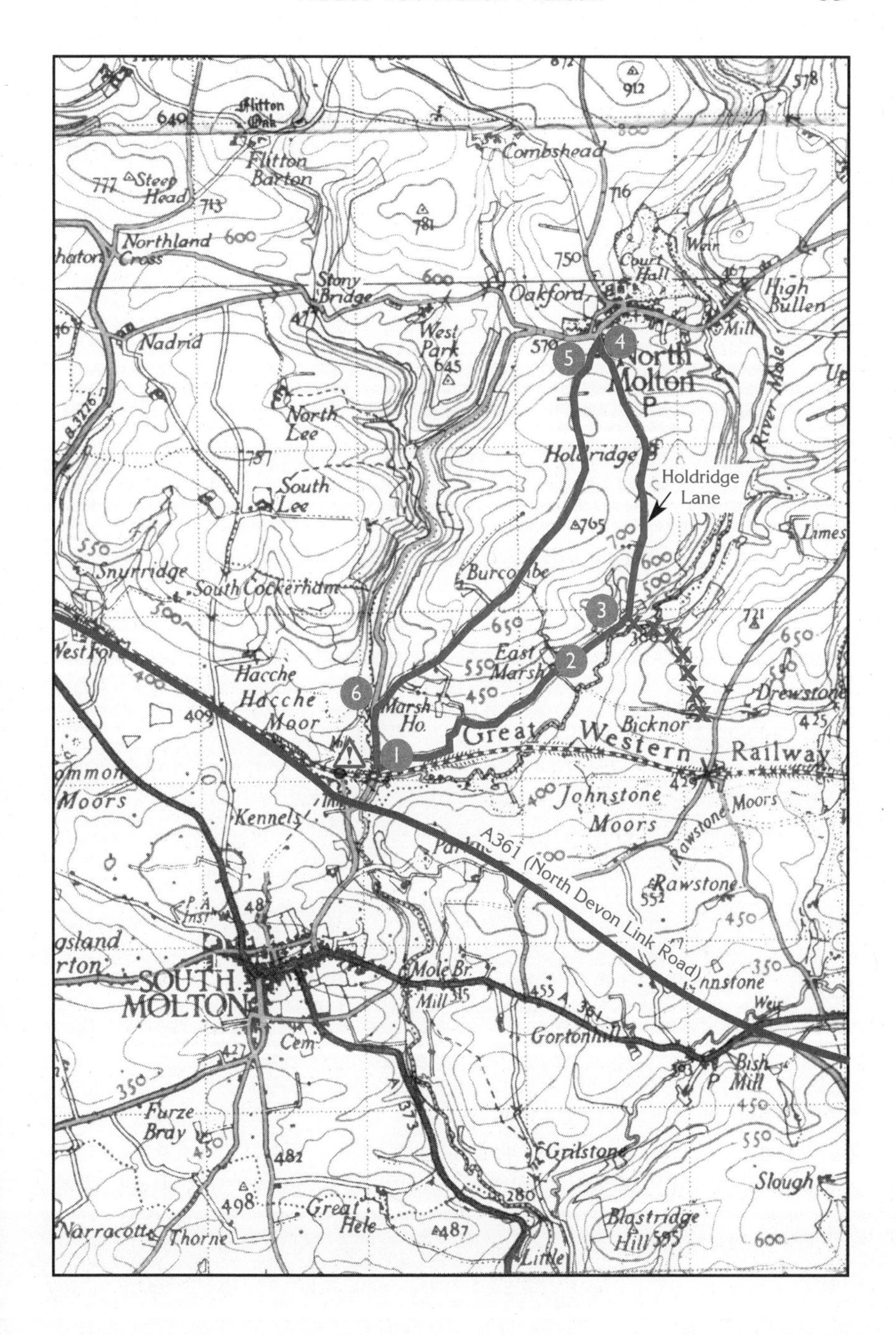

Holdridge Lane
North Molton
South Molton
Great Western Railway
A361 (North Devon Link Road)
Oakford
Court Hall
High Bullen
River Mole
Holdridge
Burcombe
East Marsh
Marsh Ho.
Hacche Moor
Johnstone Moors
Rawstone
Bicknor
Drewstone
Combshead
Flitton Barton
Steep Head
Northland Cross
Stony Bridge
West Park
Nadrid
North Lee
South Lee
Snurridge
South Cockerham
Hacche
Kennels
Mole Br.
Gortonhill
Bish Mill
Furze Bray
Great Hele
Grilstone
Blastridge Hill
Narracott
Thorne
Slough
1
2
3
4
5
6

Route 16

FLITTON OAK

OS Explorer Map OL9

This walk can be taken in almost a figure of eight, but what's interesting is how certain points – Stowford Cross, the Flitton Oak and Bampfylde Clump – move around each other in a triangular pattern throughout the walk. You are on the foothills of Exmoor, which you could see from Route 7, Rose Ash.

Conditions: Slippery and very wet in places.

Distance: 3-4 miles

Starting point: Northland Cross SS704305. There are no buses to this point, but there are plenty of parking places.

(1) You immediately begin to climb with Bampfylde Clump to your right and Dartmoor in front of you.

(2) At Steep Head the green lane to the Flitton Oak appears to your right (not signposted). There was a flock of chiffchaffs here in early spring amidst the overgrown ash hedge which, as you descend, gives way to grassy banks and tall sycamores with red sandstone and cobbles underfoot.

(3) You pass over a ford at Flitton Barns, and on your left is a monkey puzzle tree of some girth; but this is nothing compared to the 25-foot circumference of the oak which stands, supported by a metal prop, in the road triangle in front of you. The settlement of Flitton is mentioned in a 16th-century will.

(4) The oak is standing in a wooded triangle with oak and hazel coppice and holly bushes. Turn to the left and walk up to Huntstone Cross.

(5) Go straight over here, and the minor road will take you to Great Hunstone. To the right here you will see Easter Road, a private track. And why Easter? Could it have been used in some kind of religious ceremony connected to the stations of the cross?

(6) Keep to your right, but then take a sharp left up the green lane to

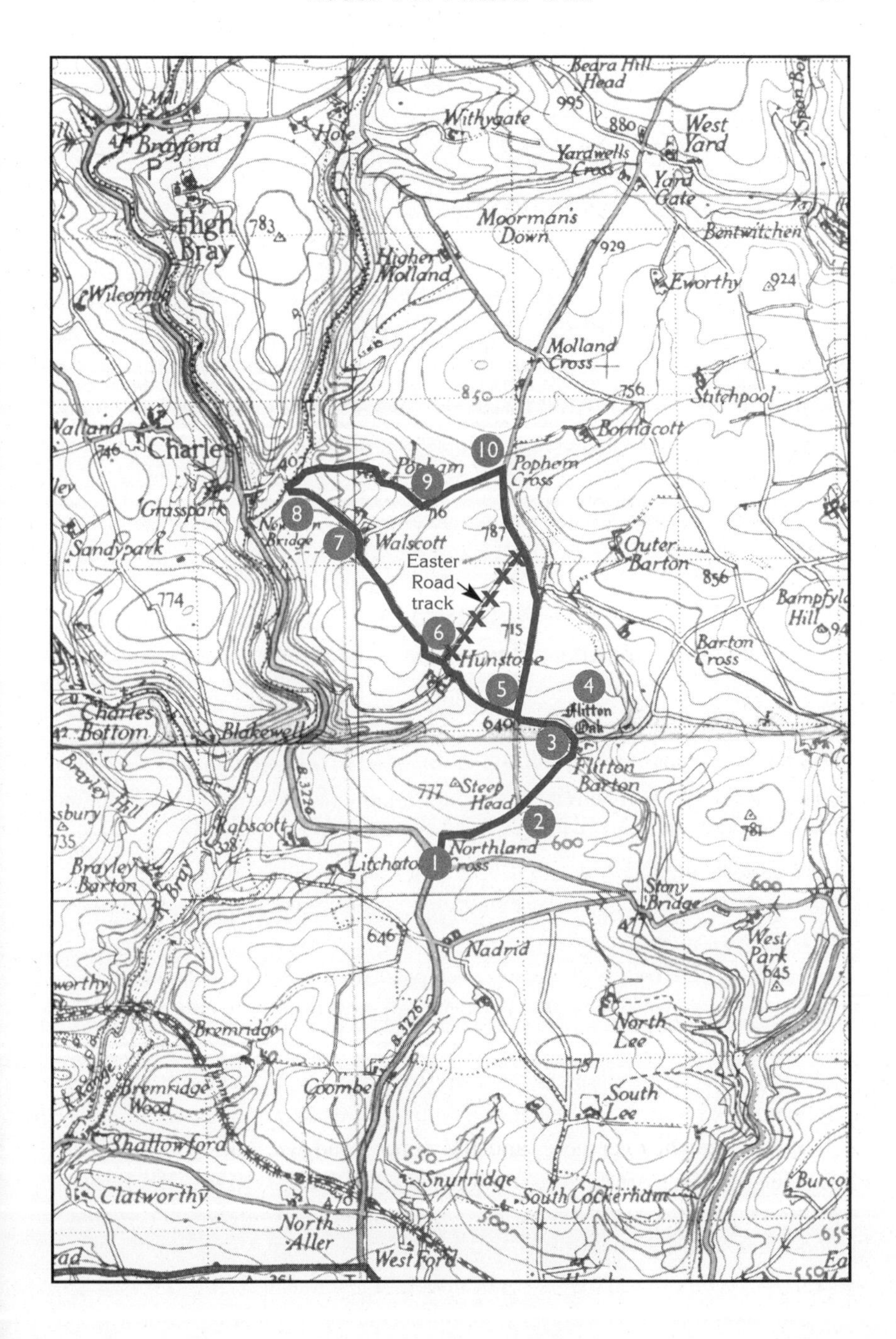
Beara Hill Head
995
880
West Yard
Withygate
Hole
Brayford
Yardwells Cross
Yard Gate
Moorman's Down
Bentwitchen
High Bray
783
929
Higher Molland
Eworthy
924
Wilcombe
Molland Cross
850
756
Stitchpool
Walland
Charles
746
10
Bornacott
Popham
Popham Cross
407
9
716
Grasspark
8
787
Newton Bridge
7
Walscott
Outer Barton
Sandypark
Easter Road track
856
774
Bampfylde Hill
6
715
Hunstone
Barton Cross
5
4
Flitton Oak
Charles Bottom
Blakewell
640
3
Flitton Barton
Brayley Hill
777
Steep Head
B.3226
2
Rabscott
735
Northland Cross
600
781
Brayley Barton
Litchaton
1
Stony Bridge
600
646
Nadrid
West Park
645
North Lee
Bremridge
757
Coombe
Bremridge Wood
South Lee
Shallowford
550
Snurridge
Clatworthy
South Cockerham
North Aller
West Ford
A.361

Walscott Farm. It is very wide to begin with, but then narrows at the top to form a very pleasant tunnel topped with hazel. You are walking towards the settlement of the 'walas' which means strangers. And so it seems, as you come out just before the farm to a view of a grey slate quarry being blasted and scraped over, with the square tower of Charles Church presiding over all.

(7) Turn sharp left downhill into another green lane without crossing the farm entrance. This is muddy and slippery with slate striations slipping down – be careful. The stream takes over in the end and you will have to keep to the middle where there is safer rock bed. You come out at Linkleyham Bridge, which is worth crossing to take a look at the Tarka Trail connection and the aptly named Rock Cross.

(8) Cross the bridge again and follow the steep road round to Popham where you will find another ancient oak tree by the road.

Notice on the left as you pass the farm buildings some sections of tumbling stone walling in the yard. Carry on to the next crossroads **(9)**. Turn left here. As you approach the next crossroads, notice on your right in the bank a rash of the lichen *Stereocaulon vesuvianum* – a grey, spongy-looking lichen with loosely branching stems clustering together (see picture above). It indicates, as you have already heard and seen, the mineral wealth of the area.

(10) Turn towards South Molton to the right and down to Northland Cross.

By the way

The triangle in which the oak stands may have something to do with how hunting practices changed in the 18th century. The fox became the big enemy, and planting small coverts to attract them became very popular. But, of course, the oak itself is much older than the 18th century, and is a boundary marker for the moor and the parish.

Other green lanes in the area

Over the valley of the river Bray to the west. Route 15, North Molton.

Links

The Tarka Trail. Buses run between Barnstaple, Exeter and Taunton into South Molton. There is a limited service from South Molton to North Molton.

Question

What's the name of the science which tells you how old a tree is by counting its growth rings?

The Flitton Oak

Route 17

PARRACOMBE

On traders' routes

OS Explorer Map OL9

This walk takes you past two churches, both of which are usually open to visit and have their tales to tell. The long lane on to the Moor itself is chosen as an example of a drovers' road which, as you will see, also includes a lane leading to a dip for the special breed of Exmoor sheep. This is not a circular walk, but merits a return run as the views are so sweeping and clear from the 1450' contour line. Because so many green lanes stick to valley bottoms and wooded areas, it is easy to forget that travelling was sometimes about visibility too.

Conditions: Surface mud in places.

Distance: 3-4 miles.

Starting point: The bus will leave you at the Inn SS667447.

(1) Look for the black-and-white post office sign, and follow this but turn sharp right before reaching it.

(2) A little way along the lane, look to your right and you can see the distinctive motte and bailey of the Norman castle of Holwell. The church of St Helen's appears to your left, standing high on a bailey itself. It is certainly not that old, having been built in 1877, but the list of incumbents inside will tell you that St Petrock himself, another Celtic saint from Cornwall, was here in 500BC. Continue up the lane and pass the school and a sign on the right for Sunnydale Farm (not Lorna Doone, as appears in my old map – was this a ruse to put literary hunters off the scent?)

(3) Cross over the bridge and you will see the second church of St Petrock on the left. Although the church is 13th-century in origin, what you see inside are the furnishings of a church 200 years ago. The smell of the plaster and the earth coming through the slates is chilling and stentorian, as

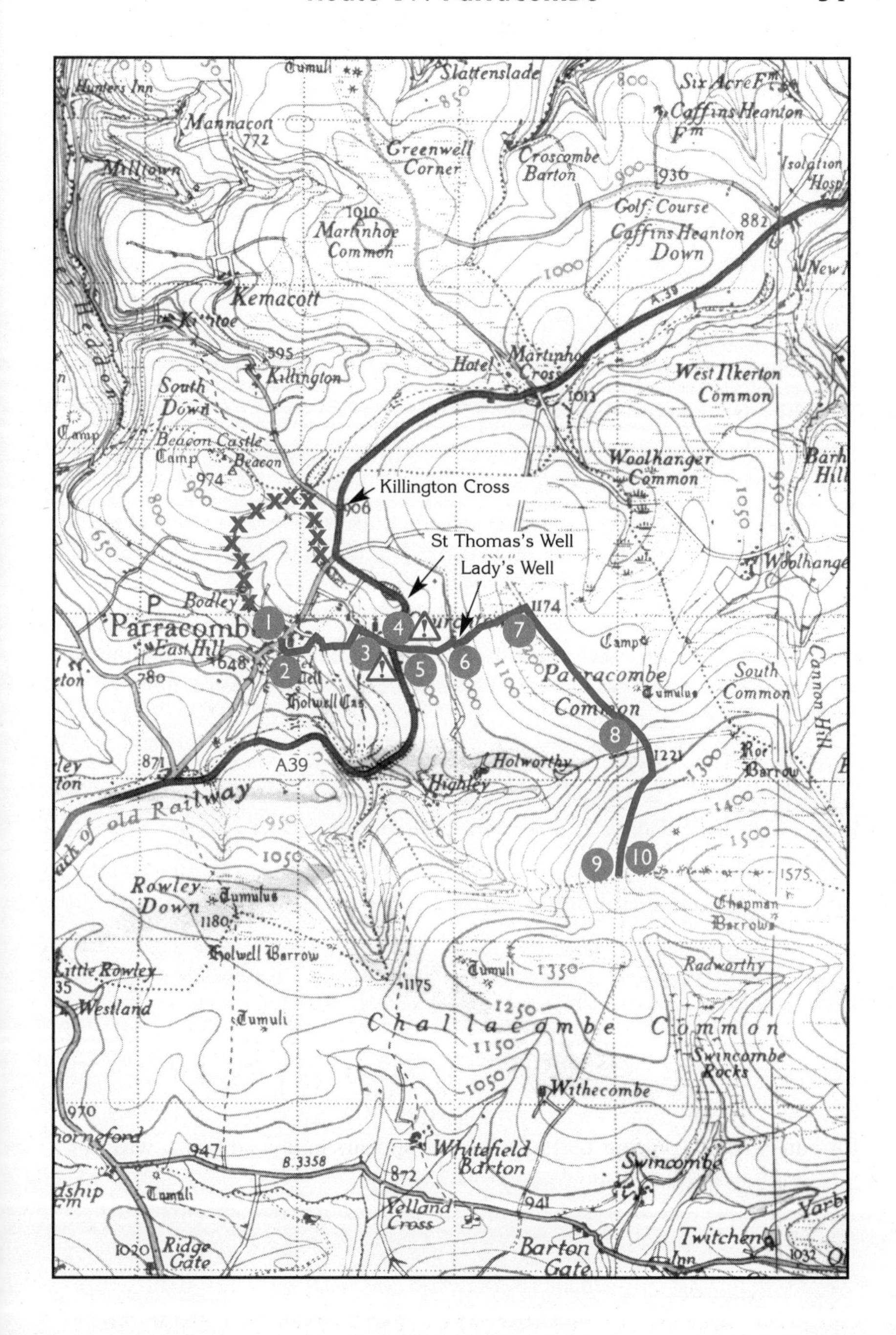
Killington Cross
St Thomas's Well
Lady's Well
A39
P
1
2
3
4
5
6
7
8
9
10
Parracombe
Slattenslade
Mannacott
Milltown
Greenwell Corner
Croscombe Barton
Six Acre Fm
Caffins Heanton Fm
Martinhoe Common
Golf Course
Caffins Heanton Down
Kemacott
Killington
Martinhoe Cross
Hotel
West Ilkerton Common
South Down
Beacon Castle
Camp
Beacon
Woolhanger Common
Bodley
East Hill
Holwell Cas
Parracombe Common
South Common
Cannon Hill
Holworthy
Highley
Roe Barrow
Rowley Down
Tumulus
Holwell Barrow
Chapman Barrows
Radworthy
Little Rowley
Westland
Tumuli
Challacombe Common
Swincombe Rocks
Withecombe
Whitefield Barton
Swincombe
Yelland Cross
Barton Gate
Twitchen
Inn
Ridge Gate
B.3358

are some of the oval plaques around the walls, but nicely placed with biblical quotations such as "Let all things be done decently and in order." Outside, again follow the bridleway sign and go straight ahead into Stony Lane.

(4) Take care crossing the road here. Continue on the lane on the other side of the A39 towards Parracombe Common. Through a gate and on your right is Lady's Well, locked up and housed in concrete.

(5) At the head of the lane keep to your left and follow the narrow pack-horse lane indicated by blue paint on the gatepost. The name of Parracombe itself is thought to have come from 'pedlar's valley'. The nearby presence of Chapman Barrows re-enforces this idea, as the word refers to traders.

The lane twists, and at **(6)** you are in a tarmacked lane which climbs up towards the Moor. There are views over to Hangman's Hill at Combe Martin from here, and a quarry which probably employed people from the village at some point in its history.

(7) Turn right at the junction and you enter a very straight piece of road hedged by beech and well-surfaced. The sea becomes visible through breaks in the beeches.

(8) (Here to the left is the way to the sheep dip, over two sets of fences to Roe Barrow lining up behind Chapman Barrows. But it is best to explore this avenue when you descend.) The lane becomes unsurfaced here and very wide, with some magnificent examples of hedge-laying involving the felling of beech branches two or more feet wide. This gives way on the left to thinner sections of sliced-off pleachers.

(9) At the top, at Two Gates, there is actually only one; you have the Moor in front of you and the way to Withycombe Gate, the second one which eventually leads to Challacombe.

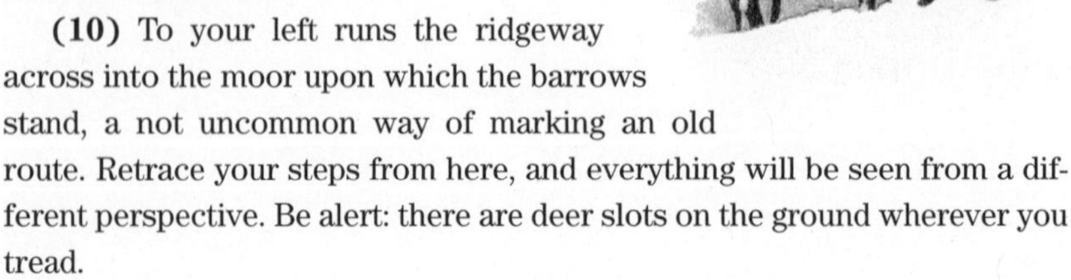

(10) To your left runs the ridgeway across into the moor upon which the barrows stand, a not uncommon way of marking an old route. Retrace your steps from here, and everything will be seen from a different perspective. Be alert: there are deer slots on the ground wherever you tread.

By the way

The conditions for farming up here were always difficult. In 1838, in a report made by the Tithe Commission, it was said that places such as High Bray were twelve miles from any form of manure, and that lime had to be brought in at the cost of £4 10s an acre. The tithe was taking 4s 6d for each acre, so arable production never made a profit. However, pasture for sheep was what was really needed. Geoffrey Grigson states that packhorses could carry up to 400 lb of manure, sand, lime or seaweed in one go. 200 horseloads per acre was standard, and a packhorse train usually had nine beasts, so there was a lot of work for the chapmen. But although arable was won back from the moor, it was the introduction of Cheviot sheep from Scotland (along with their shepherds) in 1871 on a grand scale, that determined the moor's main agricultural use from then until now. Who used these tracks – and why – will always intrigue walkers following in unknown footsteps.

Other green lanes in the area

There are those as marked to Bodley on the map. Notice the St Thomas Well, another reminder of the conscience of the nation in regard to the assassination of Thomas à Becket (see Route 49).

Here you are very close to many green lanes, which lead to the coast at Woody Bay and east towards Lynmouth and Lynton. As these are so well known and used, with many well-known stories attached to them I have not written about them here.

Links

There is a bus service from Barnstaple to Lynton passing through Parracombe.

Question

The hedges leading up to the Moor have been cut in a special way. Sometimes a chainsaw must have been used, but what hand tool has sliced its way through here?

Route 18

COMBE MARTIN

Strawberries on silver salvers

OS Explorer Map 139

At the age of five months I first opened my eyes on the beauties of Devon: it was to Combe Martin that I was evacuated from the east side of London in 1944. Accommodation was tight for this, my first holiday by the sea, and I slept in a drawer in a boarding house along the front. My father would pedal-cycle down from London to visit us at the weekends, a round trip of 395 miles in the blackout across Exmoor, where many roads were still unmade.

He arrived on Saturday morning and left on Sunday night, and still had enough energy to enjoy a stroll up Hangman's Hill. We always returned to the area for family holidays, when I must first have explored some of these lanes in this circuit. This walk is dedicated to my father and to that generation of cyclists who used their bikes just as we now use our cars.

Conditions: Rocky, watery and steep in places.

Distance: 3-4 miles.

Starting point: This village, with the longest high street in Britain, can be approached from where the 'headtowners' live around the church at SS587464, or down on the harbour SS575473, where the 'seasiders' live. This description begins from the seaside end.

(1) Take the bend of the A399 on the coast, west of the town at Furze Park. Take the footpath on the left towards Crackaleigh Farm. This is a wide, well-used green lane. As you approach the campsite the lane will take you over a stile to the left.

(2) West Park Lane begins life here as a track running up the side of the hillside. Watch out for the wonderful 1950s-style black-and-white finger-posts. **(3)** Keep following the public footpath signs, which will take you

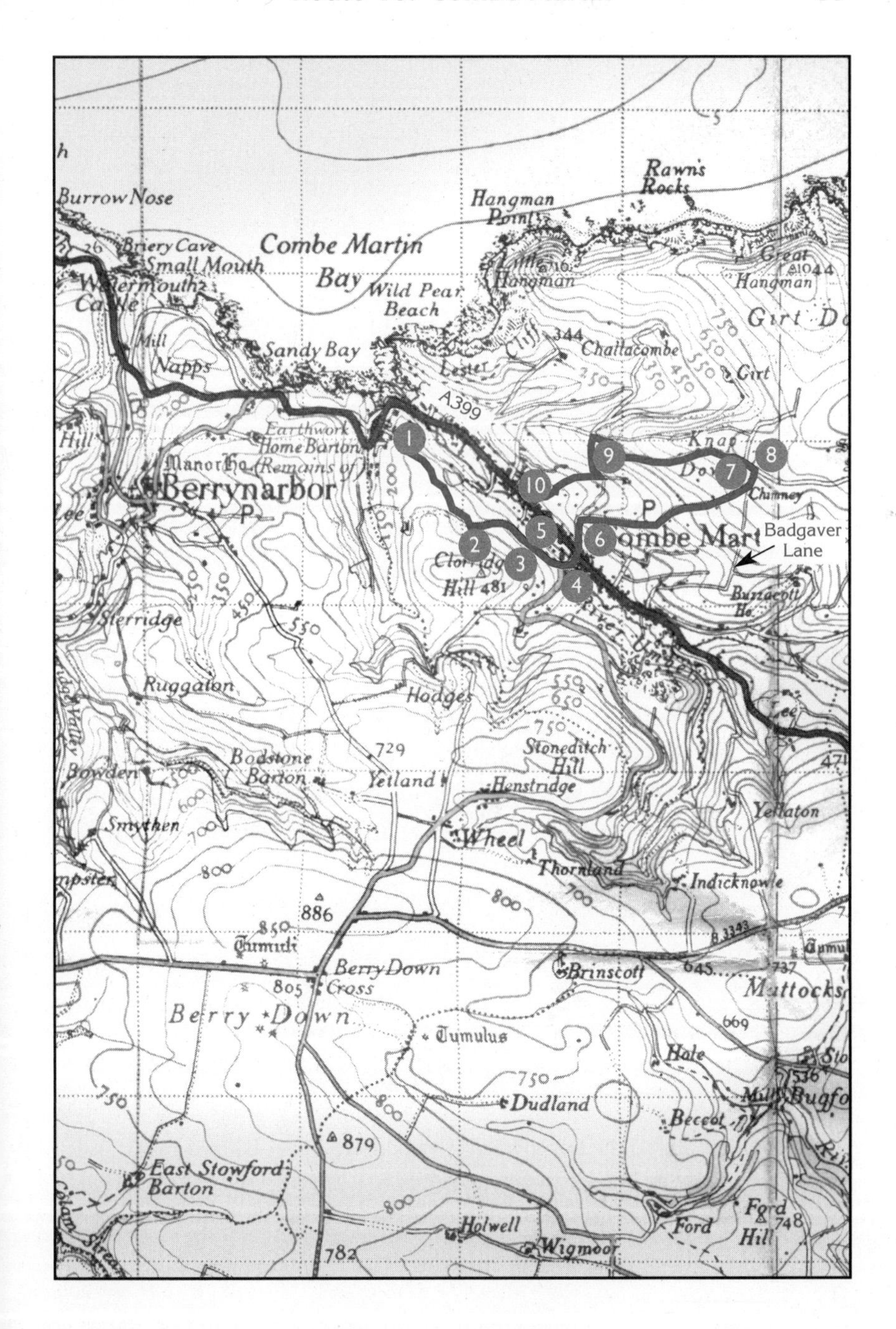
Burrow Nose
Briery Cave
Small Mouth
Watermouth Castle
Combe Martin Bay
Wild Pear Beach
Hangman Point
Rawns Rocks
Little Hangman
Great Hangman
1044
Girt Down
Mill
Napps
Sandy Bay
344
Challacombe
Lester
Girt
A399
Earthwork
Home Barton
Manor Ho. (Remains of)
Berrynarbor
Knap Down
Chimney
Combe Martin
Badgaver Lane
Clorridge Hill 481
Buzzacott Ho.
River Umber
Sterridge
Ruggaton
Hodges
Stoneditch Hill
729
Yetland
Henstridge
Bodstone Barton
Bowden
Smythen
Wheel
Thornland
Yellaton
Indicknowle
886
850
Tumuli
B 3343
Brinscott
645
737
Berry Down Cross
805
Mattocks
Berry Down
Tumulus
669
Hole
536
Mill
Bugford
750
Dudland
Becott
879
East Stowford Barton
Ford Hill
748
Ford
Holwell
Wigmoor
782
1
2
3
4
5
6
7
8
9
10

down **(4)** into another green lane which becomes a minor road and gives you good views of the mining and horticultural areas on the opposite side of the valley which you will explore later. It leads to the church of St Peter ad Vincula, with its imposing sanctuary ring on the door.

The uneasy relationship between those who worked and those who owned the land is re-enacted every year in May with 'The Hunting of the Rone'. The Rone, a metaphor for the absentee landlord, is captured in Ladies Wood, mounted back to front on a donkey and driven down into the sea.

(5) Turn into Church Street and up into the High Street slightly to the left, looking for **(6)** the public footpath to your right on the opposite side of the road at the beginning of Corner Lane.

This lane cuts its way through rock, where it becomes green and climbs up a path streaming with water. At a point just before the disused silver mines there is an interesting gully. How much silver slithered unnoticed down here? There are good views from the gates here over to Combe Martin Bay and beyond. There are also remains of little stone-faced holding areas in places, some stonewalling coming up to Knap Down Cottage and of course the disused chimney stack covered in ivy and the disused chimney.

(7) You will come to a junction here, and if you have time, before continuing your circuit go down into another deep miners' lane, strangely named Badgaver, to your right. The lane drops into a deep sunken, well-worn steep holloway lined with overgrown pollarded ash trees. The tarmac disintegrates and gives way to slippery slate striations mixed with cobblestones, up which many a weary miner must have tramped. If you go down to Skirhead Lane, you will pass a line of tiny miners' cottages.

If you stick to the circuit at the top, then turn left here **(8)** and you emerge into an almost moor-like habitat with clear views all around. Continue along to Netherton Cross **(9)** and dive down into the green lane to your left, Pentice Lane, a narrow sunken one running behind a nursery and the strip fields where once strawberries, new potatoes and other produce were cultivated for the emerging tourist industry at the end of the 19th century; in June and July schools closed so that the children could help.

By following the footpath signs to your left you will emerge at **(10)** by the Baptist Chapel into the High Street again.

By the way

The silver mines which have been used by miners trudging up here for over 700 years and were excavated to a depth of 800 feet, saw downward lane traffic carrying silver, antimony, tin and lead.

Some made fortunes, but for the miners themselves it was just a steady job in appalling conditions which did, however, pay better than farm labouring. Elizabeth Ernst, travelling through the area in 1845, notes that the mines employed 30 to 40 people in different processes. She says that:

> "One ton of picked ore produces 20 ounces of silver, antimony and lead all worth about twenty pounds."

Of the children in Combe Martin she says they were:

> "Ragged and sickly looking, the victims of hunger and disease."

Perhaps the growth of tourism – especially with the arrival of the railway in Ilfracombe in 1874 – brought some of these children out of the mines and onto the strawberry fields, a healthier if not a more prosperous life. The fruit was grown and exported from here to Wales in the 1860s. There are photographs of children gathering horse manure for the beds on one August Bank Holiday Monday in 1899. Up to 140 horses came to the village that day.

Other green lanes in the area

East Down towards Coombe and around the church.

Links

National Cycle Route 3. The Tarka Trail. Buses run along here from Barnstaple towards Lynmouth.

Question

You didn't want to be caught doing this when you should have been doing the equivalent in the mines with your eyes open.

Route 19

ILFRACOMBE

'The Call of Chambercombe': a ghostly story set in an idyllic valley

OS Explorer Maps 139 and OL9

Conditions: Rocky and slippery in places.

Distance: 3-4 miles.

Starting point: Take Ilfracombe's section of the South West Way up towards Hillsborough from Cove at SS527477.

(1) This section of the coastal path is spectacularly vertical, and illustrates how the glacial activity shaped the valleys behind. Start looking for white quartz veins, which are solidified lava. This strenuous section will set you up for the gentler valley to come. Walk along the A361 to Hele.

(2) Cross over the A361, and then go down, turning left towards Hele Business Park along the lane signed as a dead end. There is an old chapel in front of you here, now part of the industrial complex. In nearby Witheridge Place, pushed back against a wall on the right is a remnant of highway history, an old restriction sign complete with a red warning disc, which reads:

> The 1930 Road Traffic Act
> ALL LOCOMOTIVES HEAVY MOTOR CARS AND
> MOTOR CARS WITH SEATS FOR MORE THAN 15
> PERSONS PROHIBITED

The locomotives referred to here are those engines which drove threshing machines after the harvest. This restriction seems a little unfair, as the farms in the valley, unlike the tourist charabancs, really needed this service.

(3) Nearby to this the road joins another, and there is a wooden sign to Littleton and Comyn over a fast-flowing leat. Turn right here.

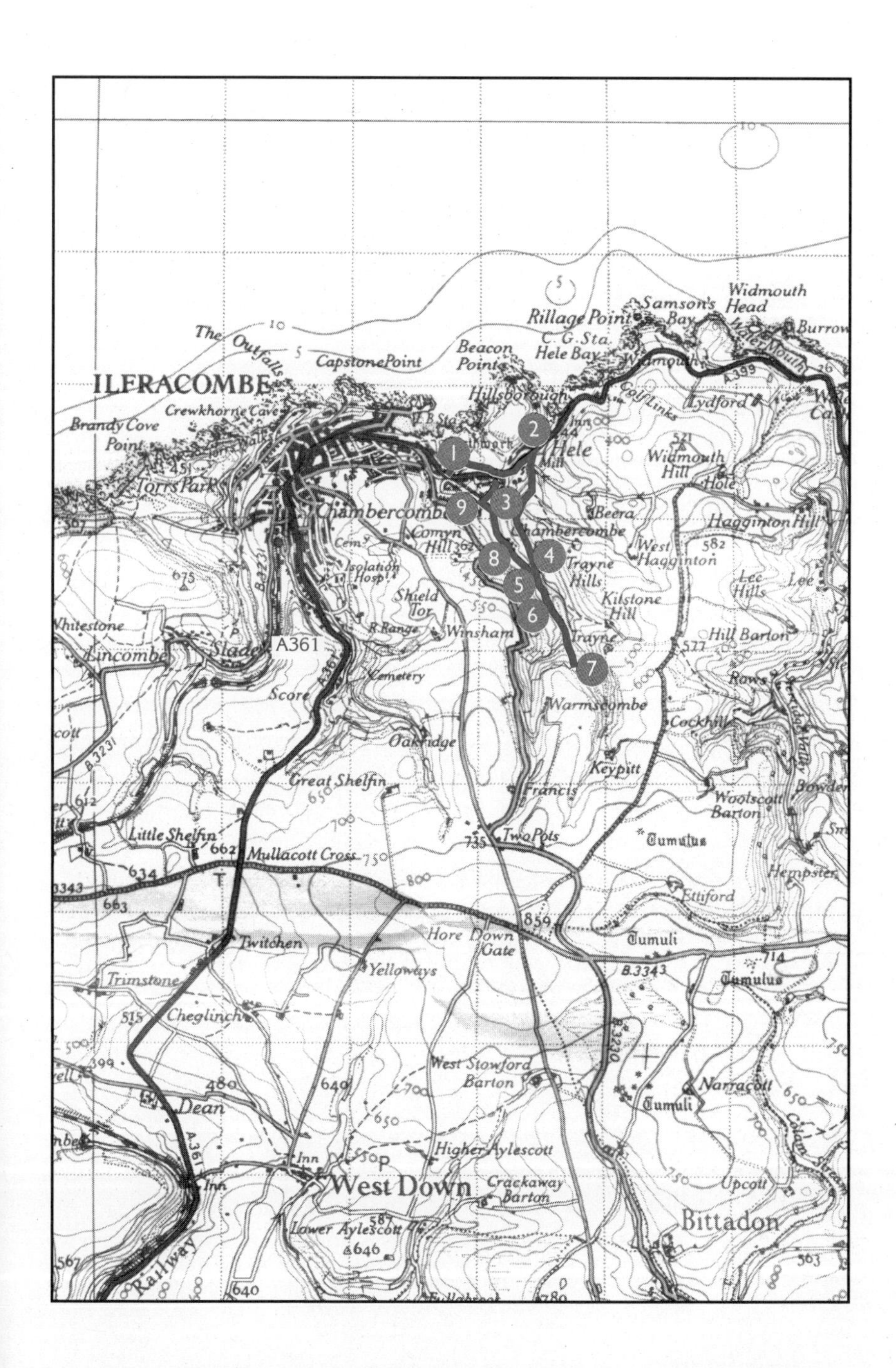
ILFRACOMBE
The Outfalls
Capstone Point
Beacon Point
Rillage Point
C. G. Sta.
Hele Bay
Samson's Bay
Widmouth Head
Burrow
Hillsborough
Brandy Cove Point
Crewkhorne Cave
Torrs Park
Chambercombe
Comyn Hill
Hele
Mill
Beera
Golf Links
Lydford
Widmouth Hill
Hole
Hagginton Hill
West Hagginton
Trayne Hills
Kilstone Hill
Trayne
Lee Hills
Lee
Hill Barton
Rows
Isolation Hosp.
Cem.
Shield Tor
R. Range
Winsham
Whitestone
Lincombe
Slade
A361
Score
Cemetery
Warmscombe
Cockhill
Oakridge
Keypitt
Great Shelfin
Francis
Woolscott Barton
Little Shelfin
Mullacott Cross
Two Pots
Tumulus
Hempster
Ettiford
Hore Down Gate
Tumuli
Twitchen
Yelloways
B.3343
Trimstone
Cheglinch
West Stowford Barton
Narracott
Dean
Higher Aylescott
Inn
West Down
Crackaway Barton
Upcott
Bittadon
Lower Aylescott
Railway
A361
B3230
A399
B3231

(4) Watch out for a sign on your left here which says Jewel Cottage, at the mouth of the public footpath green lane. Imagine bringing a steamroller up here! Although this lane begins widely as it climbs up into the valley, it is steep and sunken, and the hedges arc festooned with trailing ivy as it narrows.

Early touring car

(5) At the top of the gradient go straight ahead through a gate and into a hazel-lined green lane, known as Cat Lane. Views of the Chambercombe Valley emerge, the lane becomes narrower and grassy underfoot, and there are some dramatic sections of thickly layered sycamore hedge towards the end.

(6) There is another gate by a fine section of wall with quartz intrusions which sparkle in the sun. Turn right into Comyn Farm, then follow the footpath sign to your left and up into another green lane to the right. This farm was kept going by one family well into their old age (as was the Luxton's farm at Winkleigh), and is now being modernised, but not to be farmed as it once was.

(7) This old lane is a model of the type which led from a farm up into its top fields. There is a beech wood on your left, with some odd, thickly layered branches within. It is muddy most of the way, and the hedge-bank has collapsed. There is a fork to the right, but keep climbing to your left where the lane's slippery, grooved surface exposes the volcanic quartz.

It ends in a wooden gate, through which you emerge into a bracken-fringed meadow overlooked by the Trayne Hills. This is the place to sit and read 'The Call of Chambercombe' (see following page for details). Return by the same lane and go back through Comyn Farm **(8)**, this time taking the bridleway to the left which will take you to Chambercombe Manor itself.

(9) At the top of the drive go straight down over Chambercombe Road, passing yet another converted old chapel on your left. Within view is Capstone Chapel, high above Ilfracombe and overlooking the sea.

By the way

'The Call of Chambercombe' is one of the best spooky stories in North Devon. I precis it here, but for the full melodramatic experience of the novelette you will have to seek out a second-hand copy of the story, which was written by a Mr Pincombe in 1959 (see Bibliography). The library service can always oblige.

The origin of the story comes from a former resident of the Manor House who, shortly after moving in, noticed whilst making repairs that there were four casement windows upstairs but only three rooms. On breaking down the partition which lead into this unused room, he found a four-poster bed with the skeletal remains of a lady richly dressed and with a cross at her throat. Legend has it that she was the daughter of the last resident of Chambercombe. He was a man who had lived here as a tenant, and whose greatest wish was to own the house for himself. He achieved his dream and lost his daughter all in a stormy night when he found her body, unrecognisable and bedecked with jewels, at the end of the lane which leads to the beach at Hele. Her fine jewels enabled him to buy the house, but then he discovered who she was, and had his sad secret entombed in the house with him. Be careful what you wish for.

Other green lanes in the area

There are none really close by on this sea-dominated promontory. But to link up with Route 18, Combe Martin, there is a short circular walk from Hole at SS557474 or you can link up with the Georgeham walk, Route 24.

Links

The South West Way. The Tarka Trail. Buses run along here from Barnstaple towards Lynmouth.

Question

What kind of locomotive might you once have found here?

Route 20

SOUTH MOLTON

Swimbridge, or Swing bridge?

OS Explorer Maps 127 and OL9

This is a walk which will take you into the dark conifer rides under the sweeping curves of the North Devon Link Road and up to the high ridgeways overlooking the coast. It is very hilly country, and must always have been difficult to cultivate. Maintaining its remoteness seemed to have been promoted by the turnpike road upon which Swimbridge stands. This was improved in 1828 as it was the direct route from South Molton to Barnstaple.

However, the villages close by in the valleys and hills around remained unconnected, as the turnpike trustees considered the country:

> "Too wild and unpopular a district which cannot be expected to produce any adequate return."

It became even wilder a few years later.

Conditions: Steep and slippery in places.

Distance: 4-5 miles.

Starting point: SS636294 Kerscott Cross.

(1) Begin at Kerscott Lane, which is signed as a road 'Unfit For Motors' and begins on a dangerous bend – be careful. You are soon into this lightly cobbled lane, along with the pheasants and partridge who panic in front of you. As you proceed, there are views out to the Atlantic headlands. The jagged lines of Braunton Burrows appear to your left over the Indiwell Valley. This is the venue for spectacular light shows in the summer, and was once famous for breeding geese.

You are on top of a line of steep rounded hills which run down to the sea at least 15 miles away. The outline of Braunton Burrows is quite clear. In the

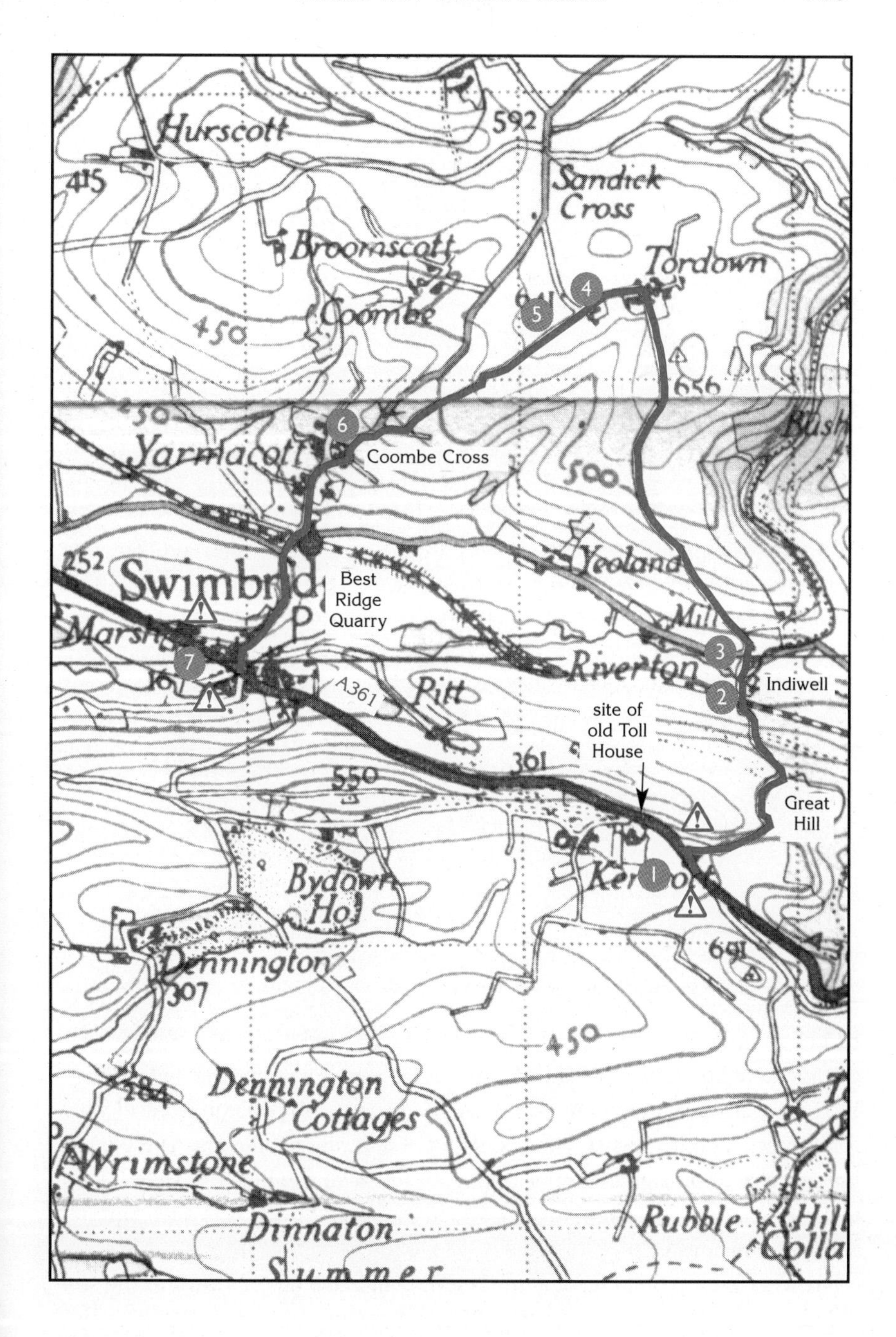
Hurscott
415
592
Sandick Cross
Broomscott
Tordown
Coombe
450
4
5
6
Yarmacott
Coombe Cross
500
Swimbridge
Best Ridge Quarry
Yeoland
Mill
Marsh
7
3
Riverton
Indiwell
2
A361
Pitt
site of old Toll House
361
550
Great Hill
1
Bydown Ho
691
Dennington
307
450
284
Dennington Cottages
Wrimstone
Dinnaton
Rubble

distance to the right the Great Hill looms. This is where in December of 1830 a group of 150 farm labourers from Swimbridge and Landkey assembled to complain about low wages and to ask for the abolition of tithes which they believed were causing their hardship. They had already visited the Magistrate Mr Nott's House at 'Bydown'. Lord Ebrington, Fortescue's son and a liberal, who was accidentally riding that way, addressed the mob. He learned that the rebels were to meet again, so he called in the North Devon Yeomanry. The sergeants had just been issued with new firelock arms known as fusils, which helped to deter any further rebellion.

(2) From here you plunge down into the Indiwell plantation along a deeply rutted 'stoggy' lane well used by 'gamers' of all descriptions. There is a double hedge-bank to your right, and the beeches on the banks give way to a dark conifer wood as you descend. You now pass under the A361 and over a bridge with sluice gates for the mills along the valley. There is a fine section of upright slate rivetments here. You are now in a tarmacked road, and a sign appears at the end of this green lane which states that it is a bridleway.

(3) At Duckslake Farm turn left, then sharp right at Fairweather Cottage. The road bears left, and suddenly loses its surface to become a green lane. You are in a five-foot-wide lane with a flat camber and smooth, worn, grey slate gulleys either side, almost a foot deep in some places. This area of loamy soil was chiefly given over to wheat a hundred years ago, which found its way to the mills along the rivers below, being transported on 'wains, drays, tumbrils, drags, sledges, or 'butts', which were crude horse- or hand-drawn vehicles. It is a long haul up this lane, but there are some gaps in the hedges where you can catch a glimpse of Swimbridge below and the ever-present Atlantic coast. There is a break on the left with some old ash layering starkly exposed.

From *The Yeomanry of Devon 1794 – 1927* (St Catherine's Press).

(4) Eventually large beeches appear to the right, and the lane curves down to Tordown House. At its end you join the made-up road where, to the right, there is a sign for tea and the Tor Down Farm Trail. Follow the cob wall road to your left to a junction showing you have traversed yet another

'Unsuitable for Motors' lane.

(5) At Long Barn, go straight into another 'Unsuitable for Motors' lane which is wide, relaxing and descending.

(6) At Coombe Cross bear left and down into Swimbridge itself at **(7)**.

By the way

Memories of the hunting parson Sir John Russell are still strong here – mostly affectionate and amusing. He set up two chapels-at-ease for the remote lands here in the south, at Traveller's Rest in 1866 (SS613273) and another in the north at Gunn in 1873 (SS634335). But think of those who had to be ready with the horses to take him, every Sunday, on his three-sermon round from Swimbridge.

In 1902 there were still four blacksmiths' forges here. These have a network of green lanes surrounding them, and provide a good example of what is involved in dating a green lane.

The fact that the lanes are still here today is a consequence of what happened after new routes were set up. In this case, it was the demise of church-going from the early 20th century onwards, the non-support of the turnpike companies in linking up the area, and the desperation of the farm labourers.

The very small outbreak of unrest at Kerscott was part of what was known nationally as the 'Captain Swing' movement, set up against rising prices, harsh conditions and newfangled machinery. It is possible that because of political implications, the leader in this case was not transported but spent 18 months in prison instead.

Other green lanes in the area

Stoke Rivers and over to Bratton Fleming.

Links

Swimbridge is on bus routes into Barnstaple, and one which goes to Taunton.

Question

What is the name of a certain breed of small dog once associated with this village?

Route 21

BISHOP'S TAWTON

Rivers, rolling waves, runner beans and routes to come

OS Explorer Map 139

Wherever you look on this walk there are spectacular views: across valleys, over rivers, to the sea, to turnpikes, to quarries, to the moors and to the villages all around. This walk is placed towards the end of the first half of the circuits, and will give you a very dramatic overview of where you have been walking. You can also see some of the Routes to come from Codden Beacon.

Conditions: Steep in places and very slippery in the green lanes.

Distance: 3-4 miles, extendable to 6.

Starting point: SS566302 Bishop's Tawton church, overlooking the River Taw, Tawstock and St Michael's School on top of the hill.

(1) Tear yourself away from this idyllic spot and take the Old Exeter Road to the right, where a sign brings you swiftly into the New Road, widened and repaired in 1828. Pass Village Street and Park Villas on your left. There is a farm nearby which spills out onto the pavement.

(2) At Codden Hill Cross turn left towards Cobbaton. Take the road to the right, passing an eco-friendly wooden house up the hill. You now have Codden Hill to your left and the Taw Valley to your right. There is a milestone to the right on the bend at the top which states that Barum is three miles away.

The strata of rocks and sands and some exposed quarry faces to your left range in colour from bright yellow to black. The furze is abundant here, along with sheep who shelter by its thorny stems. There has been some impressive tree-planting all along the bank here. To your right looms west Dartmoor, and further north the Hartland plateau tips up in the distance.

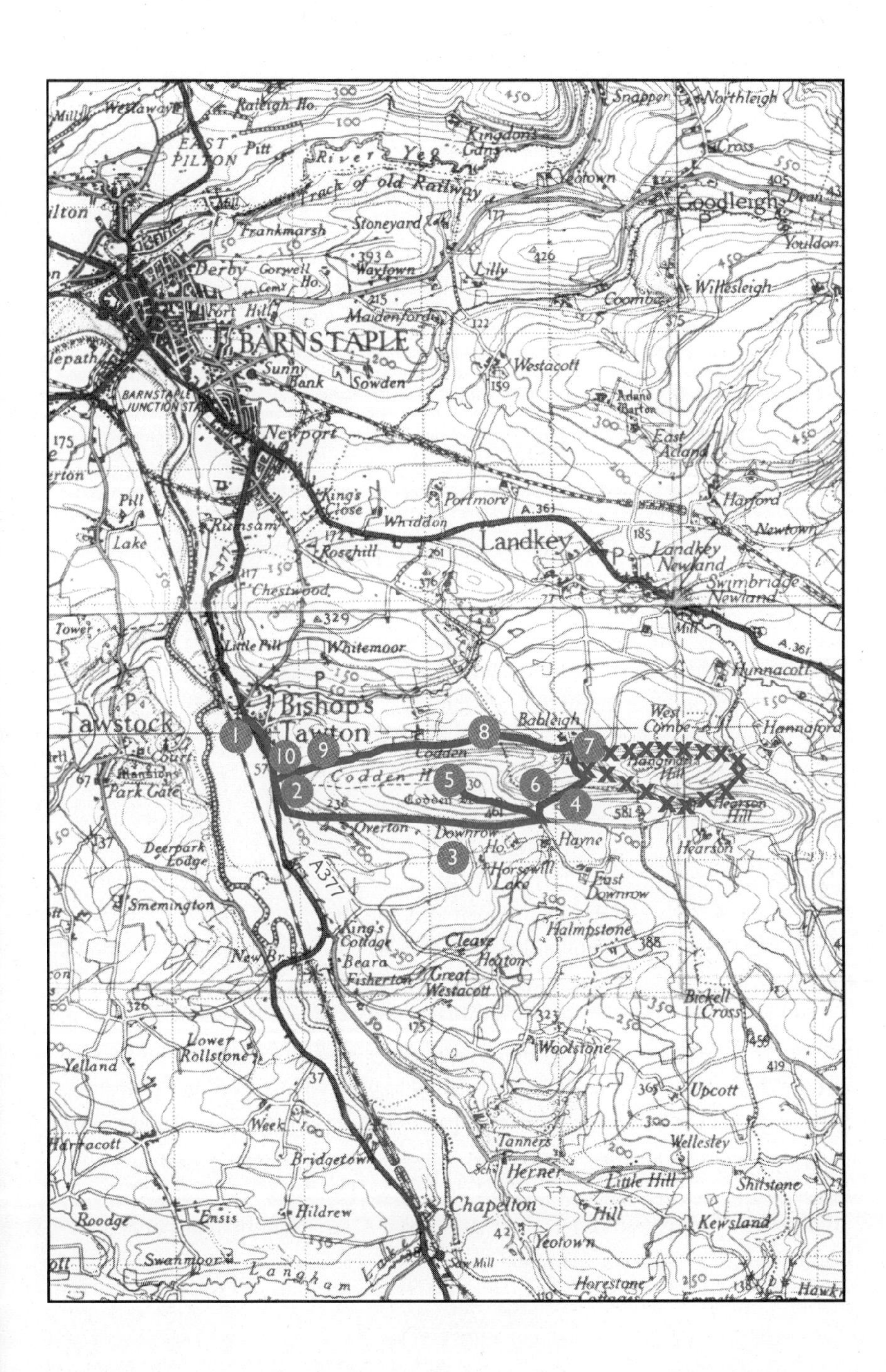
Raleigh Ho.
Snapper
Northleigh
EAST PILTON
Pitt
River Yeo
Kingdons Gdns
Cross
Track of old Railway
Yeotown
Goodleigh
Youldon
Frankmarsh
Stoneyard
Derby
Gorwell Ho.
Waytown
Lilly
Willesleigh
Fort Hill
Maidenford
Coombe
BARNSTAPLE
Sunny Bank
Sowden
Westacott
Acland Barton
BARNSTAPLE JUNCTION STA.
Newport
East Acland
Pill
King's Close
Portmore
Harford
Whiddon
A.361
Rumsam
Newtown
Lake
Rosehill
Landkey
Landkey Newland
Chestwood
Swimbridge Newland
Tower
Mill
Little Pill
Whitemoor
A.361
Hunnacott
Bishop's Tawton
Bableigh
West Combe
Hannaford
Tawstock Court
Codden
Hanging Hill
Mansion
Park Gate
Codden Hill
Codden Beacon
Hearson Hill
Overton
Downrow Ho.
Hayne
Hearson
Deerpark Lodge
A377
Horsewill Lake
East Downrow
Smemington
Halmpstone
King's Cottage
Cleave
New Br.
Beara
Heaton
Fisherton
Great Westacott
Bickell Cross
Lower Rollstone
Woolstone
Yelland
Upcott
Week
Harracott
Tanners
Wellesley
Bridgetown
Herner
Little Hill
Shilstone
Chapelton
Roodge
Ensis
Hildrew
Hill
Kewsland
Yeotown
Swanmoor
Langham Lake
Saw Mill
Horestone
1
2
3
4
5
6
7
8
9
10

(3) As you approach Downrow House notice the pattern of the market garden/smallholding green lanes in the distance on your right. There is another milestone here telling you that you are now one mile from Barum.

(4) To your left is a green lane, partly tarmacked with chippings, which leads up to a little car-parking area. Keep to your left through the gate, which will take you up and along to the beacon **(5)**, the height and views of the distance increasing as you go.

This is one of the 'whale-backed' hills of the area, formed by the collision of tectonic plates millions of years ago. It is also the site of a Bronze Age bowl barrow. You will soon reach the granite beacon, an urn on a tapering pillar, set on a grassy mound and faced on the west with stone. You are 189 feet above sea level. It was erected in 1970 in memory of Caroline, wife of the Liberal Jeremy Thorpe, and is the work of the stonemason Henry Tucker.

A large slate quarry is to your right now. This beacon must have been occupied by those who wished to see who was advancing from all sides. I will leave you to make a list of the places visible for 360 degrees around here. The dunes at Braunton and, if conditions are right, Lundy Island stand out particularly well from here.

As you return to **(4)**, notice that there is another green lane circling the glacially rounded hills, which can be added to this circuit. There is also a section of herring-bone stonewalling to your right, similar to the walling found above Woolacombe (and maybe the work of one of Mr Tucker's ancestors).

(6) Turn left down into the sunken lane, which will take you along a woodland edge to Pitt Farm Bableigh. It is steep and narrow, and the rocky striations have multicoloured layers for you to fit your feet into. Within the sweet chestnut, oak, coppiced beech and ash wood to your right are some well-mossed deer park boundary banks.

(7) Turn right here along to Bableigh Cross (at this point you might wish to extend your walk as indicated and link up to the Swimbridge circuit, Route 20), and then left again following the signpost which indicates 1½ miles to Bishop's Tawton. There is evidence of orchards in this once heavily market-gardened area, where now Christmas trees sit stumpily waiting to be snatched from the earth.

(8) This narrow lane takes you alongside Codden Hill, with its bracken and furze and newly planted rows of wayfaring trees to the left and the sheer-cut faces of Venn Quarry to your right.

(9) Where the road climbs to the right, complete your circuit by entering through a gate here to your left and take a fairly newly created green lane back to the Park area of the A377.

You are running along the back of another disused quarry here. There is plenty of bird life in the scrubby vegetation here, including Britain's smallest, and sometimes noisiest songsters, *Troglodytes troglodytes*. This is the Latin name for the wren (meaning cave-dweller), which can flit just as happily through dense brambles as in hollowed-out old quarry sides.

(10) Back on the road here, turn right and then right again along Village Street to look around this compact village which for centuries has survived, so well protected from sprawl, between river and hill.

By the way

This near perfect-looking village seems to have had quite a prosperous history, enjoying many generous landowners and charity providers such as the Chichesters and the Laws. In pre-Reformation times it was part of the See of the Bishop of Exeter. The village was set up here originally to defend Devon from troublesome Viking invaders coming in from the North. It is set back high above the River Taw, upon which its trade initially depended, and its connections with nearby Newport were handy.

The coming of the turnpikes saw an increase in its road traffic, which peaked in the 1990s when the A377 was still the main route from Barnstaple to Exeter. The railway helped in the transportation of the lime, slate and stone from the quarries at Venn.

In recent years, stone from this quarry has been used to provide highly skid-resistant top surfacing for roads throughout Devon and beyond. Back in the 1930s market gardens flourished, sending their produce to the growing seaside resorts on the coast. The green lanes by the river at New Bridge, Ford Gate and Ford must have seen a great variety of travellers and traffic in their time.

Other green lanes in the area

Leading down to and up from the river.

Links

The Tarka Trail. There is a regular bus service from Barnstaple to Bishop's Tawton.

Question

Where does the nearby railway run to and from?

Cider-making

Route 22

MARWOOD

The Oxenpark

OS Explorer Map 139

There are some green lanes, however isolated, which shouldn't be missed. So it is with Fullabrook Down Lane, which forms the boundary between West Down and Marwood, and stands on the ridgeways which run down from Ilfracombe towards Braunton. Ridgeways were in the beginning used for trade, and not just for travel. This is not a circular walk, but, because of its height and the views it gives, it can be retraced or linked with the local bus service.

Conditions: Some standing water in places.

Distance: 4 to 5 miles.

Starting point: SS542424 Centery Farm. This four-ways crossroads has its origins in the name 'Sanctuary'.

(1) Double back up the minor road which leads southwards with Crackaway Plantation on your left. You come to Burland Cross on the Old (that is, pre-turnpike) Barnstaple Road.

(2) Enter the lane straight ahead of you now, where there is a footpath sign which you ignore. The lane begins wide, and stays wide all the way with very little climbing up or down. There is some cobbling in the beginning, but a mixture of grass and stones makes it easy going all the way. Allow an hour to travel right through. The views in all directions cover both moors, estuaries and seas.

(3) At its highest point there is a very wide area with passing places and maybe a resting place for the sheep or oxen which must have been driven along here. On your left, wind-sculpted hawthorn and blackthorn cling to the tops of the banks, which in places are lined with deep-set stones similar to those at Woolacombe. Beech hedges stand to the right. The clear sound of skylarks will always be with you. In spring, you may be accompanied by a pair of buzzards indulging in some sky-dancing: dropping, gliding, swooping, gliding and rising as their wing-tips touch.

Towards its end, the lane is lined with a leggy gorse hedge; the remains of old ploughs, granite rollers and other reminders of arable farming lie overgrown by the way. Honeysuckle festoons the hedge, and suddenly at **(4)** you are walking on a minor road.

(5) Turn left towards Patsford and Marwood.

(6) Then left again to the same destinations. There once stood a chapel-at-ease at Patsford. You pass the entrances to two other green lanes on your left, which give you an added exercise loop. You pass through a few farmyard buildings before climbing a slight rise, and then on your right **(7)** is the entrance to Mare Lane, a well-grassed but damp bridleway taking you up to the field corner **(8)** which you cross to bring you to the Old Barnstaple Road **(9)**. You can follow the footpath through Whiddon and up to North Lane at **(10)**. Or you might like to turn left and go to Gypsy Corner, about which there is nothing to tell, as yet. Gypsies as green lane travellers have always been with us.

At **(10)** veer right into a public bridleway to bring you back to the road at Milltown, where once a wheelwright, a builder, an agricultural engineer and a timber merchant all plied their trades. It was here also that the Reverend Collincum wrote in 1853 that there were people living who remembered the apprentice system when the labourer who could not maintain all his children handed them over to 'the big house'.

By the way

This lane is so wide that it must have seen a lot of drovers' traffic in the past. The presence of Oxenpark Lane to the north-east and Henry Williamson's house at Oxford Cross SS469407 make this area one where ridgeways for cattle transportation must always have been important. The presence of tumuli throughout this Braunton, Mortehoe and Ilfracombe triangle is worth plotting. See also

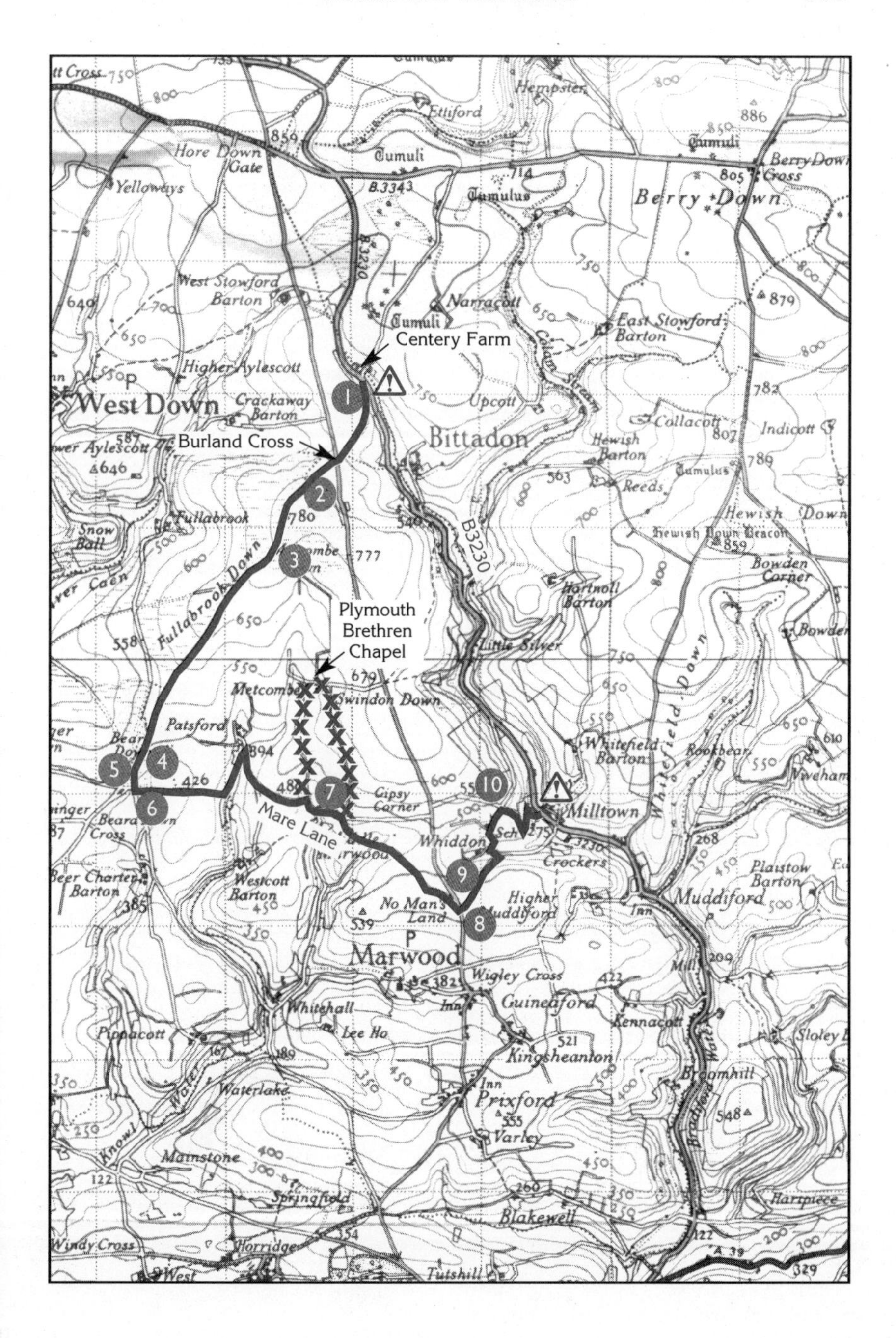
Centery Farm
Burland Cross
Plymouth
Brethren
Chapel
Mare Lane
1
2
3
4
5
6
7
8
9
10
West Down
Bittadon
B3230
B.3343
Berry Down
Hempster
Ettiford
Hore Down Gate
Yelloways
West Stowford Barton
Higher Aylescott
Crackaway Barton
Narracott
East Stowford Barton
Upcott
Collacott
Indicott
Hewish Barton
Reeds
Hewish Down
Bowden Corner
Hartnoll Barton
Little Silver
Fullabrook Down
Fullabrook
Snow Ball
Metcombe
Swindon Down
Patsford
Gipsy Corner
Whiddon
Milltown
Whitefield Barton
Whitefield Down
Rookbear
Crockers
Muddiford
Plaistow Barton
Higher Muddiford
No Man's Land
Marwood
Wigley Cross
Guineaford
Kennacott
Kingsheanton
Whitehall
Lee Ho
Westcott Barton
Beara Down
Beara Cross
Beer Charter Barton
Pippacott
Waterlake
Prixford
Varley
Broomhill
Mainstone
Springfield
Blakewell
Harpiece
Windy Cross
Horridge
Tutshill
Sloley
Viveham
Tumuli
Tumulus

Grundy's Ridgeway Map for this area (page 180), Road number 6, of which he writes.

> "The survival of its line as a modern road is remarkable because for 7 miles it runs side by side with, and close to, the modern Ilfracombe-Barnstaple road. It is also remarkable that it gets within 2 miles of Barnstaple where there is a branch ridgeway connecting it with that place. Packhorse traffic kept to the ridgeways so long as it existed in this country, and they were used for cattle traffic till the time of the making of the railways."

It will continue being a useful lane, as a wind farm is planned along this great lane.

Other green lanes in the area

Those indicated north of Middle Marwood.

Links

Braunton, Route 25. There are two regular bus services from Barnstaple to Ilfracombe, one returning via Muddiford.

Question

Towards the end of the lane is a feature which tells us that this is a parish boundary bank. What is it?

The Drovers, from Pyne's *Microcosm*.

Route 23

BRATTON FLEMING

Judge Bracton would have kept the wheels running

OS Explorer Map OL9 Exmoor

This title refers to a jurist who was instrumental in setting up England's Common Law in the 13th century. It is a pity he was not around to settle the problems of the agricultural workers who were to come here 500 years later. Happily, this is not a neglected or discontented community now.

Conditions: Muddy in places.

Distance: 3-4 miles.

Starting point: SS643377. **(1)** At the byway sign at the beginning to Haxton Lane. The green lane is tarmacked, but only patchily as it runs down then up, giving views of Stoke Rivers Church.

(2) You are on the borders of an area where the labourers suffered great hardship in the 1830s. At High Haxton, turn left into a narrow lane with a stream running in the centre, but never too deep to impede progress. It widens out at a public footpath sign on the right and becomes cobbled and firm underfoot again.

(3) Turn left where it joins the road, and just past Town Farm there are views not only towards the two rivers' estuary but also towards Dartmoor.

(4) Here at Sentry Cross you will see a sign for the National Cycle Route. There are many sentry crosses in this area; its origin as a place name is in the word 'sanctuary'. Keep walking down into the village, and notice on your right a Bible Christian Chapel built in 1854 very close to a Baptist Chapel built in 1850. This closeness must have been manageable; as we have seen, the Bible Christians called upon farm labourers as the mainstay of their congregation, whereas the Baptists probably targeted a different audience.

There were separate schools for these two schools of thought.

(5) Take School Lane to the right, and pass both school and church as you descend.

(6) At Buttonhill Cross turn left and go right down to Station House and look over the bridge here. Continue a little further to **(7)** and take the footpath to your left here down to **(8)** Button Bridge. There are some very good sections of hedge-laying, leading down to this strangely stranded stone bridge.

Return to **(7)** and take the footpath by the house called Long Acres on the right. This path runs along the edge of an oak wood to your right and the old disused railway line to your left. This is a site managed by the Devon Wildlife Trust, and there are bird and bat boxes here. Look out for the water, which in this case is piped into the holy well (Holywell) to your left.

(9) You come out on a footpath junction. Turn right here, and then sharp left before descending to the mill named after the famous Judge Bracton, whose interpretation of Common Law was used in the arguments to execute the king in Civil War times.

(10) You come out just by a viaduct, and turn left along Mill Lane and back into the village.

By the way

The lanes round here often run close to the old Lynton and Barnstaple railway line built in 1898 and closed by 1935. However, sections of the railway have been re-opened, and have been running again since 1979.

You might want to extend your walk to Loxhore and Castle Roborough. Hoskins states in his *Fieldwork in Local History* that the hedgerows in this area go back to the Domesday Book.

Other green lanes in the area

Those from number 8 on the map opposite, which will take you into Loxhore.

Links

Swimbridge, Route 20 and National Cycle Route 3.
Well served by a regular bus route from Barnstaple.

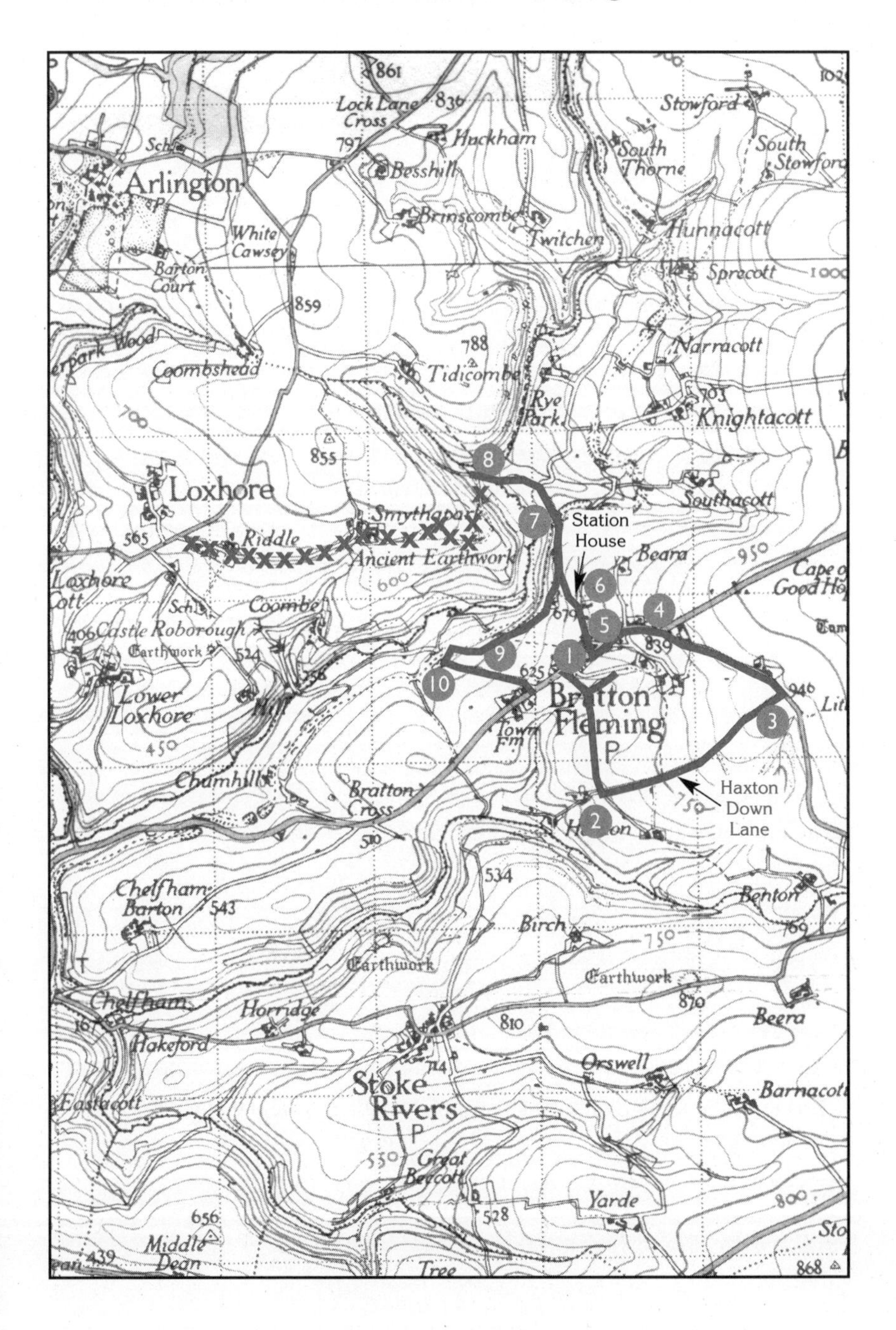
Station House
Haxton Down Lane
1
2
3
4
5
6
7
8
9
10
Arlington
Loxhore
Bratton Fleming
Stoke Rivers
Knightacott
Southacott
Beara
Tidicombe
Smythapark
Ancient Earthwork
Riddle
Coombe
Castle Roborough
Lower Loxhore
Chumhill
Bratton Cross
Chelfham Barton
Chelfham
Horridge
Hakeford
Birch
Benton
Orswell
Barnacott
Yarde
Great Beccott
Middle Dean
Narracott
Sprecott
Hunnacott
Twitchen
Brinscombe
Besshill
Huckham
Lock Lane Cross
Stowford
South Stowford
South Thorne
White Cawsey
Barton Court
Coombshead
Rye Park
Town Fm

Question

Under the bridge by Station House you will find just what kind of railway ran from Lynton to Barnstaple.

Hedge-dating theory

First put forward by Dr Max Hooper and Dr E. Pollard: count the number of different hardwood species of tree growing on one side of the hedge in a 30-metre stretch. Each species represents 100 years. Briar should be included in this exercise, but not ivy.

The leaves of dogwood, dark red after berries ripen.

Route 24

CROYDE

For the stone-breakers who paved the way for the boys from the black stuff

OS Explorer Map 139

This group of lanes up towards Baggy Point goes back to the first human attempts to cultivate the hinterland of this productive coast. This struggle was still going on up until the 1920s, when Henry Williamson came to live here and write about his fellow villagers. But he also recorded the beginnings of popular tourism and the opening up of the roads which this entailed. There was more work for the stone-breakers in their lay-bys, as recorded in his *Life in a Devon Village*:

> "There the stone-breakers, wearing gauze spectacles and sitting on the ground, tapped with their blunt double-headed hammers until the rugged piles were graded into neat rectangular heaps, when their faces, clothes and hands would be stained a browny red by the dust and the sweat."

This is not a completely circular walk, but forms part of the wider circuit represented in this and the next three walks.

Conditions: Some rocky slippery lanes.

Distance: 2-3 miles.

Starting point: From the village approach across Croyde Sands via the 'Parson's Path' SS443392, or from Stentaway Lane SS444398.

(1) Stentaway Lane at the bend becomes a green one as you cross over to Cherry Tree Farm. As you pass the yard, make sure that, as the sign says, you are wearing stout shoes, for there are puddles of standing water on this cobbled way for you to splash through. The hedgerows are draped in downward-dangling ivy here. The lane soon deepens and narrows, and the sides reveal the schists and slates in the clays of the Pilton and Baggy Beds. These outcrops are covered in grey and yellow lichens.

On the left there is a well which, although overgrown, still has signs of herring-boned walling at the back. The way becomes steep and the hedges shorter; you are crossing well-scored rock face here, the skeleton of the land which is usually covered by the flesh of grass.

A camber develops, and you can see the ruts where horse-drawn butts carried stone down and seaweed up the lane for centuries. You will pass two sections of old, overgrown green lane entrances on your left, before you reach the top crossroads at **(2)**.

If you didn't come up from the beach here, you might like to examine the stonewalling in the lane to your left. Return to **(2)**, and turn to the right into a short section of 'brambly burrow' (to use a phrase of Ted Hughes) which leads you to the stile at **(3)**.

Climb over the stile onto Putsborough Down, and enjoy views of Baggy Point to your left and Woolacombe Sands to your right. Follow the footpath round until it joins the road.

(4) Turn left towards the sands here, and keep to the top road over Putsborough Sands and Vention Lane, passing 'Clifton' to your right. There are ways down to the Sands here which are difficult to resist; one runs through a green lane. Up here, though, you are in a green lane again, with an unusual elder hedge on the seaward side and the more predictable blackthorn and bracken to your right. There were once sedge banks on the seaward side here.

At Broadsands Bungalow the lane gets steeper. Note here the ironstone quarry with its deep red stone.

(5) Take the footpath to your right up a very steep hill. It brings you to the edge of Pickwell Down. Here notice how the new gate has replaced an old narrow one which was hung on what are known locally as 'engboos', that is, end boughs or gateposts. They were often made of whole trees, wrecked ships' timbers or masts, and in the 1920s, cast concrete.

Once through the gate and on your way to the road ahead, notice how a

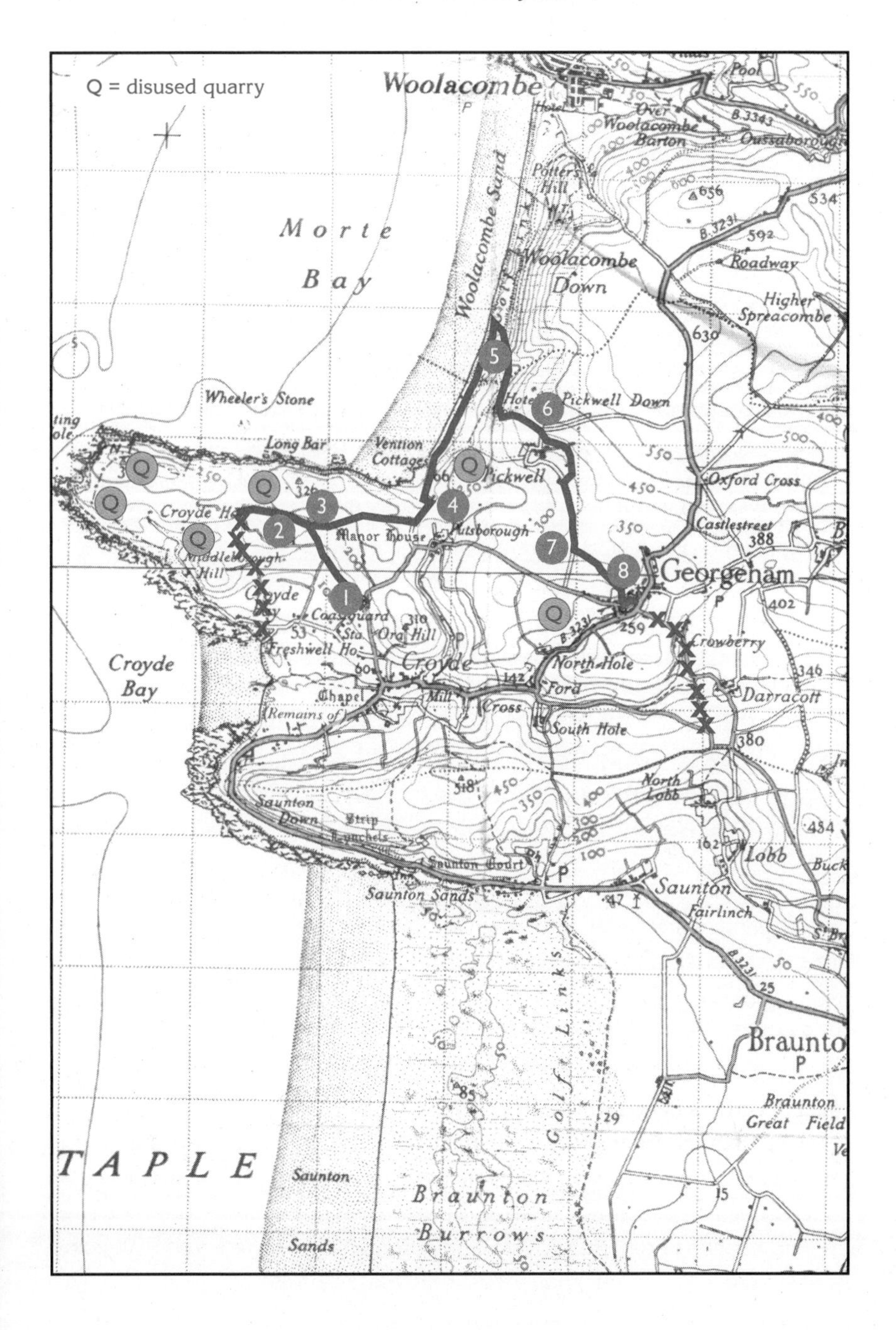
Q = disused quarry
Woolacombe
Morte Bay
Woolacombe Sand
Woolacombe Down
Over Woolacombe Barton
Potter's Hill
Ossaborough
Higher Spreacombe
Roadway
Wheeler's Stone
Long Bar
Vention Cottages
Pickwell Down
Pickwell
Croyde Ho
Manor House
Putsborough
Middleborough Hill
Croyde Bay
Coastguard Sta.
Ora Hill
Freshwell Ho.
Georgeham
Castlestreet
Oxford Cross
Crowberry
North Hole
Ford
Darracott
Croyde
Chapel
Mill Cross
South Hole
North Lobb
Lobb
Saunton Down
Strip Lynchets
Saunton Court
Saunton Sands
Saunton
Fairlinch
Braunton
Braunton Great Field
Golf Links
Braunton Burrows
TAPLE
Saunton Sands
B.3231
B.3343

cobbled surface begins to emerge; there is a distinct camber, too.

(6) Go through the gate and turn right onto the road with a salt and pepper surface, which takes you up past Pickwell Manor: follow the walled garden round. This property was once owned by John Harris, the Lord of the Manor in the Georgeham area, but now it can belong to anyone who cares to rent it on a self-catering basis for a while.

(7) Take the footpath down into the village, which becomes a green lane on a rock base again for a short section before you turn left into Church Road, passing the school and down into the village.

(8) Henry Williamson is buried in the churchyard here. His otter has inspired generations of naturalists and writers, and now musicians: a new musical, 'Tarka the Opera', was produced by local schools in 2006. You can return by bus to Barnstaple, or take another set of green lanes as indicated on the map which will take you back to Route 26, Saunton. Or you can keep up high and head north towards Woolacombe and Mortehoe.

By the way

You will see that many walks in this area owe a lot to Henry Williamson, and anyone who writes or reads cannot (or would not want to) avoid him. His records of the people who used and shaped the lanes in this area are invaluable for a green lanes historian.

Notice the number of quarries marked on these maps, which were used for house-building and road-making. They were not all for stone either: there was the Buckland iron mine to the north.

The lanes here also show how early humans struggled to farm on dry, safer headlands using infield-outfield systems, and how the medieval manors controlled farming in the area. This manorial system was to dominate farming and village life for centuries. But, being so close to the Great War as Williamson was, and being one of the few who had survived, he was aware of the changes that had been made by the absence of a whole generation in the countryside. With prescience, he felt that he was recording a way of life which was about to be blown apart yet again – and he was right.

Other green lanes in the area

There are many, and by keeping to the high contours you can work your way eastwards back to Barnstaple, enjoying the views over the estuary, the coast, Exmoor and Dartmoor as you go.

Links

The South West Way running from Saunton. There is a regular bus route from Barnstaple to Georgeham. Georgeham is on the National Cycle Network and is part of Route 27.

Question

This writer's talisman does not appear by day.

Route 25

BRAUNTON

If pigs could fly!

OS Explorer Map 139

If it is open, the church of St Brannock's is worth a visit. Look out for the roof boss with the sow and piglets, homage to the animals which St Brannock met on the way, and which told him to build his church here. This is a Celtic Christian settlement. The most interesting feature of all these green lanes is how quickly they can be reached from the roaring seaside surf-bound Barnstaple to Croyde Road.

Many still remain unclassified, most have names and, because of their adherence to ridgeways, must have served as both truss ways (a 'truss' is a bundle of produce) for arable farming and drove roads for cattle and sheep. Once you are up above the Great Field, the Burrows and the Atlantic headlands, you won't ever want to come down.

There is exhilaration and freedom here: buzzards hunt over the valley and skylarks sing high above. Depending on your time scale, the walks in this area could be made from east to west descending to the south.

Conditions: Steep, stony and watery in places.

Distance: 2-3 miles.

Starting point: The best place to begin is at the busy centre of Braunton where there the buses stop. **(1)** SS489368. Coming from Cross Tree, where traffic lights control the meeting of six ways and an elm tree once stood, look for East Street and take this minor road up to North Down Hill.

(2) Continue over the T-junction and keep on up to Boode. Halfway up watch out for a very large windswept beech to your left, which has sets of lovers' initials carved into its grey trunk.

(3) When you reach Boode House on your left, take the green lane here which is cobbled and lined with sections of stonewalling. There is an impor-

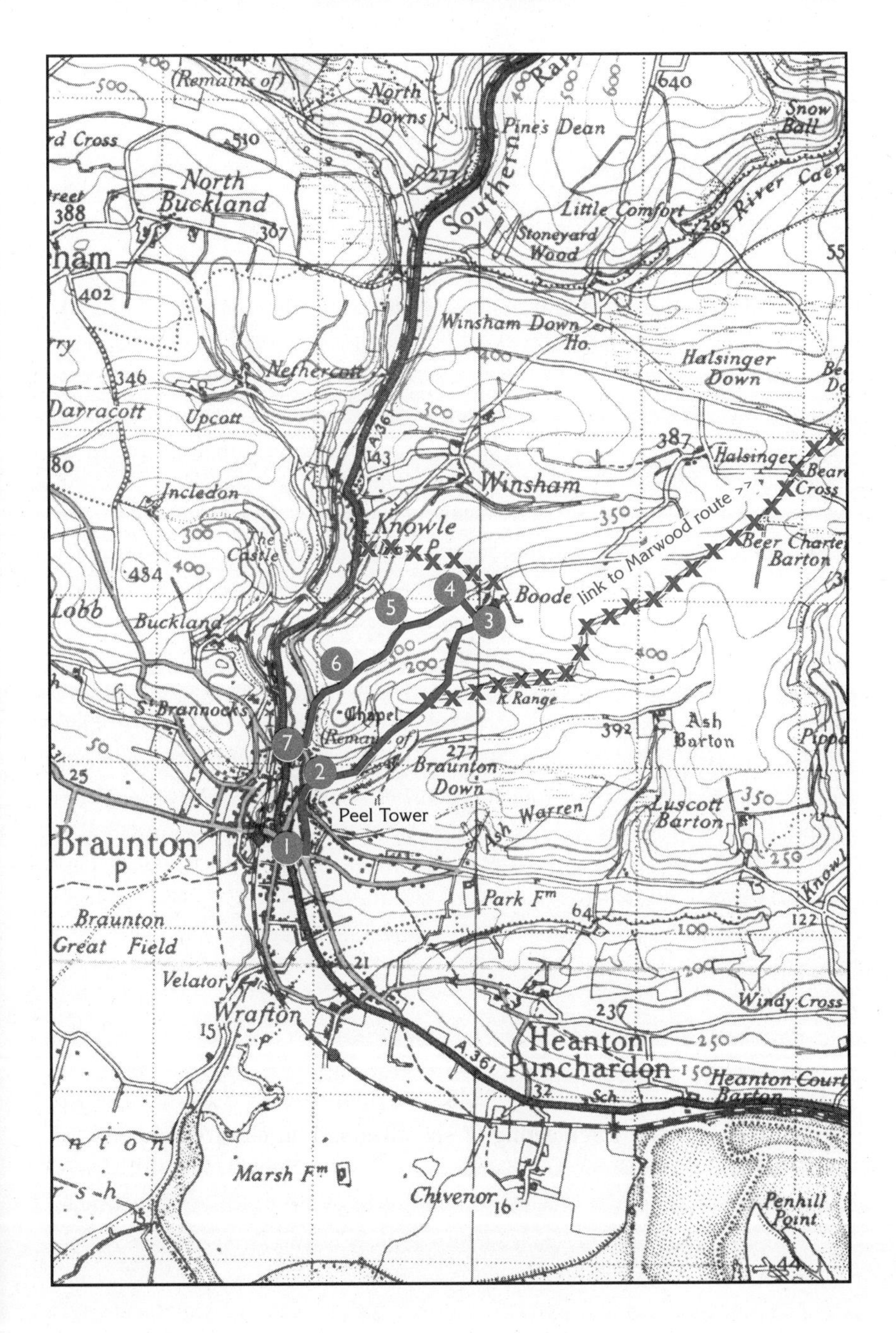

1
2
3
4
5
6
7
Peel Tower
link to Marwood route >>
North Downs
Pine's Dean
North Buckland
Little Comfort
Stoneyard Wood
River Caen
Snow Ball
Winsham Down Ho.
Halsinger Down
Nethercott
Darracott
Upcott
Winsham
Halsinger
Beer Cross
Incledon
Knowle
The Castle
Beer Charter Barton
Boode
Lobb
Buckland
St Brannocks
Chapel (Remains of)
Braunton Down
Ash Barton
Luscott Barton
Warren
Braunton
Park Fm
Braunton Great Field
Velator
Wrafton
Windy Cross
Heanton Punchardon
Heanton Court Barton
Marsh Fm
Chivenor
Penhill Point

tant protected group of beech trees well sited on the ridgeway here.

(4) At this point to extend this short walk, follow the crossed footpaths and lanes as shown on the map. Alternatively, turn left into this long, slightly muddy lane at the top and begin to enjoy the views which open out in front of you, which are breathtaking: the almost mountainous, and often purple, looming jagged profile of the Burrows beyond the Great Field, framed by the glassy Atlantic, are clear ahead. Glimpses of Dartmoor and Exmoor appear to your sides as you walk through this high rolling hill country. The trees in this lane have been managed so as to lower the level of the hedge and encourage some fine, if slightly stunted oaks to develop as standards.

(5) There is the challenge of New Lane here, which if you venture behind the gate can take you down into Kittywell and back to Braunton Church.

(6) Access to the ruins of the 16th-century chapel of St Michael's is indicated here. This church, in its exposed and hard-to-reach position, needed to be re-sited. But human weakness was not enough of an excuse to move it – only a myth had the power to do this. It was said that the church was constantly de-constructed at night by the devil, so St Brannock's prophesying pigs provided the new site below.

(7) The lane corkscrews sharply down here to a T-junction where there is an 'Unsuitable for Motors' sign. You are now coming down into Silver Street, where you will meet up with Church Street and St Brannock's. Keep to the right as you descend once more into East Street. You can extend your walk from here by taking the Carlihead Road to the right, crossing the A361 and following the National Cycle Route 27 signs up Castle Lane, another ancient track by a looming hill-fort.

By the way

Hoskins says of Braunton:

> "These churches usually became the mother-church for a big district and from this mother-church priests went out on foot along the lanes to the scattered farmsteads in the countryside converting whom they could to the Christian faith."

By climbing up above the Great Field you get a good perspective on its layout. Clawed back from the marsh behind Braunton Burrows by the Saxons, this is one of the few remaining examples of open field farming in Britain. Land was held in common, with each farmer having three strips to work in

rotation, one fallow for every two with crops. But only 140 – just over a quarter of these original strips – now remain. From up here you can see how they are divided by drainage strips; some are hedged. Looking all around you and at a large-scale map, you can also see how this method was transferred to the uplands. But here – unlike for the peasants below, who just had three strips to work and were really fully employed working for a yeoman farmer – the presence of 'cot' or 'cott' in the place names means a small farm individually owned and worked.

There is an irony here: Peel Tower lies half a mile to the east, a three-storeyed monument, now in ruins, put up in 1846 by a local working man, Thomas Mortman, to celebrate Sir Robert Peel's repeal of the Corn Laws. However, the effect of this, along with the import of foreign grain, was eventually to bring more misery and low prices for the working men who produced the wheat.

At Upcott Farm, on the extended route, there is a plaque on a great barn here stating to whom it belonged, who built it, and who owned the contents.

Other green lanes in the area

There are many stretching from the east at Croyde, to the north to Georgeham and to the west towards Barnstaple in the wooded valleys of Marwood and Shirwell.

Links

Access to the ruined church of St Michael is welcomed by DEFRA, who have a notice on the entrance gate giving details of the footpaths. Buses run from Barnstaple to Ilfracombe through Braunton.

Question

St Brannock came from across the water. From where?

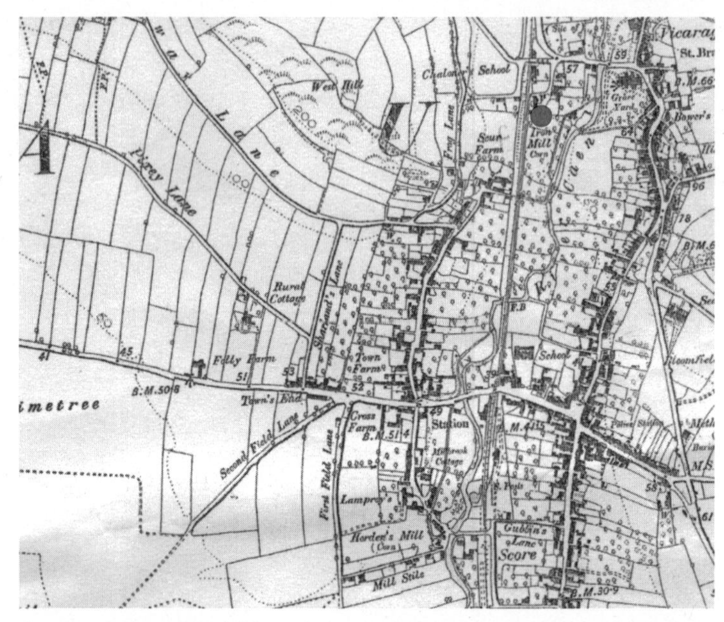

Notice the strip patterns of the fields on the map, which are pictured below, towards the sea. In this agricultural area you can see evidence of an industrial past ('Iron Mill') by the green dot and as illustrated on page 127.

Braunton Great Field, from Long Lane.

Route 26

SAUNTON

One more walk through Williamson country

OS Explorer Map 139

This walk brings you into an area and to a people whom he knew so well and whose history he respected:

> "Long before the Phoenicians came to Devon, this old lane was a way for men and horses and cattle; a track which, slowly sinking under the scrape of sleds on the soft grey rock, the peck of pack-horse hooves, and the courses of rain in winter, for centuries has remained the same." – *The Lone Swallows.*

This walk is dedicated to Henry Williamson, the nature writer and one of our first conservationists.

Conditions: Steep and rocky in parts, with cobbled, boggy and slippery surfaces, ploughed-up field edges and minor roads.

Distance: 2-3 miles or 4-6 if extended.

Starting point: SX457377. There is some parking on the Hannaburrow lane side, and the bus stop for buses to and from Barnstaple is nearby.

(1) This woodland fringe lane begins at the bend on the lane leading to Linkham House. This could be Williamson's Sky Lane which he describes in *The Pathway* as where:

> "... farmers of olden times had brought their corn from the inland valleys to be winnowed by the wind in the sand hills."

The winds which rip through from the Atlantic can certainly separate the chaff from the grain here.

You plunge into an unmade lane, overhung with ash and hawthorn trees, which rises steeply through a wooded area to the left. Saunton Court stands in the valley along with the big houses, one of which might just be Williamson's 'Wildernesse' from *The Pathway*. As you ascend, turn to catch glimpses of the seawardly undulating Burrows through breaks in the straggly hedgerow. A slate outcrop cuts across the lane, the same one which we will encounter again on descending the lanes to the east. Typical woodland-edge flora line the lane: red campion, wood avens with their burry seed balls, and umbellifers with their cream and white clusters, which turn to black burnt seed pods by late August here. At the top stands a signpost to Ford and Braunton.

(2) This 'Long Lane' to the right is a ridgeway and a boundary lane. It once ran from the Castle at Braunton down to Croyde Bay. It is wide, straight, unsunken, following the highest contour of the headland. Up here skylarks are in full throat and phalanxes of foxgloves top the hedges. To the left stretch the fields of Darracott, Upcott and Nethercott. They are empty now of farm labourers, and were even more so in 1920, as described in a piece entitled *Vacant Fields* where Williamson talks about the killer flu epidemic of the 1920s. It is not difficult to see how places up here were given names such as Little Comfort and No Man's Land. At the end of this lane you may want to explore the lanes towards Braunton for yourself, as indicated.

(3) Turn sharp right by Lobbthorn Stile Cross, have a search for the parish boundary stone **(4)**, and go down into an unsigned cobbled and sunken lane with slate outcrops. The characteristic dog-leg bend which occurs quite early in the lane shows how this access lane respected the curves of the Saxon farmer's strips, as well as over in the Great Field.

(5) On your left where the lane joins up to Cruffen Lane, there is a fine example of an overgrown lane once used as a short cut across a triangular portion of land. But continue to the right towards North Lobb and Knill's Farm.

(6) Go straight on through a cob-walled lane and through a farm gate into the corner of a field. Follow the signs across the meadows to **(7)**, where a sunken green lane is to be found. You will probably share this lane with sheep sheltering from wind, rain and sun, or decide to follow it from the hedge-bank. You continue to descend through what can only be described as a cob-built sheep's way lane. The lane is overgrown with watercress beds (fool's watercress, of course), and muddy in places. The ashes and blackthorns, stunted by Atlantic winds, cling desperately to the mud banks. When I visited, there was a sheep skull lying in the widest part of the lane where

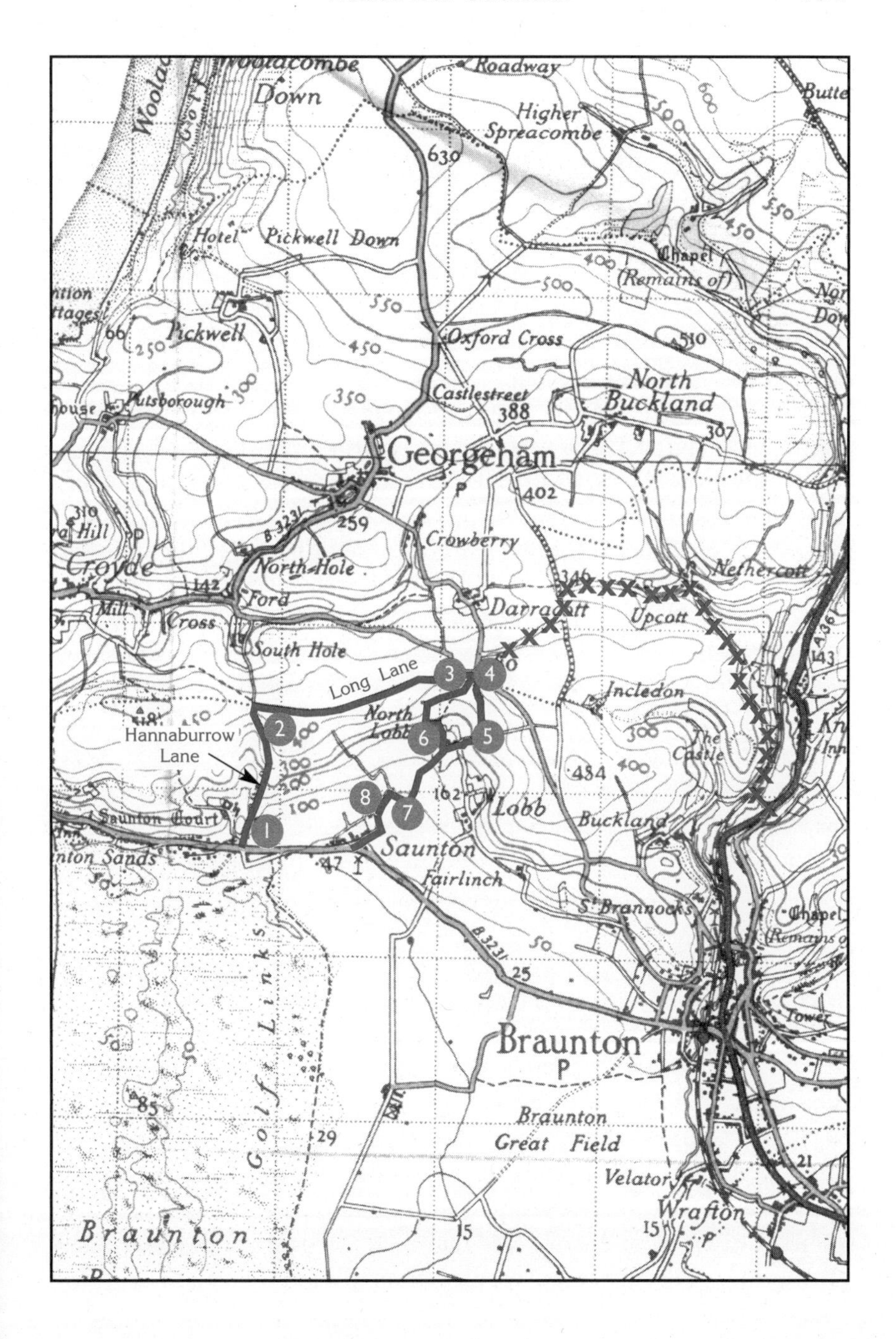
Woolacombe Down
Roadway
Higher Spreacombe
630
600
500
550
450
Hotel
Pickwell Down
Chapel (Remains of)
400
500
550
Pickwell
250
450
Oxford Cross
510
300
North Buckland
Putsborough
350
Castlestreet
388
307
Georgeham
402
310
B 3231
259
Crowberry
Croyde
North Hole
Nethercott
142
Ford
346
Mill
Cross
Darracott
Upcott
South Hole
Long Lane
Incledon
Hannaburrow Lane
The Castle
North Lobb
300
400
484
400
162
Lobb
Buckland
Saunton Court
Saunton
Saunton Sands
47
Fairlinch
St Brannocks
Chapel (Remains of)
B 3231
50
25
Golf Links
Tower
Braunton
P
85
Braunton Great Field
29
Velator
Wrafton
15
15
21
P
Braunton
A 361
143
1
2
3
4
5
6
7
8

the high mud walls had proved too steep for an escape to be made.

(8) At its end, go over a stile and left towards Saunton Farm. Notice the circular barn entrances here, and the dovecot. The roar of the surfers' road hits you once again. Finish this circuit by a visit to the Burrows – so close at hand and always able to deaden such sounds.

By the way

Much has been written about Williamson, and this part of the country which has been named after him. The basic facts are that in 1922 he came to Georgeham, having visited the area when he was a boy, and lived a life close to nature. But he was a man haunted by the Great War and the need to find a home again. He took this newly discovered countryside to his heart, along with the people and their ways. He often writes about whom he met on his wanderings and what they were doing, thus recording the last days (for a while) that these lanes saw traffic apart from for recreational purposes. The lanes above Saunton today do still belong to the farming communities, but they don't need to walk them so often.

Other green lanes in the area

Like Williamson, you could spend from dawn to dusk wandering along these evocatively-named sunken and exposed series of green lanes, such as Milkaway, Adwell, Pennywell, Eastern, Castle, to and from the sea.

Links

There are regular bus services from Barnstaple through to Georgeham along the coast.
The South West Coast Path. National Cycle Route 27.

Question

Which two parishes are marked by the boundary stone?

Route 27

BARNSTAPLE

The potters and glovers at Fremington

OS Explorer Map 139

You can follow this circuit by beginning and ending at Barnstaple railway station, and by so doing enjoy the views both towards Braunton Burrows and the sea, and inland up to Codden Beacon and Exmoor.

Conditions: Uncharacteristically unhilly, with some pools of standing water.

Distance: 3-4 miles.

Starting point: The station at SS555327.

(1) When you leave the station turn left and follow the Tarka Trail signs, but veer sharp right and go under the new bridge, following the trail towards Instow. From the beginning there are long views across the salt marshes or 'saltings' here, and the cries of curlews, whimbrels and other estuary birds rise above those of the receding traffic. To the left are water meadows, with tufts of cotton grass and standing water forming scrapes where dragonflies skim and clatter. I saw the biggest – the Emperor dragonfly – there. You pass quite a few masonry tunnels along the way from freshwater to seawater; the river Taw ebbs and flows four times a day in this estuary.

(2) Just after Tarka Trail post number 6, take the footpath signed to the left. You step over the stile and sleepers into a wide cobbled lane, and a handwritten sign reads 'Fanny Pack Lane'. Apart from potters and masons and a majority of agricultural labourers, there were quite a few outworking glovers supplied by the Barnstaple factory in the area. Records show at least three of them were called Fanny. Along the lane there is a deep drainage channel to the left, and all along the lane there are patches of purple loosestrife, mint, fool's watercress, tansy, scabious, scarlet pimpernel, false oatgrass, and, depending on the season, you will find many other species.

(3) The lane emerges at a gate into a green lanes T-junction at Clampitt Cottage. In 1851 this was a pottery, working the rich clay here to produce the distinctive Barum art pottery as well as standard bricks, sanitary ware and tiles. Turn left into a lane where the amount of elms on this walk first becomes apparent. Elm was a useful wood for those involved in the potteries. Pipes made from its timbers would have helped drain the marshy areas in which they worked. You come out into a modern housing estate, Mead Park, and out onto the B3223, formerly the A39.

(4) Turn right and cross over the B3223. Go down Combrew Lane at **(5)**. This Welsh-sounding name is partnered by the nearby Penhill and is further evidence of Celtic migrations in this area.

This lane is 'Unsuitable for Heavy Goods Vehicles' now, but once must have carried quite a few heavy goods round to the Fishley's Fremington pottery works near the farm. There are tall standing elms along here. A report on the area from 1889 reads:

> ". . . with all outward appearances of a country homestead – an illusion which is promoted by the long range of low outhouses, the call of chanticleer and cackle of hens – the pottery is the centre of an old-world picture of the life of the worker at the wheel remote from towns."

Eight men and four women were employed here in 1851 during the time of the third generation of the Fishleys.

(6) Combrew Lane comes back to the B3223, and you cross straight over with the stream and the hidden defunct workings to your right, on to a pill-side concreted-over byway at **(7)**.

Watch out for a beautifully restored green door with a medieval pointed arch, the Wills Gate, restored by Mr Atyeo in 2000 and showing the clay bricks of the area to their best advantage. There was a landing-stage for the pottery opposite the cottages here. As you advance up the creek there are unfortunately a lot of yellowing elms, but plenty of estuary birds again. This byway is also used by cars, so be careful how you go. Towards the end of the concrete there are some embedded footprints. Could this be a family and its dog recorded for posterity?

Turn right at **(8)** where you join the Tarka Trail, and views open out before you, up and down the estuary. You are close to the information point, refreshment stop and little museum here with more information on the potteries. The railway ran along here from 1846 to 1982, and it was the biggest quay between Lands End and Bristol, exporting ceramics (especially to

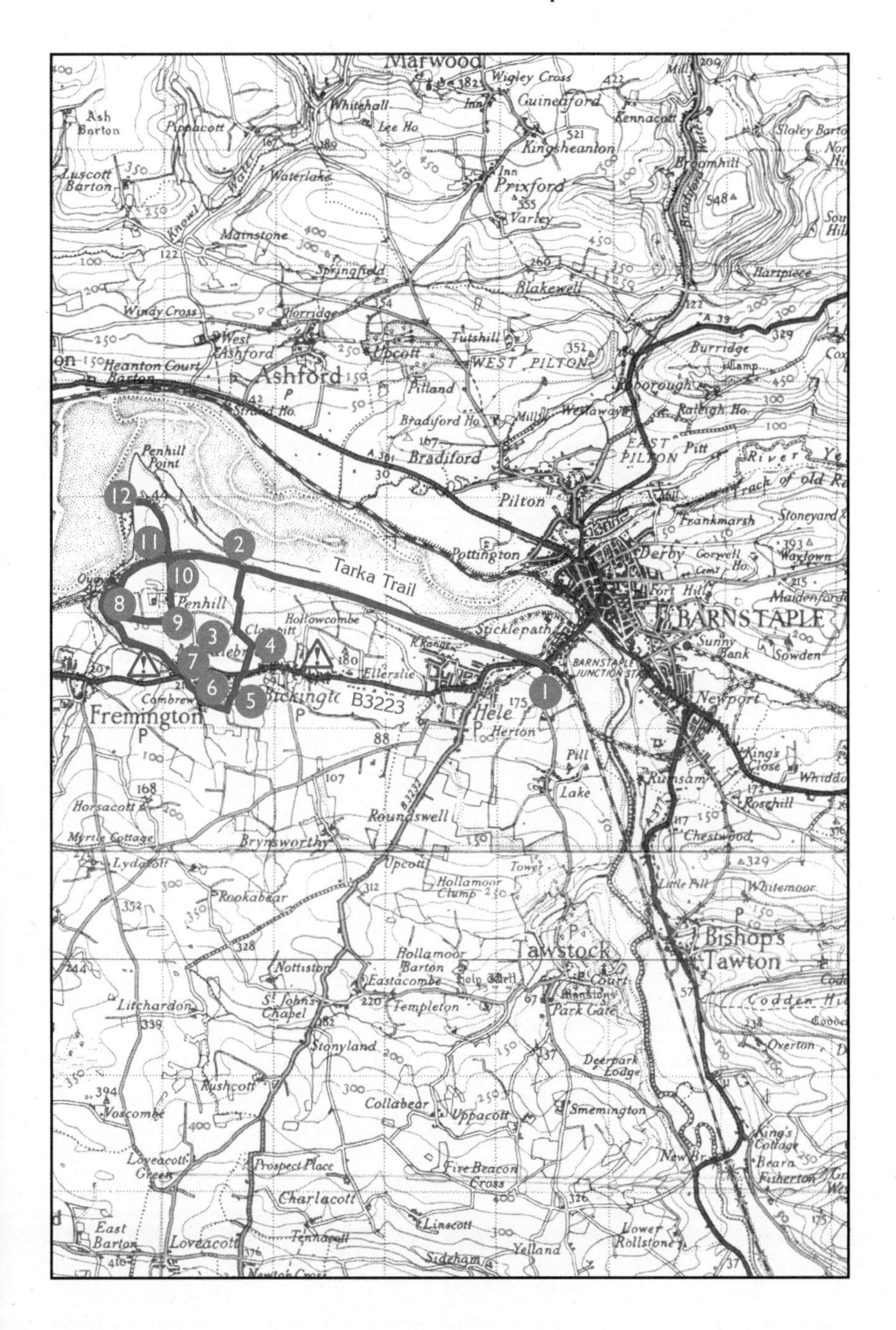
Tarka Trail
B3223
Ashford
Barnstaple
Fremington
Pilton
Bishop's Tawton
Tawstock
Marwood

Cornwall), clay and other local produce; and importing culm and coal for the railway. There are two big market lime kilns here too. In order to gain some height over the estuary and to climb just a little on this walk, at **(9)** take the footpath to the right and walk through two meadows over to Penhill. There are linnets, skylarks and starlings swirling here. In autumn they were out gleaning the parachute-borne seeds of the great hawkweed flowers.

This gives you good views out to sea and to Hartland, with a peep at Lundy. There was a quarry here, and there are ancestors of the buzzards who once hunted there soaring over you. This is a good point to compare your present-day map with the one shown here, which is only 50 years old. Penhill Peninsular, where we are next bound, was definitely wider; and the sea channels, or 'channers', have changed their courses.

(10) Turn left into a very wide clay-based lane **(11)** which crosses over the Tarka Trail and goes down to Penhill Point. There are patches of standing water here, and lots more elms, with a further variety of wildflowers including the bright yellow tall standing flowers of bristly hawkweed and timothy grass.

(12) From the small beach-cum-landing-stage here on the left, return up the lane again and at **(11)** take the steps down to the Tarka Trail and turn left towards Barnstaple. Here is all the bird life of the estuary: brent geese, greylag geese, curlews, lapwings, egrets and the occasional spoonbill. Here are the dykes created by the agriculturalist Vancouver in 1808 to keep the abundance of labourers and masons in the area busy and create more arable land. Walking back, the shape of the Civic Building in Barnstaple, housing many local employees, rises on the horizon, as does Shapland's furniture factory, built from the white clay of the area you have just walked, which was also once an important source of work for locals.

Fremington pots, a clay oven and a cream maker.

By the way

The uniqueness of the Fremington Pottery lay in a pioneer introduction of colour being applied to local clay to produce the wonderful yellows and oranges of their jugs and artwork pottery. The harvest jugs of the area are now sought-after collectors' items, bearing such mottoes as

> "Fill us full of liquor sweet,
> For that is good where friends do meet:
> When friends do meet and liquor plenty,
> Fill me again when I be empty."

Apart from these fine items, cloam ovens were one of the mainstays of the Fishley enterprise. I once found one at the side of a green lane where a house had stood which had been destroyed in a fire. There were only about 25 people employed in potting in 1851, and about ten masons. Often, as commented upon by Flora Thompson in *Lark Rise to Candleford*, a mason may just have been a bricklayer with ambition. It is a curious thing, but of the masons listed, quite a few were married to women up to ten years older than themselves. Could it be that marsh agues hit women of child-bearing age worst? This walk is dedicated to the potters of the area, but more specifically, as elsewhere in Devon, to those labourers who claimed and created the water-threatened landscape through which you have been walking today.

Other green lanes in the area

Those over the estuary at Braunton, Saunton and Croyde.

Links

There are regular bus services from Barnstaple to Bideford.
From the Tarka Railway line at Barnstaple you can get to Fremington by walking along the Tarka Trail. The Coastal Footpath. An RSPB reserve at Home Farm Marsh.

Question

What is the structure on the beach at 12 on the map?

Route 28

GREAT TORRINGTON

Gloves for the untouchables!

OS Explorer Map 126

This day-long walk will take you down to medieval field patterns where lepers laboured, and up to the ruins of an Augustinian priory and church. The ridgeways you travel were those made by generations of arable and dairy farmers living in the Torridge valley. But there were other forms of employment here too, from nail-making to an alabaster manufacturer. You may want to start this walk in Torrington itself, and link it with the Monkleigh and Littleham walk (Route 30). If so, find the old glove factory, complete with crossed glove plaques, in White Lane which was built in 1884 by Mr Vaughan, glove-maker and Bible Christian, hence its ecclesiastical style of architecture. Mr Vaughan employed 500 glove-makers here, both within the factory and as outworkers in the surrounding villages.

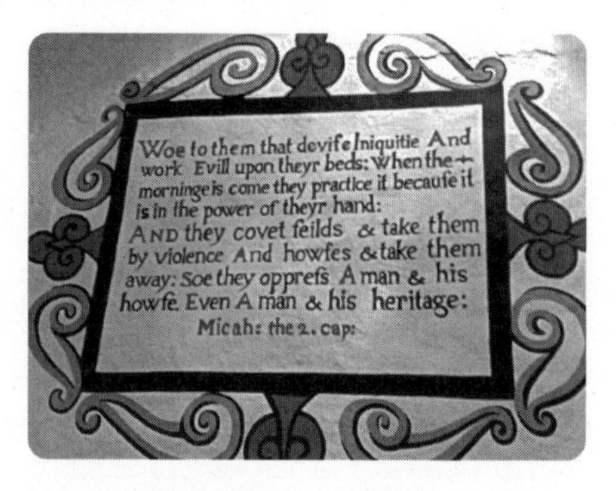

Quotation in Leper Chapel

Conditions: Muddy and slurry-bound in parts.

Distance: 3-6 miles.

Starting point: **(1)** Beginning at New Bridge on the A386, SS499185.

(2) Look for the Public Bridleway sign to your right at SS497180, and go over the gate by the bridleway, which soon climbs up into the main part of the green lane.

(3) At its end you turn right into a 'butt lane', an abutment for the lepers' field strips, which do look remarkably like very wide straps of land – or 'strapes', as they were called in medieval days. Pass the end of Mutton Lane with a sign to Oak Park Farm.

(4) Stop at the first gateway, and there you will see the boxed hedges containing narrow strips of land. The hedges have been restored and the land is now used for grazing. Continue along through a small housing development until you reach Taddiport Village Hall. Opposite here is a strape of arable land where residents are growing their own vegetables in the same plots once used by the lepers who came here in 1344.

(5) Turn sharp right and down to a crossroads, where the tiny church of St Mary Magdalen, once belonging to the lepers, hangs on the edge of the River Torridge. Its west tower is covered in ivy, the wall well-weathered; some rubble is piled behind a fence, and the leper's hatch through which they received their food is barely recognisable.

Follow round towards the bridge, once on a main turnpike route up into town, and notice the lepers' graveyard to the left. Lepers received their burial rights as soon as they were recognised as having the disease. It seems strange to us to find such contaminated land so close to running water. In front of you are the upright quoins of Taddiport Bridge (built in 1260) which resemble a set of crooked teeth and were hewn from the quarry you see later on this walk.

The two-storey tollhouse on the opposite side of the bridge dates back to the days of the canal which was here in the 1820s. Retrace your steps, and keep the Lepers' Church (founded in 1300) on your right. **(6)** Take the bridleway towards Servis Farm. This has a made-up surface, so you don't have to watch your feet as you walk by the ghostly, now redundant Unigate Milk Factory, originally known as the Torridge Vale Butter Factory when built in 1874. Its broken reflection in the Torridge reminds its former workers that change cannot be prevented. A supermarket is imminent.

You pass through ancient riparian woods here, mainly beech with some conifer planting, but with bright holly and spindle berries shining forth in autumn. Struggle on through the muddy farmyard, and at **(7)** follow the footpath through the gate which will take you across the Tarka Trail, where models of passengers sit and wait for the trains to run again. It was indeed once a model railway, running from 1925 to 1965. Go through another hunting gate with a high handle and into the meadow, where you will have to walk around the Ford **(8)**. Here at the back of the garden turn sharp right and up into the lane, which is surfaced at first but then gives way to grass. Woodlands with rhododendron breaks for gamekeeping flank this lane.

(9) It emerges at Rakeham Cross, marked with a cast-iron post with a pyramid finial bearing one 'D' for Devonshire. At the bottom of the hill to your right stands the Rothern Bridge Toll House, so called because of all the cattle (rother = ox in Anglo-Saxon) which were driven past here. I had the good fortune to see inside this house just after the last toll-keeper had died. The boards advertising toll prices had been cut down to size, and were forming part of the shelving in an upstairs cupboard. If you were a packman taking unmade gloves to workers at Monkleigh and Littleham, this might have been the route you took. **(9)** Here, if you wish, you can turn back into Great Torrington and the glove factory in White's Lane. But to continue, turn left into the ridgeway road which will lead you to Frithelstock. Notice the quarried cliffs out of which the upright quoins of the Taddiport bridge were made.

(10) The old Priory stands to the right of Frithelstock Church, and was founded in 1229 by monks from Hartland Abbey. It will have taken you just over an hour to get here, so this could have been the route favoured by the Augustinian monks who cared for the lepers at Taddiport.

(11) Frithelstock Stone stands on what once must have been a busy crossroads. Notice the village pump to your left, and the Bible Christian Chapel 1852, one where Mr Vaughan the glover may well have preached or used as a centre to collect his outworkers' finished gloves. To extend your walk into another green lane, take the road towards Bideford, the A388 to your right. You can begin to smell the sea here.

(12) Take the first on your left, turning sharply down the slurry-filled lane which soon gives way to an interesting holloway. There are ash and holly here, and some elder. The track has a sunken camber but distinct packhorse ledges, and is possibly part of the back way from the foreign-sounding River Duntz.

(13) At its end, turn right and right again down to Frithelstock Stone. Continue to the right along the A388 for a short distance until you see Hele Lane. On your left you pass a footpath green lane entrance, with good views over Exmoor.

(14) Turn to the left into a lane marked with a dead-end sign, pass Leaside and then to the right into a well-cobbled lane. This leads towards Priestacott. Back in Torrington you will see a plaque by the Vicarage stating

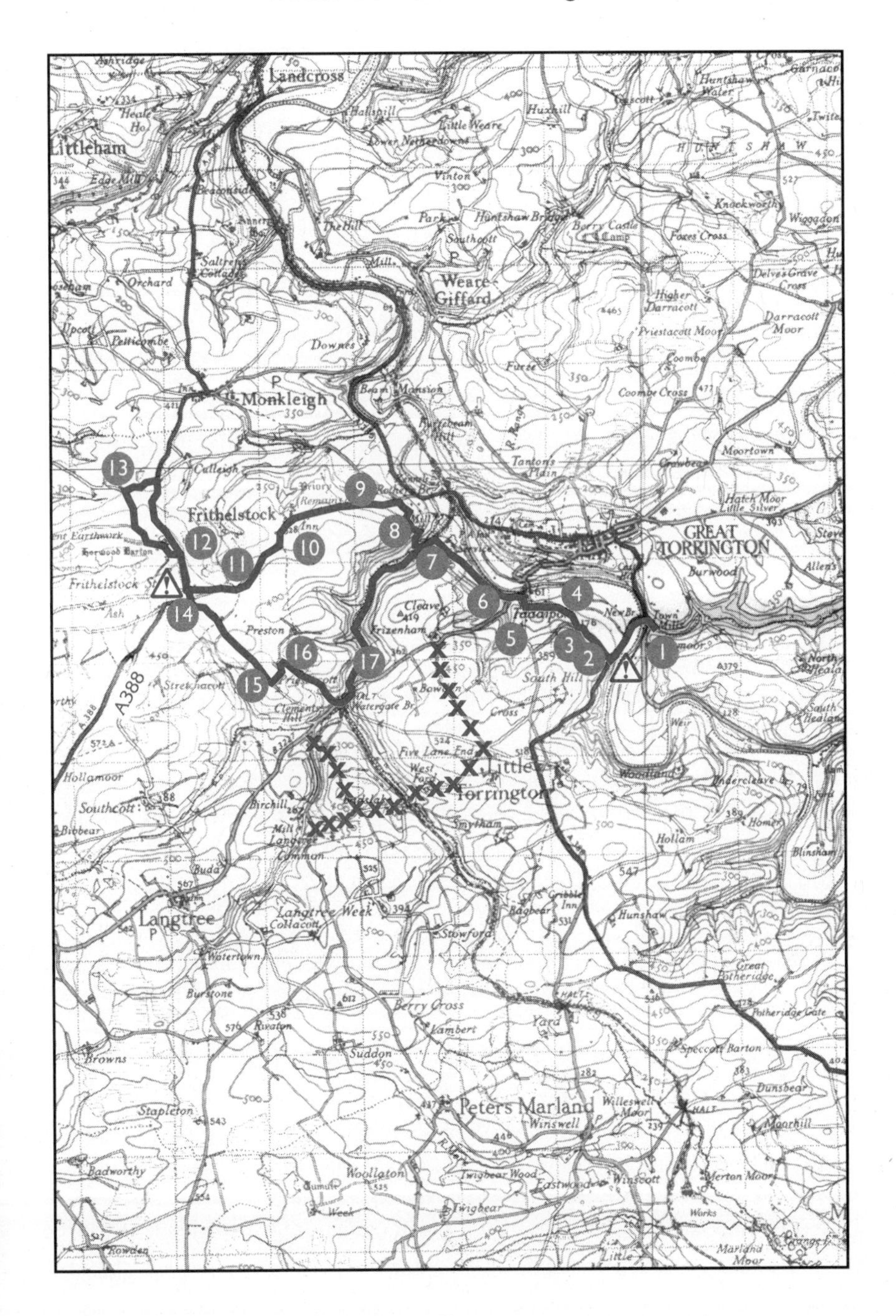
Landcross
Littleham
Monkleigh
Frithelstock
Weare Giffard
GREAT TORRINGTON
Little Torrington
Langtree
Peters Marland
A388
1
2
3
4
5
6
7
8
9
10
11
12
13
14
15
16
17

that in 1491 the residence of the parish priest had been built here so that he did not have to tramp up to church too often along these muddy ways.

Turn left into the footpath here. **(15)** 'Tramp' is the word here again: just as you pass through a gate into a rambling farmyard there is another gate on the right with a Torrington Tramp number disc attached.

As you descend, notice the very wide drovers' green lane ahead of you on the opposite hillside: the green lane which runs from Five Lane End – a common drovers' way place name – to Frizenham.

(16) You drop down through the woods to the Tarka Trail again.

(17) Follow it to your left at Watergate Bridge, and this will take you back to Rothern Bridge, which is said to have been designed and built by the monks of Frithelstock. This is close by the old Torrington Station, with its large station yard where cattle were corralled before boarding. Eggesford and King's Nympton have similarly large yards.

By the way

Although this walk is particularly overshadowed by ecclesiastical monuments, it is also a tale of shifting fortunes. It begins with the original Saxon strip fields and the Torrington Commoners' Lands, given to the people by Baron Fitz Robert of Torrington in 1194 whilst his monarch Richard I was at the Crusades.

You keep close to the river, where there was an important transport system for quarried stone from Rolle. Changing fortunes bring changing travel patterns. It is ironic that the success of the glove industry in a town which was so fiercely Cromwellian came about because, after the Restoration of King Charles II to the throne, it was the fashion to wear very long silk gloves to the elbow. Some Torringtonians must not have wanted to touch this industry any more than the lepers at Taddiport.

The going rate for glove-making was 3s 6d for twelve pairs. It took between ten and twelve hours to make two pairs. Glovers had a reputation for being gadabouts and flighty, as many worked from home. But at these rates it seems that they would hardly ever have had time to even look out of the window.

Other green lanes in the area

The triangle of lanes at Gortlage/Barley Hayes/Little Comfort, and Watergate Bridge.

Links

There are buses through Great Torrington from Barnstaple, Bideford, Exeter, Hatherleigh and Holsworthy and Plymouth. The Tarka Trail. Mill Lane towards Buckland Brewer.

Question

The sanctuary ring: where can you find a ring of protection on this walk?

Images on Vaughan's glove factory.

Route 29

PETERS MARLAND & BEAFORD

Clay workers and the freer-footed drovers

OS Explorer Map 127

This walk is dedicated to the stuggy-footed (see page 42) clay workers of Peters Marland who worked these pits by hand and on foot from the 17th to the 19th centuries. The conditions in which they worked must have been appalling, with no wellington boots to protect their feet. Wellingtons were first brought into popular production after the second world war (although they had already made an appearance in the first one when the army issued 12 million of them). It was Wellington's preferred design, rather than what we consider to be wellingtons today, which gave them their name. The Hunter Wellington Boot Company was founded in 1946, and went into liquidation in 2006.

This is a mysterious part of west Devon, where glimpses of the bald-headed plateau of the clay works still come as a surprise amidst the rolling hills and woodlands of the Torridge Valley. This is not primarily a circular walk, but can be made so if you wish. It links two bus routes: one from Exeter to Barnstaple, and one from Plymouth to Bideford.

Conditions: Some minor roads and some stuggy green lanes.

Distance: 3-4 miles.

Starting point: SS553151.

(1) Take the first of the lanes which is actually called 'green' here, and which runs behind the church and the Beaford Centre. Turn left, and begin to descend towards Beaford Mill. Notice to your right the beginning of another series of green lanes which can take you back to the village.

(2) The Torridge's riverside meadows open out before you as you cross

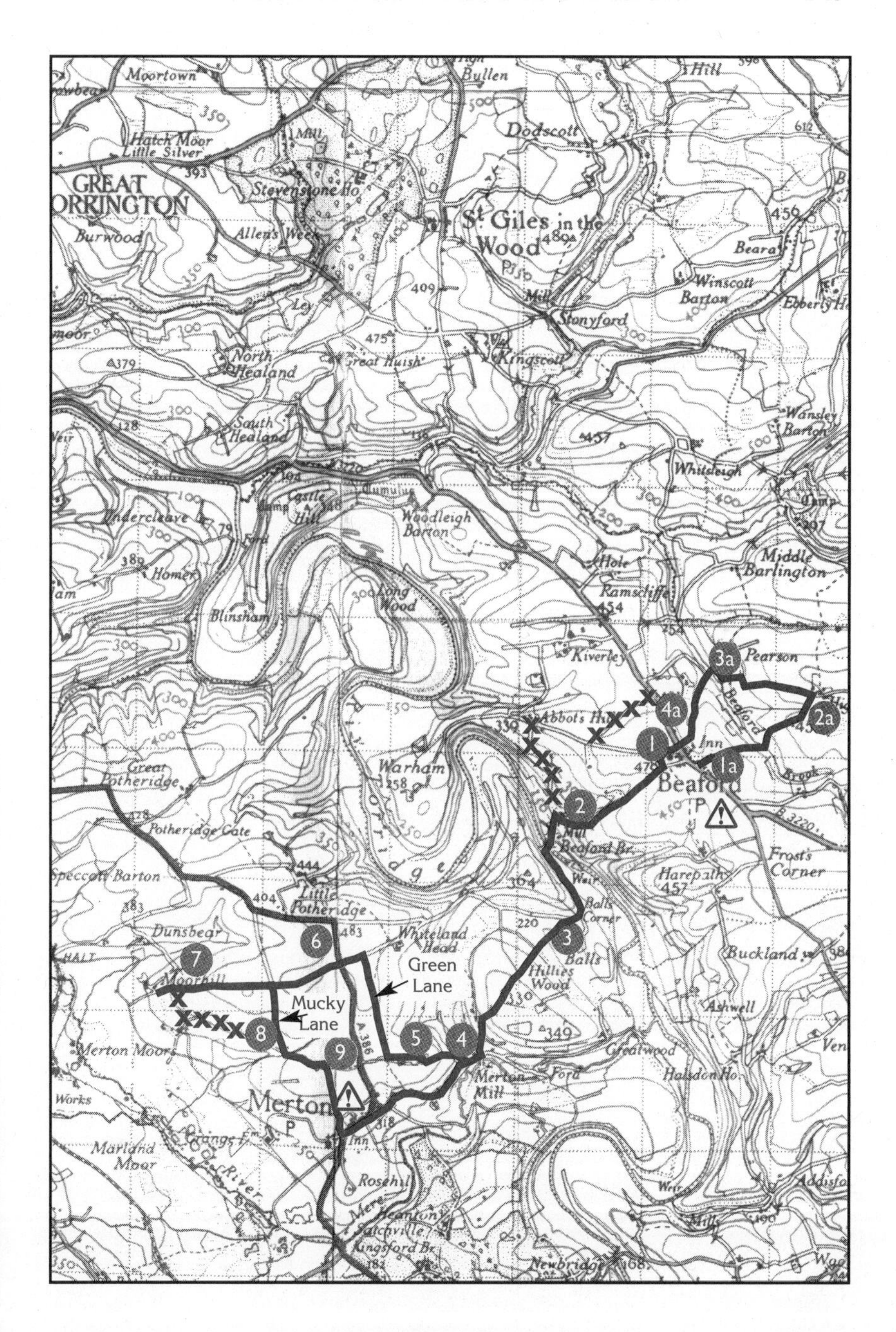
Moortown
Bullen
Hatch Moor
Little Silver
GREAT
TORRINGTON
Dodscott
Stevenstone Ho
St Giles in the
Wood
Burwood
Allen's Week
Beara
Winscott
Barton
Stonyford
Great Huish
Kingscott
North
Healand
South
Healand
Wansley
Barton
Whitsleigh
Castle
Hill
Woodleigh
Barton
Undercleave
Homer
Middle
Barlington
Hole
Ramscliffe
Long
Wood
Blinsham
Kiverley
Pearson
Abbots Hill
Inn
Warham
Beaford
Great
Potheridge
Potheridge Gate
Beaford Br.
Frost's
Corner
Harepath
Speccott Barton
Little
Potheridge
Dunsbear
Whiteland
Head
Balls
Hillies
Wood
Buckland
Moorhill
Green
Lane
Mucky
Lane
Ashwell
Merton Moors
Greatwood
Merton
Mill
Halsdon Ho
Merton
Works
Marland
Moor
River
Rosehill
Heanton
Satchville
Kingsford Br.
Newbridge
Addisford
3a
4a
2a
1
1a
2
3
4
5
6
7
8
9

over the wide span of the Beaford Bridge, built in 1845. There are woods of oak and beech to one side, and spruce woodlands to the other. Along the banks here, and those of the Taw too in many places, there are coppiced stands of alders, purple-headed in winter. If you're here on a rainy day, these words by Kathleen Jamie will haunt you:

alder, who unfolded
before the receding glaciers
first one leaf then another
won't you teach me
a way to live
on this damp ambiguous earth?

Climb up to Ball's Corner **(3)** then turn left towards Yeory Farm and Merton. The fields have a square pattern as you climb up once again. This is where the first group of Monterey pines appears on the horizon.

These giants, to be found all over Devon, were first introduced into Britain by David Douglas from the 1830s onwards. They were often used as marker trees for droveways.

(4) From this dark pine valley, take the bridleway to the right through the woods which soon leads up towards the Old Rectory, now known as Merton House. This is yet another of the huge rectories in this area, which seem out of all proportion to the size of the congregations. In 1871 there were only just over 300 people in the parish. Follow the lane round, passing a group of farm outbuildings on your left then at **(5)** take the wide footpath which is in part a green lane and in width very much a drovers' lane. Turn left at its end, noticing the clump of pines at Towell Farm to your right.

(6) Go straight across at these crossroads into the bridleway known as Mucky Lane. On a windy wet day in January I didn't find this completely the case, as the lane runs quite high and is flanked dramatically by more pines. The most noticeable building, standing high and white on the horizon to your right, is the former Bible Christian Chapel founded in 1870 which now bears the plaque of the United Free Methodists and is dated 1907, the year when many nonconformist groups were brought together. But its positioning here by the Bible Christians would have attracted those working on the land, in the clay pits, or droving cattle. These people were the mainstay of their congregation; they were ready for anything which would lighten their loads.

(7) Go straight across at these crossroads and, if you have not heard them before, this is where the sound of the lorries working in the clay pits clanks across the hills. Gaps in the hedges reveal the clay pit plateau to the left. In 1889, 75 workers came here each day from 6 a.m. to 1 p.m. to extract clay from the open-cast pits and roll it into 18lb balls. Fifty percent of the clay was exported, and all was sent to Great Torrington by tram. The pine trees decrease in number. Perhaps they were not put there for drovers, but by the kindness of the Holwill family, who ran the Marland Brick and Tile Works and the North Devon Clay Company, to guide their workers to work. Ivy House on the right is built from Peters Marland clay bricks.

The dynasty and the works closed in 1942, but, as you hear and see, clay continues to be extracted. Keep on descending towards Moorhill Farm, and from the bank at the beginning of the green lane you get a very good view of the works, whatever the weather. To return, retrace your steps and take the footpath up the steps to the right which will lead you to **(8)** Tythecombelake Cottage and on up and over to **(9)** Limers' Lane. There were also lime kilns in the clay pits. Descend towards Merton. From here you can make the link with the Plymouth to Barnstaple bus.

If you decide to make your way back to Beaford, then there is an additional two- to three-mile circuit which has been inserted here under numbers **(1a)** to **(4a)**.

Beaford

Nowhere better than in this area do you meet the hidden changes within the landscape of mid-Devon. You are on top of a series of moors: Cherubeer, Stafford, Dowland, Cudworthy, Merton, and, of course, Beaford itself. The curtain of grey skies brought in from Dartmoor can suddenly change as the sun reveals the folds of the valleys around, from which the mists are coming up from the river – and the biggest miasma comes from the Torridge below. From the A3124 onto the old turnpike road leading into Great Torrington and built in 1835, take the footpath sign at **(1a)**. This lane will take you down to the Beaford Brook and up towards Higher Upcott, where you will not be able to see the remains of St Clement's Chapel, as indicated on the modern OS map.

(2a) At Higher Upcott, turn left into a lane lined with tall beeches. There are extensive views over to Dartmoor here.

(3a) Turn left into a green lane footpath here, which immediately divides. Take the path to the right through a stand of small leafed lime, coppiced long ago, by the Beaford Brook. There is dog's mercury growing here too; both the lime and this plant are indicators of ancient woodland. As you proceed up the surprisingly well-cobbled lane you will see **(4a)** a concreted-up well to the left. This was one of two which served this village, because although there is a ford in its name it stands high above the water courses below in the valleys which flank it.

By the way

The clay pits here have been quarried since 1680, when working in such stuggy conditions must have been dreadful. Apart from the clay-ballers themselves, there were many others too who worked: running, making and repairing trucks and horse-drawn transport around the site. 'Marl', as in Peters Marland, is a subsoil which contains lime, so there were lime kilns working here and producing fertiliser for the area too.

You will find some old workers' cottages at Yarde, near the Gribble Inn on the A386. The school shows that in 1872 there was room for 80 children, but the average attendance was always around half this number. For those who couldn't afford shoes to walk to school in, there were some things which were easier to do without them – maybe puddling clay. Nearby Potheridge Hall is the birthplace and dream home of George Monk, who never seemed to have time to enjoy it. He was active throughout the Civil War, and was well known for his sense of justice and philanthropic outlook. He died in London in 1688, helping to revitalise the city after such devastation. Had he been at home, you feel sure that he would have made sure that the clay workers' conditions were improved. This would have met with the approval of Ernest Bevin, from Route 1.

Other green lanes in the area

Some to the north of Beaford. An established walk south-westward towards the Torridge from Abbot's Hill, Beaford. From Dolton there are the riverwards routes to New Bridge, Huish and Merton.

Nearby Hollocombe has many green lanes running through this deer park. There is a publication about walks in this area, available from

Winkleigh Post Office.

There are countless lanes in this area which remain truncated as a result of changing farming methods, charting the gradual change from arable to pasture; the tipping point in favour of pasture was 1889. For example, if you carry on in a westerly direction from Upcott Barton in the Beaford walk at SS564155, you will see the pattern shows deforestation, then an arable use, moving to complete pasture land. The lanes remained throughout all these changes.

Links

The Tarka Trail. The Plymouth to Barnstaple bus route. The Exeter to Barnstaple bus route. There is a Barometer Museum at Merton.

Question

What colour are the bricks which are made from Peters Marland clay?

The clay railway which ran for six miles from Peters Marland to Great Torrington, now part of the Tarka Trail.

Route 30

OFF THE TARKA TRAIL AT LITTLEHAM

Tales of poaching and pestilence at Monkleigh and Landcross

OS Explorer Map 139 or 126

Along the length of the Tarka Trail there are various footpaths and minor roads to entice you off the beaten track. It's difficult to choose. Here is a diversion into some surprising stories, hidden wildlife treasures – and from time to time, spectacular views. Besides the Trail itself, there are three bus routes running along the valley here.

Conditions: Muddy and slippery in lanes and footpaths. Some steep climbs and descents.

Distance: Full circuit 5-7 miles.

Starting point: I have given the Chapel at Landcross SS455237 as the middle point for starting, but it is not essential.

(1) Turn left off the A386 and, although you are still on a fairly busy road, by keeping to the left and dodging into gateways which overlook the river this is a good route to look out for the herons, shelduck, noisy orange-legged whimbrels and little egrets which dine in the dense mud below. You pass a house with a warehouse-look about it, called Belle Vue. Next there is a sign for Whitehall, and some riverside houses with an industrial warehouse feeling about them. On your right as you approach the tollhouse there is a milestone with its plaque missing.

(2) Turn sharp right up what was once the way from Bideford to Torrington used by the turnpike, and is signed as being 'Unsuitable for Heavy Goods Vehicles'.

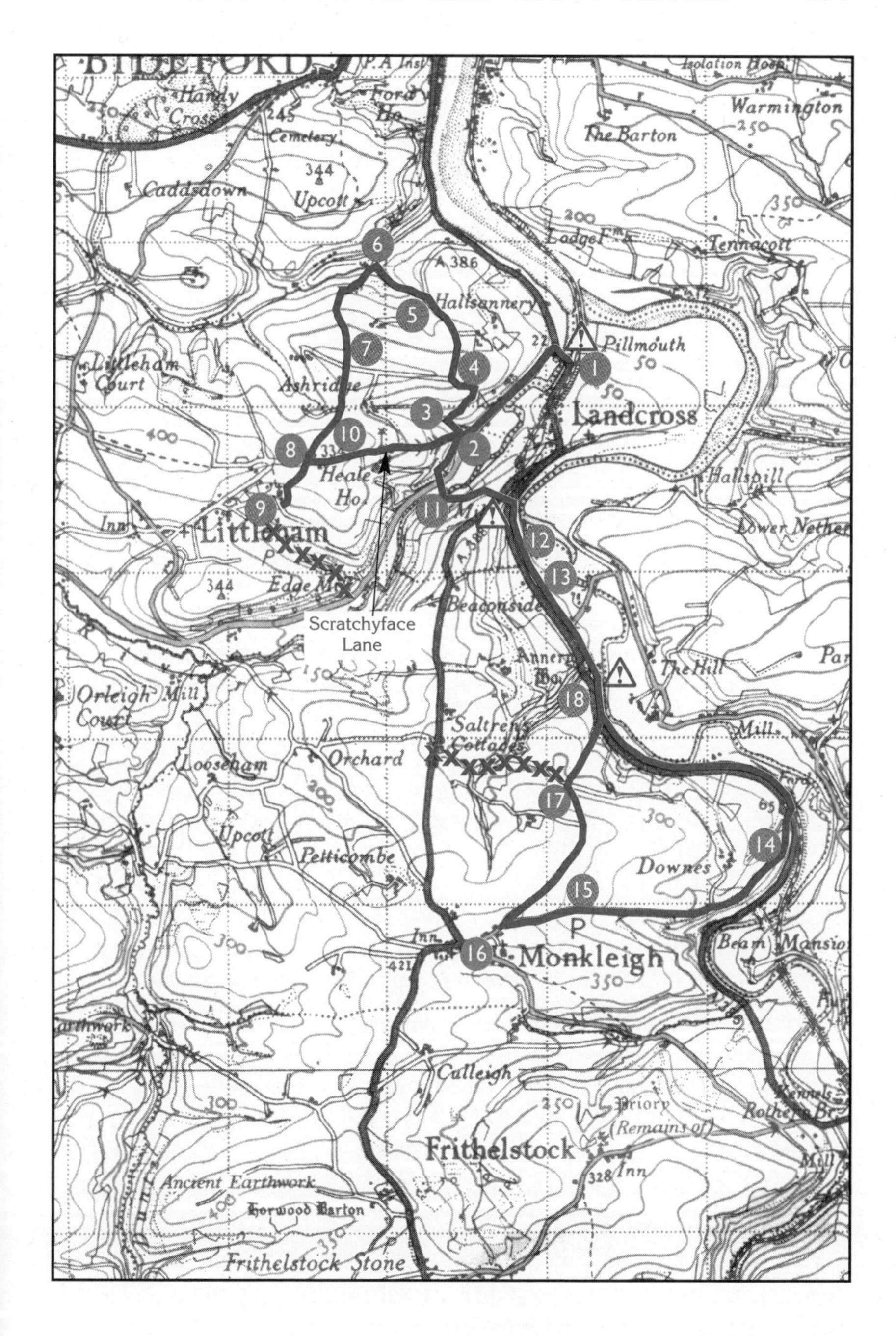
Scratchyface Lane
Bideford
Landcross
Littleham
Monkleigh
Frithelstock
Pillmouth
Hallsannery
Ashridge
Heale Ho.
Beaconside
Saltrens Cottages
Downes
The Barton
Warmington
Lodge Fm.
Tennacott
Hallspill
The Hill
Littleham Court
Caddsdown
Upcott
Cemetery
Edge Mill
Orleigh Mill
Orleigh Court
Loosebam
Orchard
Petticombe
Culleigh
Priory (Remains of)
Ancient Earthwork
Horwood Barton
Frithelstock Stone
Beam Mansion

(3) At the top bend, by Spinney Cottage, go straight over into another lane with a 'Restricted' notice, which soon becomes green and is towered over by sycamores. Towards the top there is a line of once-layered ash trees, huge and hollowed round their roots, where shrews and voles now live.

(4) Turn right here and follow the lane up, enjoying views to the right over the river valley with the square tower of Landcross Church to your right, the slopes of Exmoor, and a view of Bideford and its two bridges below, with Baggy Point in the distance.

(5) You pass Hallsannery, once a pottery, and then at the end of a slope you plunge into a dark watery public bridleway to the left. There is some tarmac at the beginning, which gives way to cobbles, and a view of Ashridge to the left. There are indeed a lot of ash trees growing in the spinneys through which you pass. Tarmac comes back at the wide end of the lane, and you come out into a road with a mill to your right. Continue round to the left at **(6)** and up into the ash woods again. The lane climbs narrowly up with more wide-ranging views through the hedgerows.

(7) At the top there is another 'Unsuitable for Heavy Traffic' notice, and on your right a sign to Ashridge Farm. Continue to the right, then straight down towards Littleham.

(8) At the crossroads where the Village Hall stands, go straight over and into the public footpath towards **(9)**. The church is in an idyllic position amongst the cedars of the imposing rectory. Look for the children's graves in the churchyard. The background to some of the scarlatina victims you will find here has been touchingly commemorated by Liz Shakespeare in her book *A Story from a Devon Churchyard* (see bibliography).

At this point you can take the footpath through the churchyard and go down to Edge Mill or retrace your steps to the crossroads at **(8)** and turn left into **(10)** Scratchyface Lane, also once turnpiked; and deemed, as so many in this circuit, to be 'Unsuitable'. It passes the backs of some large houses, Heale and Summerhill.

Turn right again as you pass by **(3)** again. When you reach the A386 at the toll house, again turn right for a while and then **(11)** left again opposite Heale House Lodge. You soon come to Landcross Cornmill bridge, where there is an almost guaranteed sighting of kingfishers – cross the bridge and watch out for them. From here you can either go straight up Mill Lane or take the footpath to the left by the river Yeo, bordered with purple sedge, which climbs over the fields.

(12) The footpath takes you onto the Tarka Trail. I suggest that you turn right here and enjoy the ease of walking along a straight surface for a while.

(13) However, you can choose to go over to Landcross and the beautiful little church where Henry Williamson was married in 1925, in an area where the idea of Tarka was first born (1927), and to whom the trail you return to will always belong. If not, carry on down towards Great Torrington on the track and at **(14)** Loxhore Cross go under the track on the right to come up on the minor road to Monkleigh, passing Downes to your right. Continue straight on here to **(15)** Monkleigh for a look around the church at **(16)**. Then back on to the track to **(17)**, this time keeping left. There is a green lane to your left here, which was once part of the Annery House Estate, perhaps the escape route for the gamekeeper who shot his master over 500 years ago (see *By the way*). Follow the footpath sign ahead and down through the fields, keeping the stream to your right as you go and using the shuttering which keeps you out of the mire. You come out into a lane by the A386. Take great care as you cross here.

(18) Climb back onto the trail here by a drainage channel-cum-waterfall and a seat. Turn left and back towards Landcross.

By the way

At Monkleigh we have the story of the unfortunate death of Sir William Hankford of Annery Hall in the 1430s, who lies buried in the south aisle of the church. In his zeal to stop poaching, he ordered his gamekeeper to shoot on sight anyone suspected of the crime. One evening Sir William himself appeared in a lane by the river, and was indeed shot on sight by his gamekeeper. Annery House itself, a Tudor mansion, is long gone. But in its plans there were a series of very small rooms with plain doors and small windows. Spy holes through which to spot poachers, maybe?

Apart from otters, the Two Rivers have always been frequented by poachers, however hard landowners have tried to protect what they saw as their rights. In 1828, a new law stated that anything which swam or flew over a landowner's land was his or hers alone, thus adding to the hardship of those who were only trying to keep their families alive by claiming what God had created, yet only some people could legally claim.

In Littleham in 1871 there was a scarlatina epidemic. Study the gravestones and you will see young children amongst its victims. These lanes were walked by the poet postman, Edward Capern, on his route from Bideford to Buckland Brewer. Living here also was a William Williams, a blind coal-carrier who supplied the villagers with fuel from Bideford. Let's hope he used the locally available water-borne transport to help him in this task.

Other green lanes in the area

Many going back to Torrington or northwards towards Bideford.

Links

The Tarka Trail. On three bus routes, from Exeter, Barnstaple and Plymouth.

Question

Which of the two rivers of Tarka country are you passing by here?

Route 31

BIDEFORD

Defending the Quay

OS Explorer Map 139

The overpowering presence of the high Bideford Bridge gives this walk a threatening edge, which fits the history of the area. A stone marks the spot where Hubba the Dane gave up his Raven Standard and his life to King Alfred the Great in battle. It reads:

> "Stop Stranger Stop
> Near this spot lies buried
> King Hubba the Dane
> who was slain by King Alfred the Great
> in a bloody retreat."
> – The Anglo-Saxon Chronicle Chappells Record, 878 A.D.

The Danes, having come back for the body of their leader, doubled back into some of the lanes you will walk today before being harried out to sea. You are walking in an area which once swarmed with provisions coming in and out of the busy quay.

Conditions: Steep in places with some stony surfaces and narrow paths.

Distance: 3-4 miles.

Starting point: The Lundy Island Offices SS457276 Bideford Quay.

(1) Follow the Quay northward away from the Bridge passing the statue of Charles Kingsley and the skateboard ramp. Great Torrington Council offices are on your right, and the site of the cattle market to your left, which will be covered by more new houses soon, no doubt.

(2) Veer left into Chircombe Lane, passing the entrance to Chircombe House, once inhabited by General William Crichton. The lane has cobbles and is deeply sunken – obviously for centuries the way to the river.

(3) Turn right at Riverford Hotel into the bottom of Limers Lane. Resist the temptation to stick to the river here, and take the footpath inland by Cleave. This moss covered alley-like lane takes you between houses which crowd together by the river, where you will find an abandoned ruin of a house and a striking copper beech tree.

(4) Follow the footpath down again towards the river.

(5) Here you will pick up the Coastal Path again through what seem like back gardens, but will soon take you into a green lane hedged with coppiced hazel and some large beeches. When you reach the T-junction, with a well in front of you, think of the hordes of Saxons and Vikings crashing along the lanes in the ninth century. Take a detour and follow the lane to the top where it merges with an estate lane, and turn back down. Once again at the well follow the lane round, where you will be confronted by reminders of another conflict. The lane has a row of anti-tank pyramids across it, through which you will have to squeeze.

(6) You now start a pleasant stretch of walking through National Trust oak woodlands at Burrough, where Charles Kingsley once lived as a child. The cries of curlews and whimbrels are in the air below. There are glimpses of Westleigh Church over the water.

(7) Veer left up into woodlands and then into a green lane known as Windmill Lane, which gradually merges into a housing estate. The windmill here was first recorded in 1609 in a will made by Thomas Leigh, but no ruins remain. There are some windmill ruins in Bidna Lane, further north at SS457296, where the letting was advertised in 1806 stating its capacity: "With a brisk wind it would grind twelve bushels of corn in an hour." Veer right into Greenacre Close, and take the footpath over a field, stopping at the top for sweeping views over Northam Burrows.

(8) Turn left into the green lane at the foot of the hill, and along to the main road to find Hubba's Stone. Turn back along the green lane again and go down into the estuary.

(9) At the river's edge, turn right. There are glimpses of the ruined windmill at Instow from here. Retrace your steps back to the Quay, keeping to the well-marked Coastal Footpath as you do so.

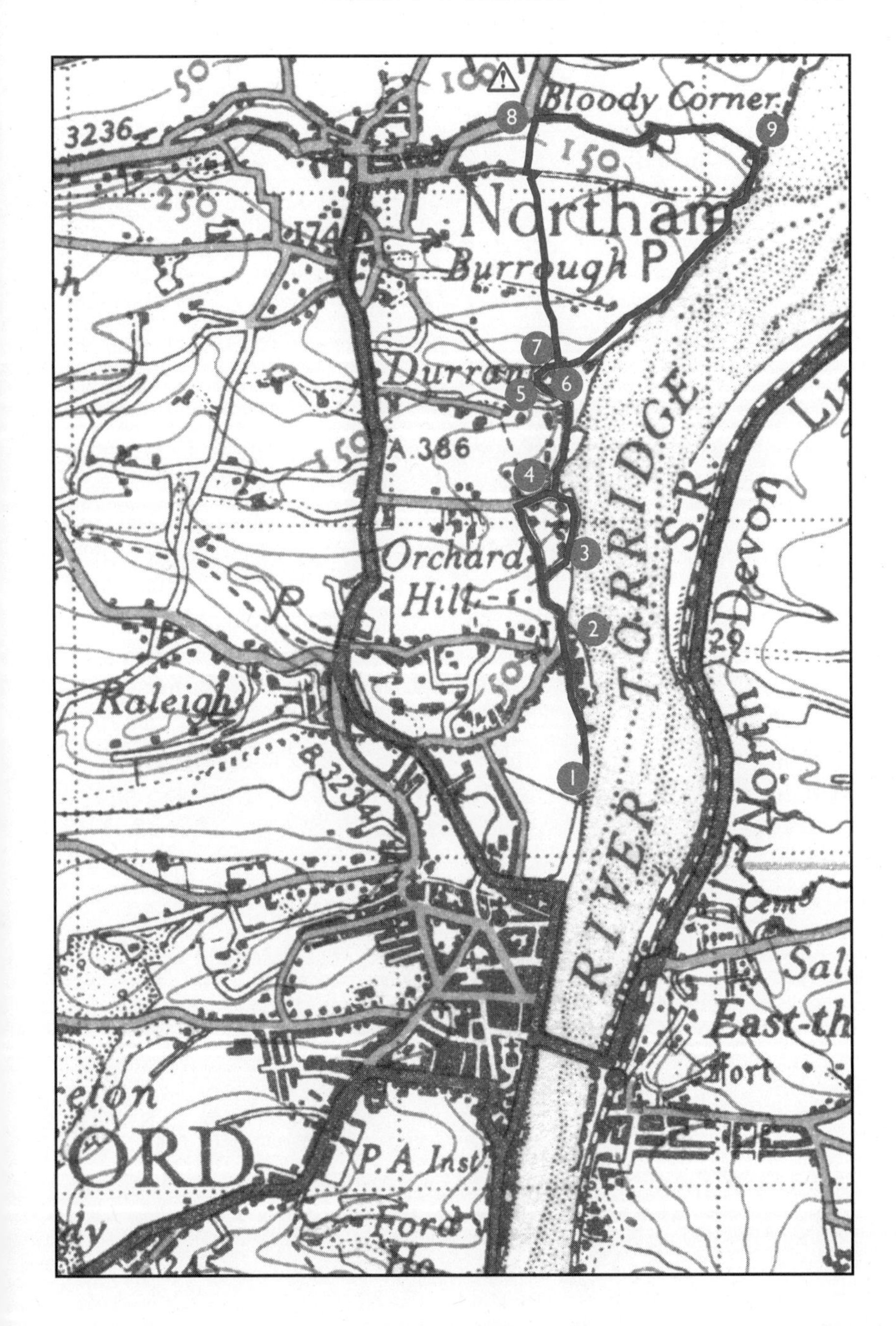
Bloody Corner
3236
Northam
Burrough
Durrant
A.386
Orchard Hill
Raleigh
B.3234
RIVER TORRIDGE
ORD
P.A Inst
East-the
Devon
North
50
100
150
250
174
1
2
3
4
5
6
7
8
9

By the way

At the outset we pass an area known as Orchard Hill. The apples which once grew there included such local names as Barum Wonders, Annie Elizabeths, Scarlet Leadingtons and Lane's Prince Alberts. The town and port of Bideford was well provided for by provisions of all kinds coming from the hinterland and destined for export. However, some of these provisions were desperately needed at home. Because of the high price of corn, many raided local mills to demand a just price for bread, or took to eating potatoes when they could. However, here in 1816 there were 'potato riots' on the quay, when hungry Devonians tried get their hands on outgoing shipments of produce which they had grown. The North Devon Yeomanry were not called out on this occasion (see Route 20 for when they were). This was partly the result of high corn prices during the French Wars 1795–1815, which enabled potato-eating to become well established amongst all classes.

Links

There are many buses which pass through Bideford in all directions.
The Tarka Trail.

Question

There was something burning here by the river before it was carted off inland.

Abbotsham Riflemen (see Route 32).

Route 32

ABBOTSHAM

A stronghold now sidelined

OS Explorer Map 139

This walk will take you to the site of Kenwith Castle, which Hubba the Dane was hoping to conquer in the ninth century. When thinking of the common man in this period, it has been said that he was involved in one of three things; agriculture, fighting or praying. It's the fighters who feature most prominently in our imagination, but taming the land and working the sea have always been more of a priority here.

Conditions: Some rocky and muddy surfaces.

Distance: 3-4 miles.

Starting point: Abbotsham Church. SS426265

(1) Rural trades are illustrated on the church's roof beam ends, and the tools of these trades are shown on some of the bench ends; but look out also for the juggler and death.

(2) Cross over and climb up to the Post Office on your right and follow the signpost to Greencliff. You will pass the Rebohoth Chapel, a Bible Christian chapel on your right. This strange word comes from the Hebrew, and means a wide space, implying room for all. Before you is the sea framed by Exmoor as you plunge down into a narrow green lane **(3)** 'Unsuitable for Motor Vehicles' on your right. This sunken, twisty lane must have hidden many a smuggler and wrecker. It has deeply worn slate steps in places. When the green lane meets the minor road, continue straight ahead into the green lane opposite. This can be watery, but has some fine examples of overgrown hedge-laying.

(4) At the top turn left, and follow the minor road along to **(5)**. Here at the entrance to Abbotsham Court is a fine example of the kind of pine tree that thrives so well in coastal areas.

(6) You now take the way indicated towards the sea by a furze and gorse hedgerow down to Abbotsham Cliff.

(7) On your right roll the breakers at Saunton, and to your left Clovelly is sketched tumbling down into the sea. You may see Lundy ahead. Below, ravens and kestrels wheel round the ruined lime kiln. Turn left and follow a short section of the Coastal Path here to **(8)**. A footpath is indicated to Greencliff on the left, and you climb up, reaching a recently planted group of trees popular with finches, whitethroats and linnets.

(9) You enter a short section of lane; the name Rixlade here refers to the industry of rush-growing and cutting along the stream and river banks. The lane is cobbled in places, reflecting its former heavy use. It brings you out over a stile and into the minor road at **(10)**. Turn left and you will find yourself back in Abbotsham once again. (You might want to reverse the order of this walk, and link it up with the previous walk in Bideford).

By the way

The obvious pleasure of this walk is the Coastal Footpath section, but don't forget the threat of invasion which would have come from the sea. Two hill-forts – Kenwith, where Hubba the Dane attacked Alfred the Great in 878, and Godborough – stand close together here.

You can return to Bideford by following the direct line on the high ridgeway road which runs back down into the Torridge. This must once have been the way to work for those involved in another kind of revolution – the rise of the white-collar worker. In the 1870s there were no less than three collar factories in the Kenwith area, employing over 1,000 people. This once important pedestrian way has been replaced to the west by the Kenwith Viaduct from Bideford built in 1987. It is an eight-span box girder bridge. If you take this minor road back to Bideford, look out for the Wade hedge-banks which were built here as part of the Atlantic Highway landscaping project. They are metal A-frame cages, constructed as hedge-banks and now flourishing with plants and wildlife.

You come out at the top of Bideford by Edge Hill School, founded by the Bible Christians as a girls school in 1884.

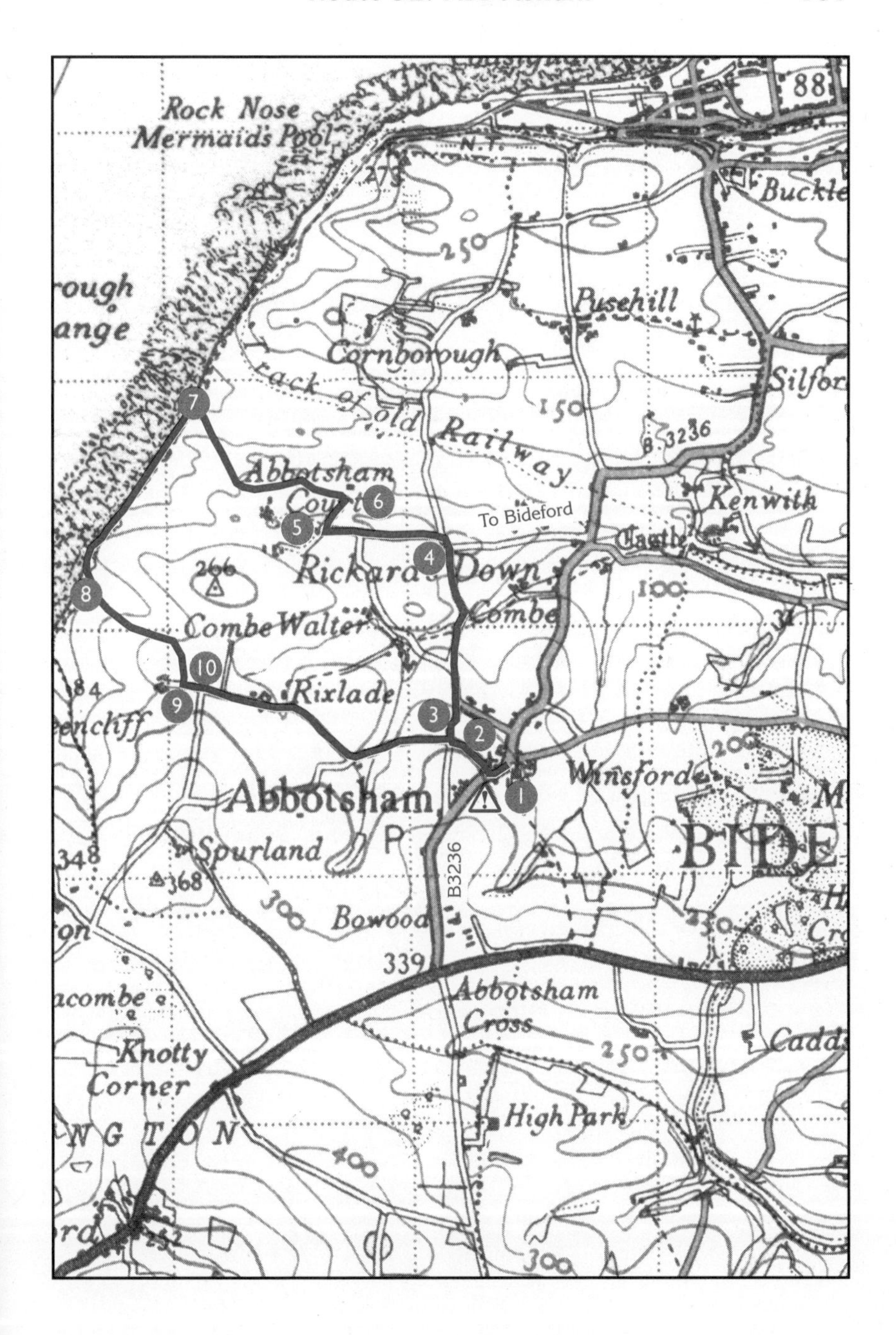
Rock Nose
Mermaid's Pool
Buckle
Pusehill
Cornborough
Track of old Railway
Silford
B 3236
Abbotsham
Court
Kenwith
To Bideford
Castle
Rickard's Down
Combe
Combe Walter
Rixlade
Abbotsham
Winsford
BIDE
Spurland
B3236
Bowood
339
Abbotsham
Cross
Knotty
Corner
High Park
250
300
400

By the way

From *Industries of North Devon* by Strong (1889) reprinted by David and Charles with notes by B. D. Hughes (1971).

> "The linen which we may call the raw material of the collar-maker, is, for the most part, received from Ireland, and the calico from Manchester. The bales are stored in a room at the further end of the old factory, from whence linen and calico are given out to the dozen or so cutters employed in the cutting-room next to it. The cutting is done by hand, with a knife very much like that of the leather-cutter, but with a trifle bigger blade. The linen is first cut to the necessary lengths and widths at the head of the cutter's room. Above the head of the workman who stands at his table, there runs a shelf on which are arranged the numerous wood patterns of the various collar, cuff and front shapes. Selecting the pattern required, the cutter fastens it down upon his layers of linen and runs his knife around the edge of the pattern, on the raising of which we detect the shape of the collar that is to be. Here the linen backs and calico strips of the collar are also cut."

Links

The Barnstaple to Hartland bus passes through Abbotsham.
The South West Coast Path.
Bideford, Route 31.
Buckland Brewer, Route 33.

Question

Is the pine tree growing at the entrance to Abbotsham Court a Scots or a Monterey Pine?

Mr Brown of Holwell Farm, Buckland Brewer with R. Bowden, Plymouth Branch Fascist, at the 'Danger Zone!'. From the *Western Times*, 20th October 1933 (see Route 33).

Route 33

BUCKLAND BREWER

A black tale of one rick of corn and one rick of hay

OS Explorer Map 126

It was at Holwell Farm in Buckland Brewer during 1933-4 where farmers refused to pay the old Church Tithe in kind. In 1933 their resistance was aided by around 40 members of the British Union of Fascists who set up camp, built trenches across the road, and felled trees ready to block the bailiffs. They were there to collect tithes in kind, and ricks of corn and hay. However, these suddenly started to disappear from the fields.

The fascists went the same way, so the case was dropped. Buckland Brewer was also the home of the poet-postman Edward Capern, who worked his way to and from Bideford twice a day for 15 years on foot. This walk sticks to the outskirts of the village, which you might like to explore later, along with the Duntz Valley.

Conditions: Some stoggy sections in lanes.

Distance: 2-3 miles.

Starting point: SS454187 at Frithelstock Stone.

(1) Mind how you negotiate this stretch of the A388 on the corner. Walk round to the minor road signposted to Tythecott and Thornhill. You will soon come into views of Exmoor again and Buckland Brewer church to your right. There is a lot of furze and holly in the hedges here.

(2) There is a small cemetery to your left here. As you descend, the large earthwork known as Hembury Castle is in view, but you might not think it. Its rounded contour is covered in beeches, oaks and ashes; unfortunately there is no access. Although this part of Devon seems treeless, remember that it was not always so. The Romans noticed that the ancient Britons often built forts in impassable woods, and this could have been one which they took over.

(3) This is where you enter Ashbury Lane and the long green lane which leads down to Stibb Cross. From a strategic point of view, this is obviously a way as old as the hill-fort, and a back way in and up towards Stibb Cross and beyond. In the beginning it is surfaced, and at the top of a steep incline through woods becomes green and an 'Unsuitable for Motors' sign appears when once past the farm. Just after **(4)** Cholash Farm, you come to a junction with a footpath to your left, a bridleway to your right and a minor road to Stibb Cross. This was heavily guarded by both Blackshirts and police in the 1930 incidents of tithe collecting. Slogans were daubed in white paint along here encouraging other farmers to UNITE AGAINST TITHES, THE TITHE WAR FARMERS WILL NOT SURRENDER.

(5) Take the bridleway to your right, and you will soon come to a grassy road triangle on a bend. Over 600 farmers camped out night and day in 1934 to support their fellow farmers.

(6) Follow the bridleway sign down into the wooded area, glancing to your left towards **(7)** Holwell Farm as you pass. Through a metal gate curves a sunken grassy lane, a holloway well below the level of the fields – you are hidden, protected. There is a stream at the bottom, which is easily forded and takes you up through the wood again where there are remains of a quarry and a flat area ideal for parking and camping. No doubt some of the farmers' supporters, including the Blackshirts, would have used this area well away from the 60 policemen who were stationed between Stibb Cross and Clovelly during the incident in 1934. On this occasion the bailiffs were successful, and took away the cattle. The Blackshirts suddenly departed for an important rally, leaving the Holwell farmer to pay a fine and penalties amounting to £70. Follow the footpath over the field to the right at **(8)**.

At Thornewidger, turn right and follow the road towards **(9)** Hoarestone and up to Buckland Brewer or back to **(3)** and your starting point. It is a minor road, and not so dangerous for walking. If you decide to visit Thorne Moor, now open through the C.R.O.W (Countryside and Rights of Way Act), or Thornehill Head where there is a Bible Christian chapel dating back to 1830, remember those farmers who had been so desperate that they put their faith in being rescued from their tithe-paying by a fascist organisation.

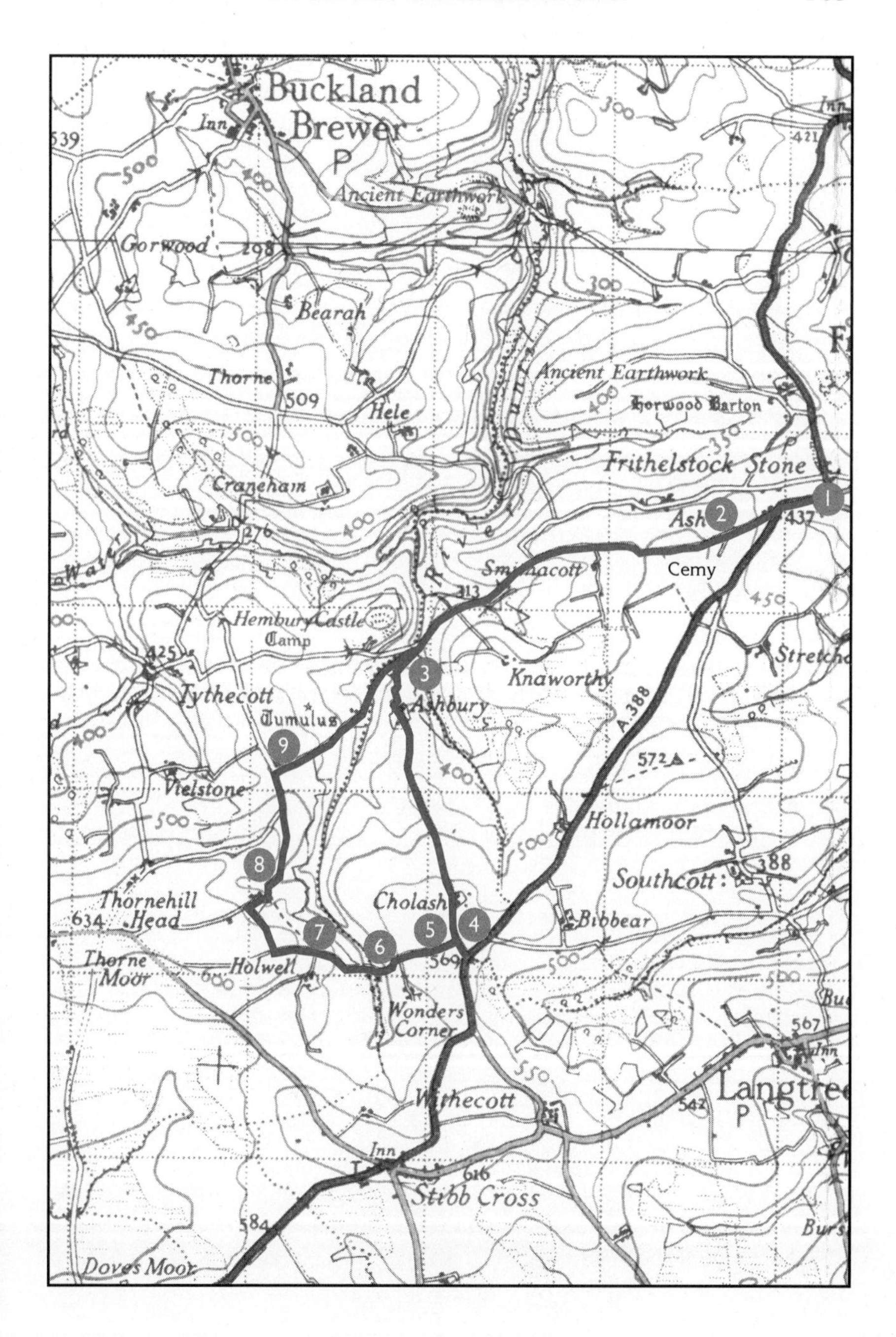

Buckland
Brewer
Inn
P
539
500
400
300
Ancient Earthwork
Gorwood
298
Bearah
450
Thorne
509
Hele
Ancient Earthwork
Horwood Barton
350
Frithelstock Stone
Craneham
276
400
Ash
437
Cemy
313
Hembury Castle
Camp
425
Knaworthy
Stretcho
Tythecott
Ashbury
Tumulus
A.388
572
Vielstone
500
Hollamoor
Southcott
388
Thornehill
Head
634
Cholash
Bibbear
Thorne
Moor
Holwell
569
600
Wonders
Corner
567
Inn
550
Withecott
Langtree
542
P
Inn
616
Stibb Cross
584
Doves Moor
1
2
3
4
5
6
7
8
9

As Todd Gray in his book, *Blackshirts in Devon*, concludes:

"History can repeat itself, and it is also possible to overlook and forget it."

By the way

Forget Dartmoor, visited by thousands every year: this north-west corner of Devon is the last wilderness. Buckland Brewer has been steadily farmed since Saxon times, and steadily subject to the paying of tithes both to the Vicarage and also to the Rector, as it came under Barnstaple Archdeaconry and Hartland Rural Deanery, and had once belonged to Tor Abbey in south Devon.

Throughout the country, tithes – a tenth of all produce – had to be paid annually. 'High' tithes were levied on corn and hay, and 'little' tithes on livestock, wool and non-cereals. These were stopped, and substituted by a monetary payment in 1836. But this was not so in this corner of north-west Devon when, in 1933, some of Mosley's Blackshirts from London, together with local recruits, came to defend Holwell Farm against the collection of one rick of corn and one rick of hay. They were also called in in 1934 against the collection of twelve cattle. In the latter event, members of the British Union of Fascists withdrew from the situation in order to attend a big rally in Olympia, London. Their presence is remembered more than the cause which they temporarily championed.

Other green lanes in the area

Great Torrington, Route 28, and other routes to Taddiport as indicated.

Links

There are links with the Great Torrington and Parkham walk here but the links with bus services are tenuous. There is a service from Barnstaple to Buckland Brewer but you need to study the timetable carefully.

Question

What is the original meaning of the word tithe?

Route 34

PARKHAM TO PEPPERCOMBE

'The gap before me'

OS Explorer Map 126

This walk is dedicated to all those who once walked this countryside on their way home from working in the fields and scouring the shoreline, and in particular to those from this village who went to serve in the Great War, believing it to be a 'Great Adventure'. It was their sense of duty which was appealed to in such Biblical quotations as this one displayed on their memorial in the church porch:

> "And I sought for a man among them that should make up the hedge and stand in the gap before me for the land." – *Ezekiel 22:30*

94 out of a population of approximately 750-800 did just that. Luckily only three were killed. However, the horror of the new experiences the survivors brought back to the village must have had a great impact on future generations.

Conditions: Prolonged steepness and rockiness in some parts; some rocky, hunched lane scrabbling in others.

Distance: 4-6 miles.

Starting point: SS389215. Beginning at the church, take the road to your left towards Chapel Lane.

(1) There is a public footpath signposted 'Unsuitable for Motor Vehicles' to your right, which runs down to the valley, passing the farm to your left. It is extremely wide and grassy, and feels like a drovers' route.

(2) At the bottom, turn left into the road over Newhaven Bridge and climb up this minor road, first reaching the hamlet of Goldworthy. Descendants of the poet John Gay once lived here. There is a chapel here. The farm has the date of 1918, and R.T. scratched above its roadside mounting-block. These were built for the convenience of not getting plastered in mud when mounting your horse.

(3) You will come to the Coach and Horses Inn at Horns Cross, standing on the opposite side of the busy A39. Cross with care by the Inn, which in the past was part of an old coaching route.

(4) You are now on National Trust land. Take the footpath to the right which leads down to Peppercombe. This runs down over cobbles through lines of layered ash accompanied by the rushing of the stream alongside.

(5) Take the right hand fork to Peppercombe by passing to the right of the wooden summer house painted in GWR (Great Western Railway) brown and cream. Go through the gate into a mysterious sunken section of lane where pollarded beeches have fallen across to form a tunnel, like diplodocus necks.

(6) Having emerged, you find yourself on a beach of grey and black rocks with bright red sandstone cliffs to your left towards Bideford, and the white slab of icing that is Saunton Hotel almost facing you. Clovelly tumbles down to your left, and Lundy might make an appearance in front of you. The ragged lumpiness of Peppercombe Iron Age Fort Castle looms beside you, from which peregrines and kestrels hover and dive.

(7) Now return straight up the path to your right, signed to 'Coastguard and Coombe Cottages, Northway ½ mile'. Towards the top here there is a section of the path which is drained using a central drainage channel, which seems to be made not out of concrete but stone. This form of highway management, which channelled the water into the middle of the road was popular in the 18th century, but this seems a much later development. There is a well to the right at the top here.

(8) Back up again to Horns Cross, where you will have the choice of crossing over and walking a few yards to your right and seeking out the footpath to the left which will lead you down eventually through West Goldworthy Farm; or you can return via the minor road from **(3)** to **(1)** down to Parkham Farm again.

(9) If not returning, follow the footpath signs down, then turn right into an oak-lined green lane. This is muddy in places and opens out into a field. Follow the field edge to your right, and dive down very deep to enter the hawthorn and hazel green lane which runs along here. Angry thrushes and blackbirds will flit by you, enraged at your discovering their hideouts.

(10) At the end you will find a field gate. Go straight across the meadow

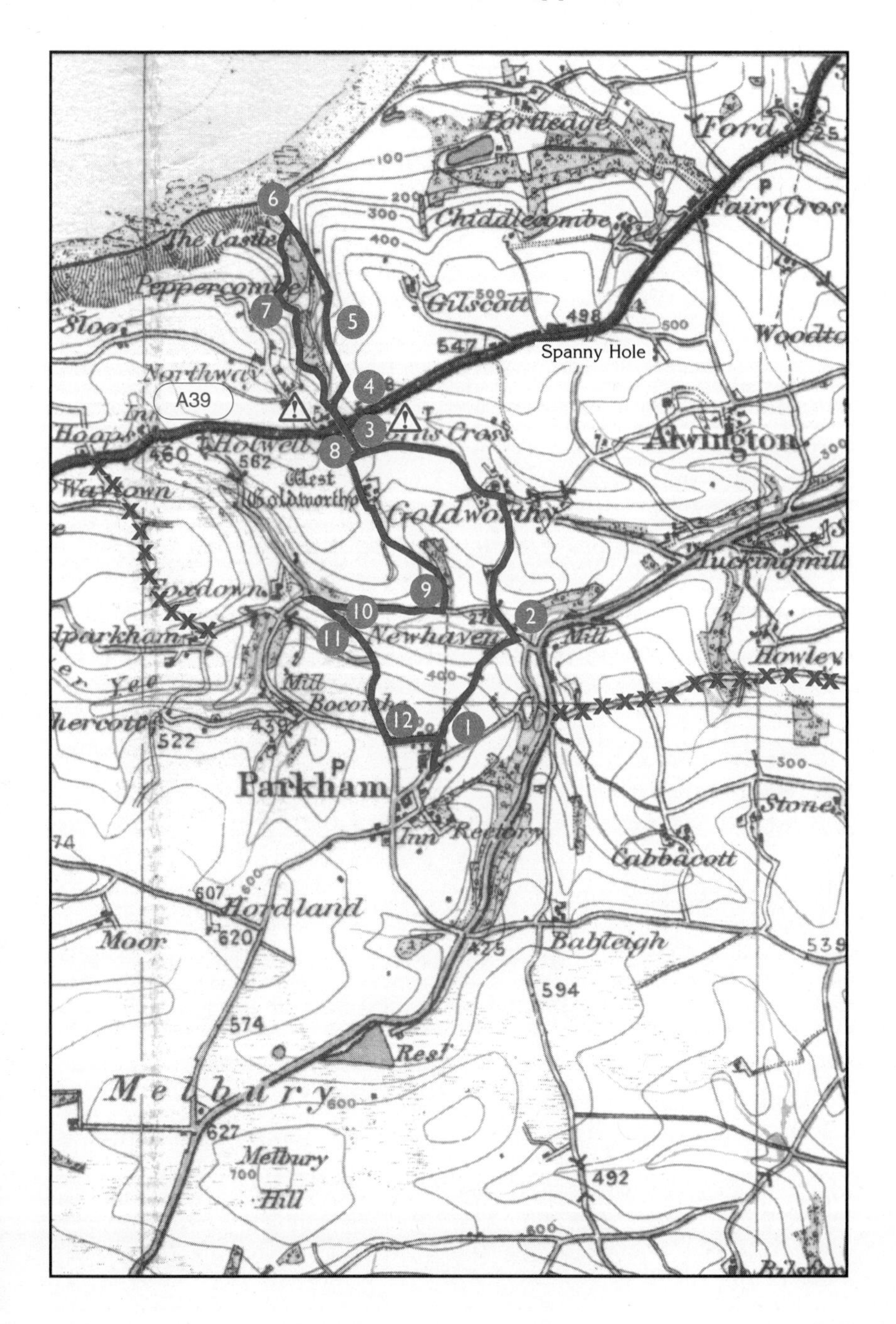
Portledge
Ford
Fairy Cross
Chiddlecombe
The Castle
Peppercombe
Gilscott
Spanny Hole
Woodtown
Northway
A39
Hoops Inn
Holwell
Horns Cross
Alwington
West Goldworthy
Goldworthy
Waytown
Foxdown
Newhaven
Mill
Buckingmill
Howley
River Yeo
Bocombe
Parkham
Inn
Rectory
Stone
Cabbacott
Hoddland
Moor
Bableigh
Rest
Melbury
Melbury Hill

towards a stile and into a rocky, low-ceilinged green lane.

(11) Turn up left and fight your way through to the road – a little more perpendicularity will be possible than in the previous lane.

(12) Turn left and follow the road around to Chapel Lane on your left. From here take the footpath which runs round the back of the church and in front of the magnificent Wesleyan Chapel (1888), its window bedecked with white icing-cake ribbon plasterwork.

By the way

The number of green lanes in this parish and its neighbour, Buckland Brewer, give plenty of speculation as to why this kind of lane has survived un-tarmacked. In the 1920s and 1930s, when the main tarmacking initiatives took place, these lanes were not considered economically important, yet the population was still quite high. As you walk, the call towards the sea is always strong.

This is what one London reporter from *The Daily Telegraph* in 1871 had to say about travelling by coach along this spectacular coastline:

> "A genuine coach and four leaves the aerial village on the Lyn every morning for the pleasant town on the Taw, I say a genuine coach and four by way of distinction from the aristocratic playthings now known to Londoners. The North Devon 'Vivids' and 'Lightnings' are unquestionable remnants of the system of locomotion which George Stephenson superseded, and like many another remnant they have made the hills their final stronghold. Along the wild uplands and down the deep combes which I traversed, the coach and four takes its way with the proud confidence of absolute sovereignty; no whistle frights the bucolic inhabitants into excitement, no thunderous roar startles the deer on distant Exmoor. The coach and four with its uncertain hour and its uneasy racket of hoofs and wheels is master of the situation. You run over the breezy moorlands, not under them, and inhale the pure air which comes from the Atlantic laden with ozone, while the eye feasts upon miles of golden gorse and purple heather, or wanders along a coast made beautiful by nature and classical by art. Anon you descend almost precipitately into the depths of some leafy combe, and cross its 'troutful stream' by a rude bridge, around which lie scattered the picturesque though, I should say, most incommodious cottages of a quiet hamlet. At length the way runs for miles along

a fat valley where the pretty little Devon cattle crop the greenest of herbage, and – I may as well out with it – suggest thoughts of junkets and of cream. This is Barnstaple attained, and thus ends a journey to be remembered."

Other green lanes in the area

Buck's Mills to Higher Worthygate, Lower Worthygate to Broad Parkham.
The previous walk at Buckland Brewer.

Links

There is a bus from Bradworthy and Barnstaple direct to Parkham. You can reach Parkham from the Bideford to Hartland service.
The National Trust.
The Coastal Footpath/The South West Way.

Question

What year was the Goldsworthy Chapel built?

Route 35

HARTLAND (A)

Penguins and saints

OS Explorer Map 126

The travelling penguins in this book come from a 1939 edition of the Penguin Guide to Devon, price 6d (see clue for further information). I suppose there is nothing quite so endearing as penguins on the march. If you find walks in this wild, far-flung area of Devon daunting, then just remember those penguins marching across the ice to spend months in darkness incubating their eggs.

This walk is one of three linked green lanes walks in Hartland. You will see that you can explore the crossed roads and invent your own green lanes circuits back and forth to the all-surrounding sea.

Conditions: Muddy and overgrown in places.

Distance: 2-3 miles or 4-6.

Starting point: SX258245.

(1) This was once a well-used carriage run from Springfield in Hartland through the Vale to Hartland Abbey. The Abbey probably became a missionary centre, with the many roads around it leading forth into the wild country settlements all around. We begin in Hart Lane, which takes us back to the 13th century, when harts roamed this deer park. The steep double boundary banks are further proof of its former use.

(2) You come into an area of wide open parkland, where falconry or archery would have been practised. There are large parkland trees here: oaks, ashes and limes. In the 18th century, the Stucley family took over the Abbey, created the parkland and opened up the links between its grounds and Hartland village. Follow the wooded area to your left then up over a stile and into a wide green lane with a cobbled camber.

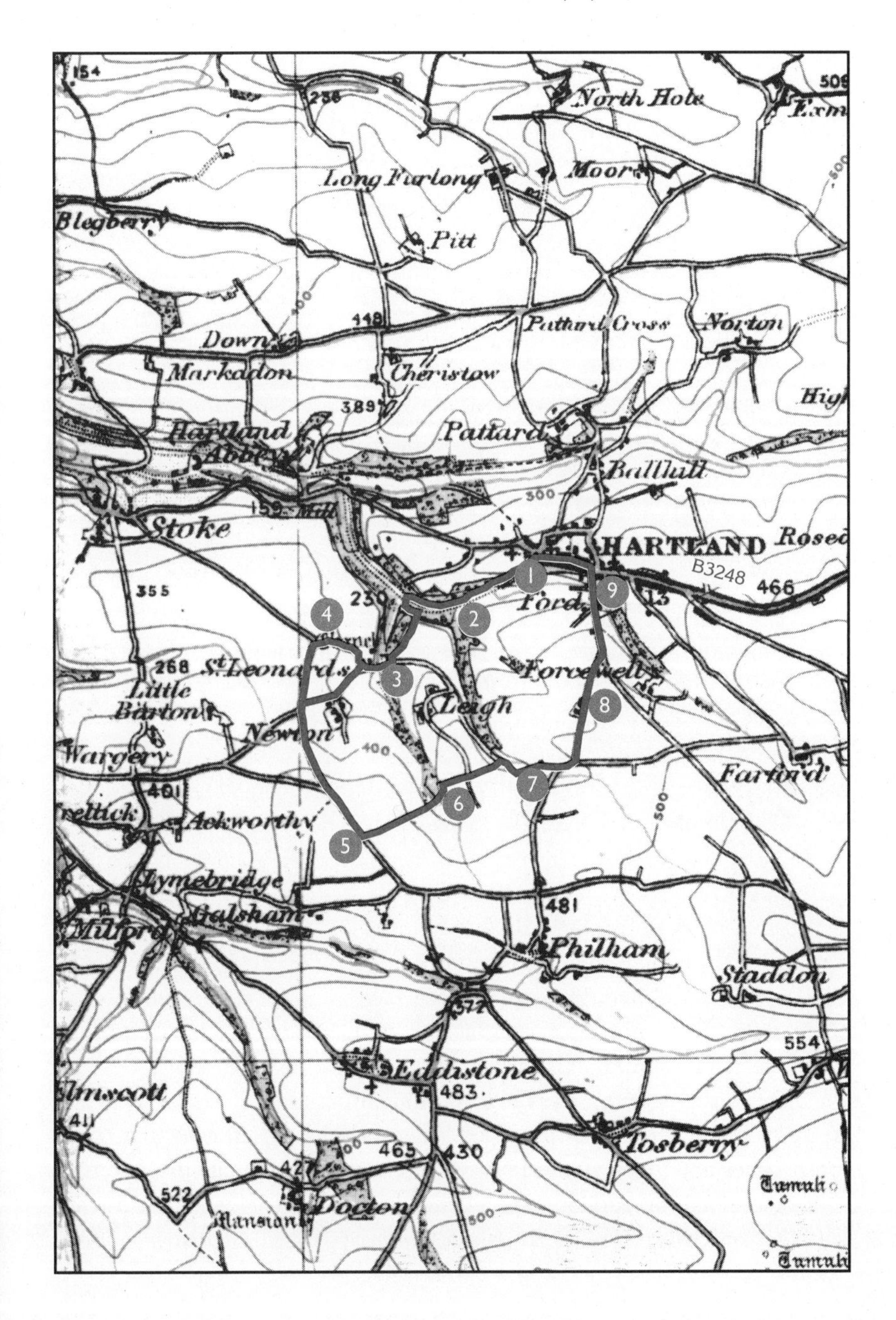
North Hole
Long Furlong
Moor
Blegberry
Pitt
Down
Markadon
Cheristow
Pattard Cross
Norton
Pattard
Hartland Abbey
Stoke
HARTLAND
B3248
Ford
St Leonards
Forcewell
Leigh
Little Barton
Newton
Wargery
Farford
Ackworthy
Philham
Staddon
Eddistone
Elmscott
Tosberry
Docton
Tumuli

There are tall standard trees to one side and a managed hedgerow on the other.

(3) You come out onto a surfaced lane. Pass up this fairly steep lane to the right by St Leonards. There are remnants of this former densely wooded area bordering your every step, just as there are references to the many Celtic missionaries who have passed through from Wales and Ireland. Their former presence was seized upon by prosperous landowners seeking immortality by dedicating a chapel to one or other of them. This would ensure themselves, and their families, a place in heaven.

(4) At the top turn left into the minor road, which has some grass growing in its centre and which makes the going easier. The verges here are full of wild flowers which flank their straight lengths. Here in midsummer are staggered rows of foxgloves, like drops of red blood along the way. It was believed that wherever they bloomed, this marked the trail of the martyred St Nectan, a sixth-century Celtic missionary commemorated in Stoke, whose church spire you can just see in the distance.

Up until twenty years ago, her martyrdom was celebrated by filling the church full with red foxgloves which represented the blood of the martyr scattered over the countryside after her death. All along this lane there are still single-wire telegraph poles looping low over the hedgerows. There are also patches of gorse which have welded their way into the hedgerows and have given them a domestic appearance. There is elm here too, which always seems to survive in maritime climes. This is a flat, windswept landscape. Pass Liberty Stile Cross and look for the green lane to your left.

(5) This lane is easy going until you descend into a hollow tunnel which does, however, have enough cobbling to keep your feet dry as you cross and re-cross the Abbey stream. There are outcrops of black basalt here, which you will find on the beaches all around, and a wide variety of ferns fill the hedgerow sides.

(6) Go straight across and into another green lane. This one passes a strip of former deer park wood, and there are many fine oaks here, which have remained small owing to deer browsing and furious winds from the Atlantic. In the damp patches, brook lime, fool's watercress and water forget-me-not grow. This lane is very wide in places, and has a drovers' feel about it.

(7) You come out onto the road and turn left into the bend of a narrow surfaced lane, with a ditch on one side brimming with white blooms of bittercress and meadowsweet, topped with a sculpted beech hedge.

(8) Turn left passing Sutherland Farm on your left, and return to

Hartland by way of Ford, with its Millennium Stone, and another crossing of the Abbey stream.

By the way

Hartland Abbey was founded by Emma, daughter of Richard I of Normandy in 1296. She was the mother of our last Saxon King, Edward the Confessor. This part of Devon, with its extensive woodlands, was a great hunting ground. This land was prized by generations of hunters, but also by traders because of its proximity to the sea. Hartland market held a charter from 1286 into the early 19th century, when road transport had just started to become viable through Devon. The name Hartland has its origins in the personal name 'Hert', which still survives in the name of the 'Heard' brothers who run the bus company in the village today.

Other green lanes in the area

The lane which leads from Wargery up to Stoke and others northwards to Hartland Point provide an alternative route to the Coast Path, easier in stormy weather. You can go by green lane and take the long way round from Rosedown to Clovelly. From St Nectan's Abbey to Norton and back, or up to Brownsham and Mouthmill Beach.

Links

There is one service from Bude to Barnstaple via Hartland. Other Hartland walks (Routes 36 and 37).

Question

Search for the answer to this clue after walk number 36. It depends when you decide to visit Stoke church. You've found the saints outside the church. Now look for the penguins inside.

Route 36

HARTLAND (B)

Shiploads of barley and lead for the roof

OS Explorer Map 126

This is one of the many circuits running from valley to seashore all around you in Hartland. We shall never know the details of how many tons of barley for brewing fine ale were ground or shipped out from here, or the multitude of other goods that were – legally and illegally – shipped in and out, and blessed by those who prayed in the many saints' chapels throughout this block of wild land. In transport history terms, the sea was of primary importance, as the many green lanes leading to it show. Hartland was not cut off by the sea, but connected.

Conditions: Very muddy and slippery in places.

Distance: 5-6 miles.

Starting point: SS246247.

(1) You can walk out from Hartland to Stoke along West Street, or take the footpath running down over the valley. However, there is quite a lot of up hill and down dale in this walk, so you might want to save yourself at the start.

(2) As you pass Horton Millennium Stone, notice the bridge plaque which states that it was built by Clements and Sons in 1898 – no doubt over an earlier crossing, as the Manor here goes back to Saxon times. One of the two spans forms a dry bridge, a very popular landscape garden feature of the 1800s. A little further down the road at Bow Bridge Crossroads, turn right and take the footpath at **(3)** into a woodland edge path. (You might like to carry on a little further on this lane and take the Cheristow Farm green lane to Pattard Cross.) I have chosen this streamside walk as it has a good surface and a carriage-run feel to it, or at least one which speaks of prolonged commercial use, as it leads to Tucking Mill in the east. There are rhododen-

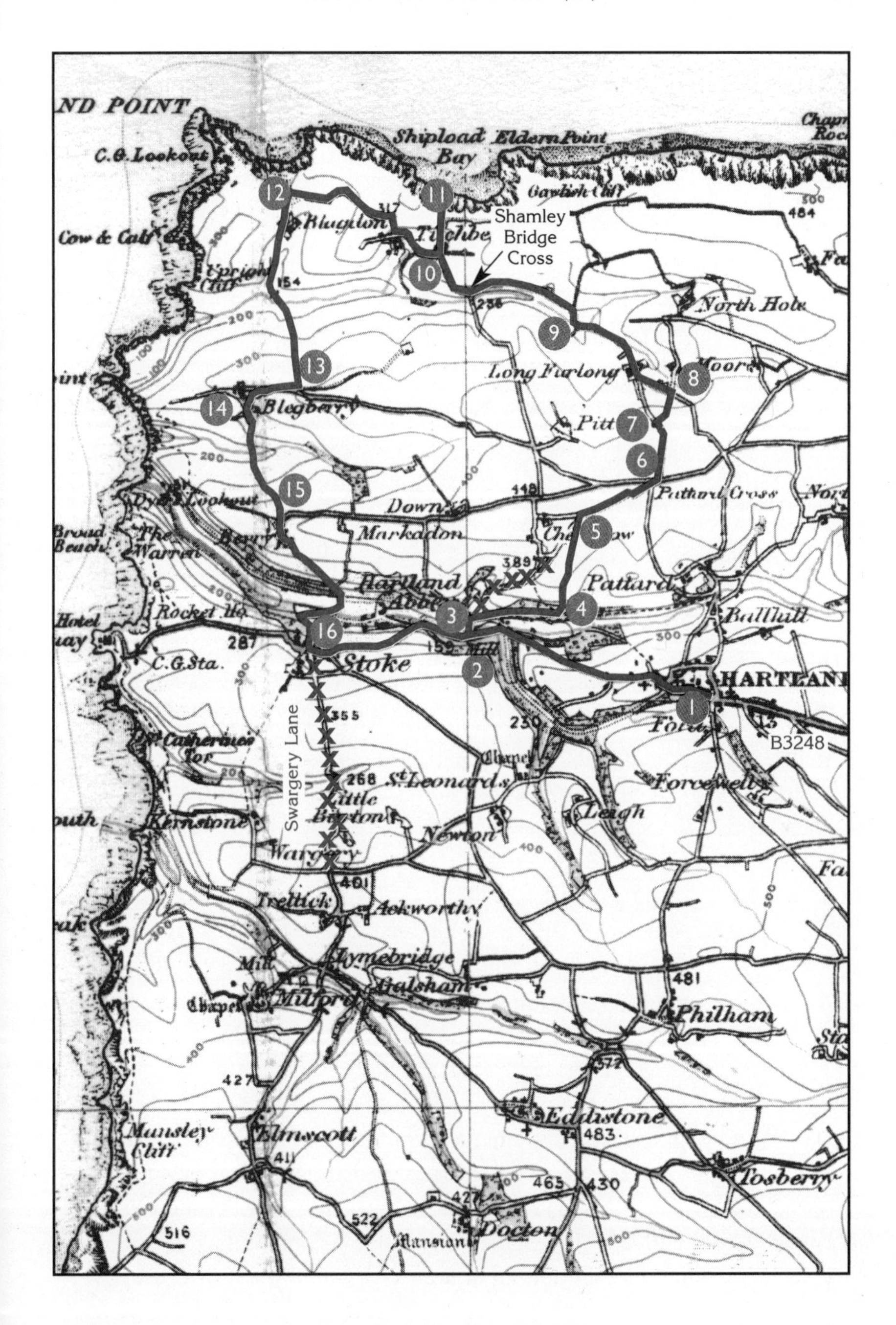
Shamley
Bridge
Cross
Swargery Lane
B3248
Shipload Bay
Eldern Point
Blagdon
Tithe
North Hole
Long Furlong
Moore
Pitt
Blegberry
Down
Markadon
Hartland Abbey
Pattard
Stoke
Mill
St. Leonards
Newton
Leigh
Philham
Eddistone
Elmscott
Docton
Milford
Tosberry
Forcewell
Acworthy

drons here for game cover, and a small group of ancient yews to the right by a ruined barn. The new OL map won't tell you that you are in the area of a former chapel dedicated to St Wenn (or St Wenna), which is very close to the Cornish Christian name Morwenna. This would have been founded by one of the early Celtic saints who came over from Ireland or Wales. 'Stow' (= holy place) in the name Cheristow denotes this, and it is indeed the site of the first church in Hartland.

(4) Go through a stile, then take the path through a gate to the left which has been laid out by DEFRA. This is well marked by a series of hillocky field edges by small gates. You have climbed quite high now, and can see Hartland footpath field below. The final gate at the top will take you through a meadow with a dew-pond in it to your right.

(5) Turn right and join the Cheristow Farm Green Lane, which has a camber and cobbles, and often great puddles of standing water.

(6) From Pattard Cross, turn left into a minor road with wide and watery drainage channels either side. There is a house on the left down here, and opposite **(7)** a short section of green lane – once more it is well cobbled. **(8)** Turn left at its end, and follow the road down into an oak-treed valley.

(9) The lane swings round to Long Furlong, which once had a chapel in its grounds, and then down to Gawlish Bridge. As Emma was Edward the Confessor's mother and the founder of Hartland Abbey, it is no wonder that one or two of her fellow religious countrymen might choose to live in the area. You pass Laburnum Cottage on the right, and then go down to Shamley Bridge. As you climb up to the right there is a triangular stone on the left set into the bank, which could just be a 'C' stone (see page 58).

(10) There is a National Trust sign here for East Titchberry Farm. Go through the yard, with its close collection of old buildings including the historic malt-house, and enter a short section of green lane straight ahead towards the sea and **(11)** Shipload Bay. The lane has a short section of horizontally laid stonewalling. Returning to the main lane, continue to the right down along past West Titchberry Farm. There are pennyworts in the lane here as big as saucers. The lighthouse appears in front of you, with its Buckminster Fuller-style dome. On the right is a group of tarmacked but now re-greening lanes. A radar-cum-radio station was first set up here in 1941, which was used into the 1950s.

(12) Take the lane to the left marked as a public bridleway, which tells you that Blegberry Hill ('bleak hill') is a mile away. You pass through a farmyard with 'H.H. 1915' inscribed in concrete on a stream outlet. From here you can see before you where your path lies up a well-boxed-in green lane. The hedges in this area of Hartland are wide and square, and look like chunks of a flower arranger's oasis snaking up the hillside. There is metalling on the one hedged lane by the farmyard. You descend into a beautiful little glen, which has snowdrops and wild daffodils in the spring, then up into a slippery, narrow lane with gorse, stunted blackthorn and hazel, for a long mile.

(13) Turn right for a short stretch along the lane, and then at **(14)** turn left passing the farm and holiday cottages of Bleak Hill. This lane is muddy in the beginning, and widens out towards the top where there is a gate **(15)**.

Go straight on and veer left through the farmyard and newly restored big house at Berry. The lane snakes down through woodland and into the Abbey Valley, where there are standard trees growing in the parkland by the bridge. You climb up towards the side entrance of St Nectan's at **(16)**, and if there is a wind (in Hartland, why wouldn't there be?), you will hear the whistling oak timbers of the church sirening you to enter and solve the question given in the previous walk.

Other green lanes in the area

There are many green lanes as indicated in the north of Hartland, and you can link through to Clovelly on the Coastal Footpath. The Hobby Drive is now an SSSI, and is stunningly beautiful whatever the weather conditions. This was constructed between 1811-1829, times of great hardship for those working the land and those returning from the Napoleonic Wars. Thomas Roberts was one of the supervisors for the laying of the drive. He had lost his hands when a midshipman, and had been taken in by the Hamlyn family as a tutor for their family – shades of Blind Jack Metcalf of Knaresborough, the great road engineer.

By the way

The Malt Mill at Titchberry was just one of eight working in the parish when corn and barley production was very important, not least of all for providing fuel for horse-drawn transport. For centuries Hartland Quay, just below the point, saw many important shipments safely into the parish. Mr Jackson in his book *Roads and Bridges of the Torridge Valley* refers to how Stoke Church got hold of a ton of lead for the roof in the years 1616-7. It came from

Tacliffe Hill in Bristol, bought for £12 then sent to Northam, Clovelly and Hartland quays. It was stored in a cellar at Docton Mill near Elmscott but at least a mile from the church, and then brought back – down Wargery Lane maybe. The transportation to several local quays points out how important it was to keep overland transport hauls as short as possible.

Links

There is a bus route from Barnstaple and Bideford to Hartland, and beyond to Bude.

Question

Just where is the helicopter going from here?

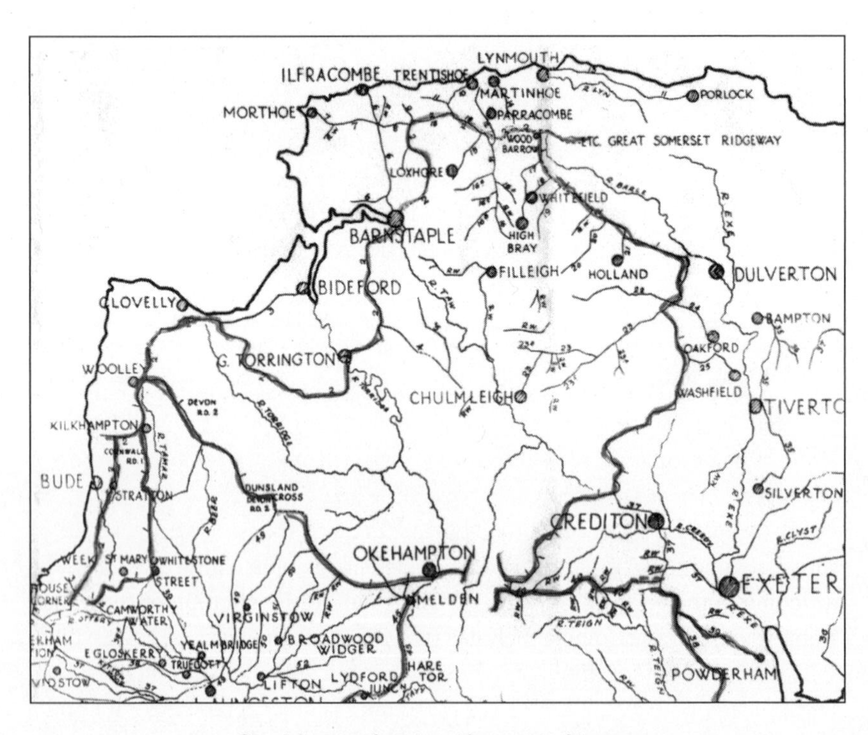

Grundy's map of ancient ridgeways in this area.

Route 37

HARTLAND (C)

Bursdon Moor's Green Lane

OS Explorer Map 126

As you work your way through this book exploring green lanes, you may sigh as you enter, once again, what looks as if it is just going to be another mirey, stoggy, sunken way leading from some small farm or settlement to another. Magical as they all are, their purpose and story only becomes obvious after a lot of research and seasonal observations. But sometimes a lane will appear which just doesn't seem to fit its location, and then you begin to ask wider chronological questions. Such a one is this purposely named Green Lane in Hartland. You can link it with others in this book, or prolong your puzzling by walking both up and down its length.

Conditions: Mainly on the level, with one or two climbs and some running water.

Distance: 2-3 miles.

Starting point: From the A39 between Summerville Cross and the Westcountry Inn, SS269195.

(1) This is a minor road which branches off immediately onto Bursdon Moor, a beautiful wild area which once was common land and is so once again, as it is now an SSSI.

At Lighthouse Cross on the B3248 leading into Hartland stands a pair of gateposts put up by James Berryman of The New Inn at Clovelly in 1902, to welcome in the reign of Edward VII. He refers to the creation of the world from Alpha to Omega, and concludes that Omega is the West. His verse talks about how the commons have been changed to grassland:

> This field was once a common moor
> Where gorse and rush grew free
> And now it grows green grass all o'er
> As all who pass may see.

So here we have a common which will not be turned into grassland – well, that's what today's legislation says, but who can say what will happen in 100 years' time? It is difficult to say whether or not Berryman regretted this grassing over, but it is worth seeing these columns proud in the open landscape, as they might not stand for another 100 years.

On Bursdon Moor Common now you will be greeted by skylarks sheering off into the heavens to distract you with their panicky sound. There are curlews, as we are still close to the coast. They nestle in the cottongrass amidst the marsh plume thistle, bog bean and devil's-bit scabious. There are marsh orchids and heath spotted-orchids here.

(2) Turn left, and notice the deep drainage channel to the left of the lane where bog asphodel and plenty of invertebrate life can be found. Whilst walking along here, check the number of tumuli, beacon points and enclosures in the area. It is a reminder that this has not always been a landscape settled with individual farms. The fields to your left have some interesting humps and bumps on their slopes. Pass the Lutsford Farm buildings and **(3)** turn right on the corner. Follow the road along, passing a strip of hazel coppice to your left, strangely pigmied by the Atlantic winds. Just beyond here in a bend on the road is the Green Lane at **(4)**.

The lane is fifteen to twenty feet wide, and has cobbles and a camber from the start. The stunted beech on the banks have wild, frizzy, backcombed hair-dos on both sides of this straight lane. They are on the banks in places, but have grown into the ditch at the bottom too as you proceed.

The significance of trees on top of banks is that by dating them we will know that the bank beneath is even older. And as the bank to the right becomes double, it could indicate a form of ha-ha common in deer management. The lane seems deeper because of this, but it has not sunk and will not do so until its end. For this to happen it means that some trouble has been taken in its maintenance, by the owners of Lutsford and Egar's-ton (Eddistone), or by much earlier residents perhaps.

(5) There is a break in the hedgerows here over a stream, but continue

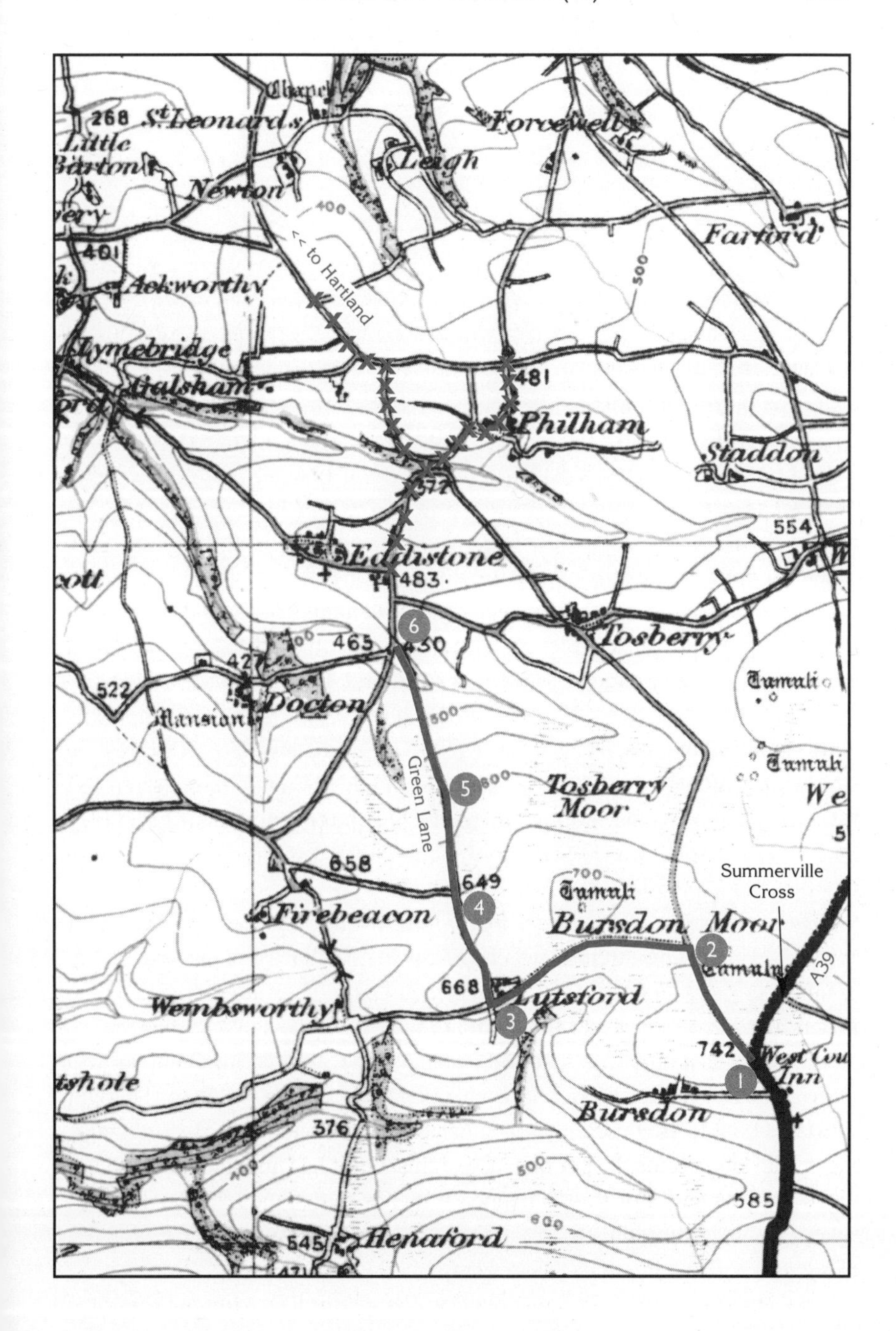

St. Leonards
Little Barton
Newton
Leigh
Forcewell
Farford
Ackworthy
Lymebridge
Galsham
Philham
Staddon
Eddistone
Tosberry
Docton
Mansion
Tosberry Moor
Burscott Moor
Firebeacon
Lutsford
Wembsworthy
Bursdon
Henaford
West Country Inn
<< to Hartland
Green Lane
Summerville Cross
A39
Tumuli
Tumulus
1
2
3
4
5
6

on keeping to the left where the lane slightly narrows. There is more hazel here, which gradually gives way to gorse from the moor. Some holly appears; this was often planted to control the movements of deer, or is it here just a sign of ancient woodland? As you reach the end, the lane drops over some stone outcrops and Painton Water spills out over the wide horning out of this still well-cobbled lane.

(6) There is an 'Unsuitable for Motor Vehicles' sign at its end. Turn right here towards Eddistone Cross, and decide on your route: either back to the left and the sea, or straight on towards Hartland. There is another 'Unsuitable for Motor Vehicles' lane at Philham, as indicated. There is yet another holy well dedicated to St Cleer, and a Canon's Chapel to St Nectan on private land here.

By the way

I have suggested walking this lane in both directions, as it does have a remarkable feel to it and is puzzlingly well-built and maintained. Studying its plant life through the seasons may reveal further clues as to its age.

Other green lanes in the area

From **(6)** you can link up to Hartland, Route 35 as indicated northwards. There are many lanes in all directions, as shown by crosses on the map. However, for a similar style of cobbling take a visit to The Hobby Drive at Clovelly detailed in the previous walk.

Links

There is a bus which runs from Hartland to Bude on the A39. Other Hartland walks (Routes 34 to 36).

Question

Apart from the sudden flying upwards of birds here you might be frightened by something larger in the skies. Where are they coming from?

Route 38

WELCOMBE

A watery welcome

OS Explorer Map 126

This is a very small circuit but one which you can choose to enlarge using the many well-indicated green lanes in the area. There is a bewildering contrast between walking in these, furry, tropical lanes and clambering up to come face to face with the wide buffeting Atlantic coast. The enclosed, lush nature of these lanes is nowhere better expressed than in Edward Thomas's poem 'Lights Out' – doubly appropriate as within the church you will find no form of electricity.

> "Many a road and track
> That, since the dawn's first crack,
> Up to the forest brink,
> Deceived the travellers,
> Suddenly now blurs,
> And in they sink."

Conditions: Some standing water in the lane leading to the sea.

Distance: 2-3 miles.

Starting point: SS227184 St Nectan's Church.

(1) Take the lane which leads down past the well-preserved clear waters of the well to the left dedicated to the Celtic saint. From now on, the sound of the stream rushing to the sea on your right is with you all the way down.

(2) Take the lane to your right; it is like walking through a furry green tunnel, where mosses and ferns cover every inch of ground around the Atlantic-stunted bank oaks. Willow and alder grow vigorously along the watercourses and feeder streamlets. Along here are one or two idyllic-looking dwellings wrapped in green and bound by ribbons of sea mists.

(3) At Strawberry Water go straight over into the green lane towards the sound of the sea, which has now drowned the whisperings of the stream. You will see it again tumbling and shining over black rocks below you as you descend to the beach.

(4) There is an information board here put up by Devon Wildlife Trust, as this is one of its specially protected sites. The rocks here were folded and put away in these cliff drawers 320 million years ago. From here you may wish to climb precipitously up the cliff and extend your route to run close to the Cornish border and return via Darracott. However, for this short circuit return to the road at **(3)** and take a fairly steep climb up towards Mouhay. The lane has groups of twisted hawthorn and holly in regular ranks along its banks.

(5) At the top, turn left towards Welcombe House where the centre of the lane begins to grass over again.

(6) Go straight over at the crossroads and up to the Welcombing church once more. To take a detour here, turn right to the Pottery, but before arriving at **(7)** take the green lane to your left known as Well Lane.

(8) Take a left at King's Cross to bring you back to the church.

By the way

Once again we find ourselves in a remote corner of the county where what we now consider to be some form or other of extreme religious fervour took place. For close by is Morwenstow, where the eccentric Parson Hawker practised. Equally bizarre, the Chapel at Darracott crossroads was where a very devout Bible Christian would have prayed seven times a day. There is a feeling of barely clinging to the land, as you are surrounded by the pounding of the Atlantic waves and the constant trickle of water. Close by, in this parish, the great rivers Torridge and Tamar begin.

Other green lanes in the area

Those to the south, as indicated, which lead to the Welcombe and Marsland Devon Wildlife Trust Reserve. Here you will find such rarities as pearl-bordered fritillary butterflies amidst the coppicing and woodland glades and marsh orchids in the spring.

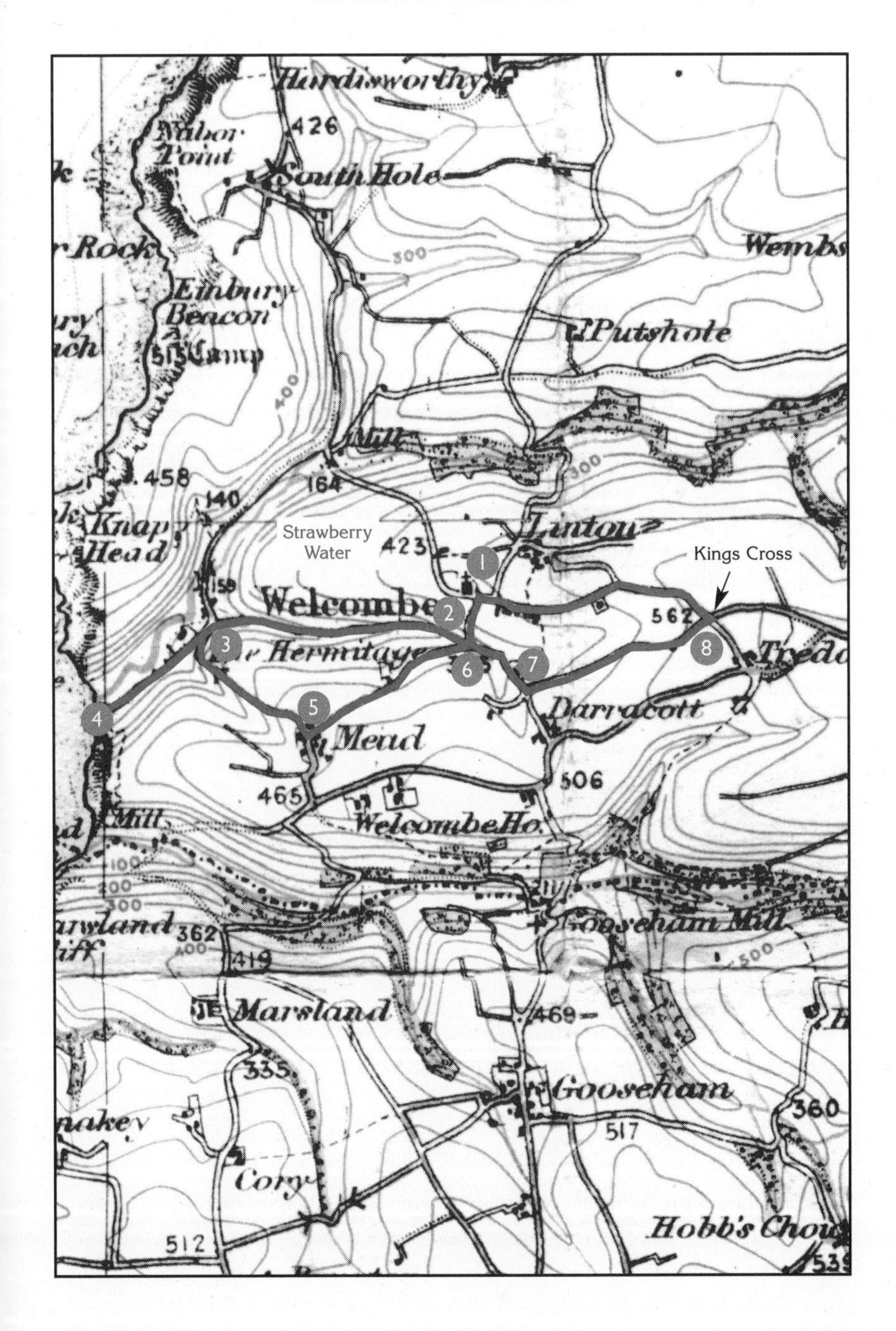
Hardisworthy
426
Nabor Point
South Hole
Rock
Embury Beacon
515 Camp
Putshole
Mill
458
164
140
Knap Head
Strawberry Water
423
Linton
Kings Cross
Welcombe
562
The Hermitage
Tredo
Darracott
Mead
465
506
Mill
Welcombe Ho.
Marsland
362
419
Gooseham Mill
469
335
Gooseham
360
517
Cory
512
Hobb's Chou

Links

There is one service which runs from Bude to Barnstaple via Hartland.
The South West Coastal Path.

Question

To which Saint is the well at **(2)** dedicated?

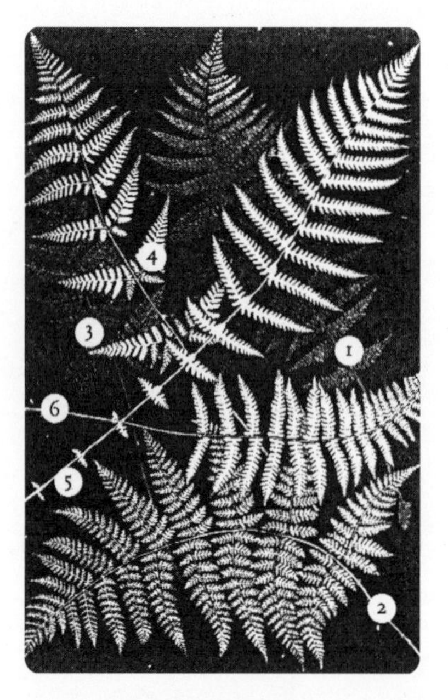

The Buckler Ferns
For example (2) Broad Buckler Fern

The Single British Ferns
For example (3) Lady's Fern

(See the author's book *Discovering Green Lanes*.)

Route 39

HOLSWORTHY

Left on the line

OS Explorer Map 112 (and Map 111 – the corner only)

This walk is very close to the Cornish border, and there are clear views all around. When I visited on 27th October 2006, I experienced what was known as the Bude boom. At about 12 o'clock there was a great explosion. On returning to the town I was told that buildings had cracked, animals panicked and people had run for cover – a mystery which to this day has not been solved.

Conditions: Muddy in some lanes and waterlogged in some meadows. You will need wellies to ford the streams.

Distance: 2-3 miles.

Starting point: SS339035. This is the point where the National Cycle Route Number 3 leaves Holsworthy along the disused railway line. Take the back road to the viaduct.

(1) Take the road to the new supermarket and into Underlane, passing the famous cattle market on your left. Turn right at the end here and onto the A3072 to the traffic lights, and there you will see it: the viaduct for the Holsworthy to Bude railway. You go through a wooded section of the line, which looks out over the Derriton Valley and is home to many finches and buzzards.

At **(2)** you climb up off the track and take the lane through the gate and over a fletton-brick-built bridge to the left. This brings you out onto the Derriton and Pyworthy Road **(3)**. Turn right and you are walking from east to west, with views of a supine Dartmoor to your left.

(4) The Pyworthy church spire and that of Bridgerule soon appear in front of you. You can begin to feel the urgency of your mission, as you are walking towards the very first home of the Bible Christians. It was from

Bridgerule that they set out on their missions in 1815, coming up from Cornwall, covering miles and miles on foot, and taking every opportunity to talk to those they met. Don't let this deter you from visiting Pyworthy church, dedicated to St Swithin, with its own special toilet by the lychgate. The floor tiles are from one of the Barum (Barnstaple) potteries.

(5) Returning to the crossroads, take the footpath marked to Burnard's House, which is where the lane straight ahead of you is going – but don't take it. Turn sharp right and pass down the back of some new houses. There are some cobblestones here, then you come out onto a brief section of tarmac road before reaching a house called Kittywells. Pass to the right along the back of this house and to a stile which takes you into a waterlogged meadow. Go straight across and into another field. Follow its perimeter to the left and then you will be aware of the green lane which follows you to your left.

(6) This is, in fact, the railway line again. **(7)** Pass through a gate at the field edge and keep **(7)** to your left. There is a footpath sign ahead of you, which brings you out into a tarmacked lane to your right. Growing cropped and trimmed in the hedge are some holly and pedunculate oak trees.

(8) Pass Killatree ahead of you, and follow the road round to **(9)**, to a T-junction where a long bench seat has been placed. Turn right into the A3072, and walk carefully along for about ten minutes before turning into the lane at **(10)** on the right by what is now The Rydon Inn, and once was just a farm. This waterlogged lane with spaced oak and hawthorn sapling plants atop the left side of its hedge-bank contrasts with the density of the hedge to the right.

Given that this valley must always have been difficult to cross from north to south, hedge-dating (see page 118) will give a rough guide as to how long the farmers of Holsworthy and Pyworthy had been engaged in this struggle. Back at **(2)** you can turn onto the cyclepath back to the viaduct.

By the way

At the end of Victoria Hill there is a plaque set in the wall and dated 1930, celebrating the arrival of the Western Road into Holsworthy. Unfortunately this economic asset has made the market town nothing more than a very busy crossroads for traffic both commercial and touristic. However, for a piece of peace and quiet, try the green lane which runs down by the side of the church and leads to the site of a well, as indicated.

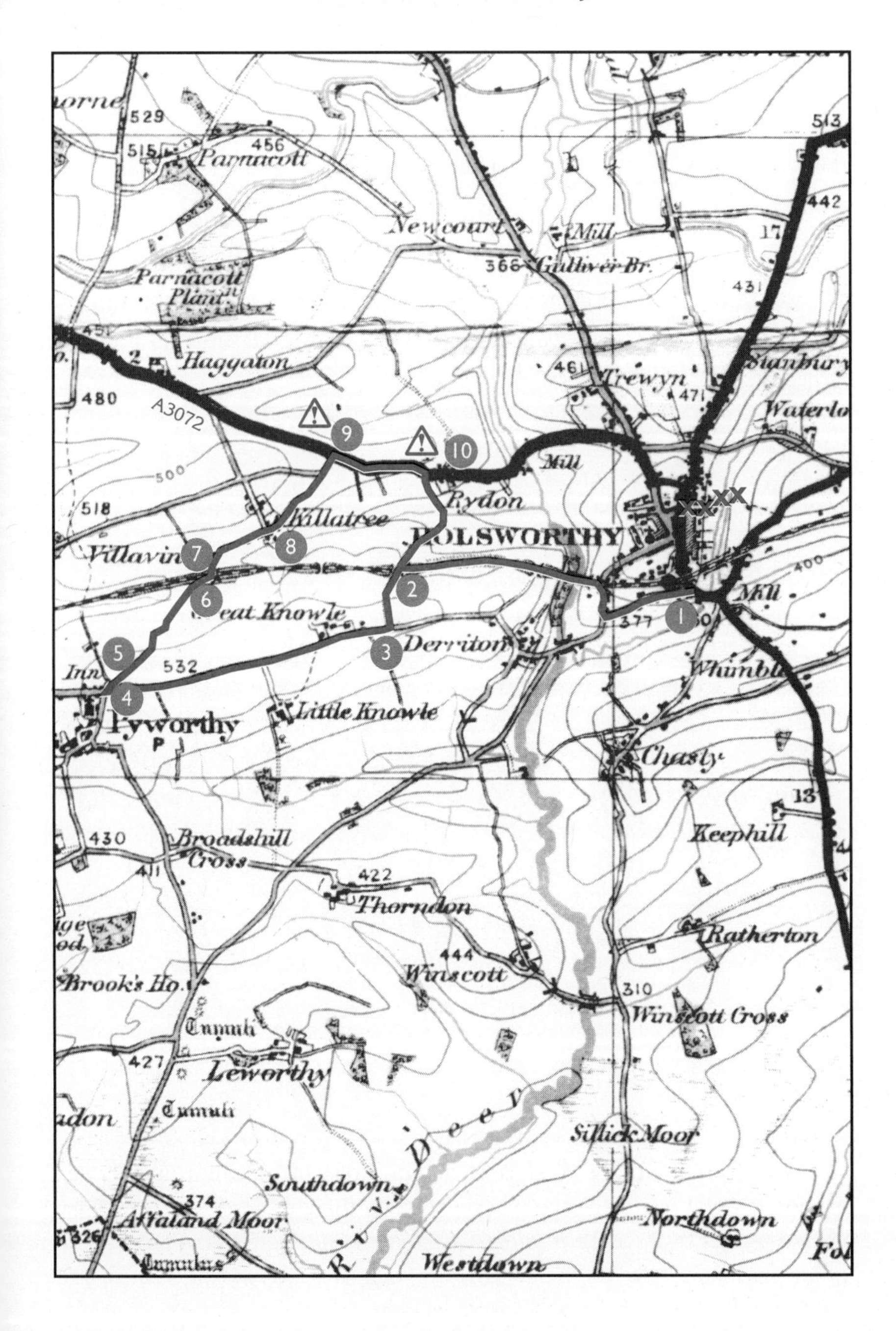
529
456
515
Parnacott
Newcourt
Mill
366 Gulliver Br.
Parnacott Plant.
Haggaton
480
A3072
461
Trewyn
471
Stanbury
Waterloo
Mill
Rydon
Killatree
HOLSWORTHY
518
500
Villavin
Great Knowle
Derriton
377
Mill
400
Whimble
532
Inn
Pyworthy
Little Knowle
Chasty
Keephill
430
Broadshill Cross
411
422
Thorndon
Ratherton
444
Winscott
310
Winscott Cross
Brook's Ho.
Tumuli
427
Leworthy
Tumuli
Sillick Moor
Southdown
374
Affaland Moor
Northdown
Tumulus
Westdown
513
442
431

Other green lanes in the area

There are some to the north of Holsworthy in Holsworthy Hamlets close to the Bude Canal.

Links

There is one bus service which runs from Bude to Barnstaple, another from Holsworthy to Exeter, and quite a few local services from Holsworthy. National Cycle Network No. 3.

Question

When was the viaduct built?

A 1920s tarmacking gang – about to change the appearance of green lanes for ever.

Route 40

HIGHAMPTON

The carpenter's store

OS Explorer Map 112

This short walk can be extended to take you on further north through land which was once woodland. Place names such as Beara, Longwood, Wooda, Totleigh and Buckland Filleigh confirm this – all providing useful material for local carpenters.

Conditions: Stuggy underfoot in places.

Distance: 3-5 miles according to the circuit you choose.

Starting point: SS489047.

(1) The church stands away from the A3072, which swings round here on its way from Holsworthy to Hatherleigh. The lane on which it stands is a quiet one set up high over Hollow Moor, with an expanse of Dartmoor to the south. The landscape seems to be dotted with trees in this direction, map-like in their distant appearance. Looking towards Torrington in the north, there is a fine view of Sheepwash over the Torridge, showing ancient field patterns just in the lee of Sheepwash church tower. These fields, laid out in Anglo-Saxon times, had provided enough food for generations. But by the mid-19th century agricultural labourers were leaving this area and migrating not just to the new world but also to the east and north of Britain. Between 1860 and 1880, a quarter of the population of Shebbear sought a better life elsewhere.

(2) The green lane, signed as a footpath, starts just past The Old Rectory on the right, and you cross over two stiles and into a most unusual form of green lane. This is formed by a corridor of north to south standing large oaks with a smooth grassed holloway at the centre and the occasional patch of furze. You are walking along a medieval woodbank, which now marks the edge of the wood but in the past was just one of many holloways running through the great forest here.

(3) At Venton there are two bridges made of railway sleepers to cross. You go out again into an even more exposed stretch of woodland ride, where the roots of the oaks which line the way have in places been pollarded to stumps, the wood having been taken to work into a house for a medieval farmer. Rackham calculates that 150-200 smallish trees, usually oaks, were needed to construct a family house. You go out again over another stile and sleeper bridge into an area of almost wood pasture, which thins towards the road.

Just before **(4)** you cross over the dismantled railway line which once ran from Halwill Junction to Hatherleigh and on up to Bideford from 1925-1965. Turn right and follow the road very carefully along to another footpath sign on your right **(5)** which will take you back and over Parker's Down to Town Barton and the church again. As you enter by the back way and pass by the carpenter's headstone again, you might like to continue down to his dwelling-place at Sheepwash Bridge as indicated.

By the way

In the churchyard to your left as you enter is a headstone for the carpenter who lived at Sheepwash Bridge and died in 1845. Here was a man who worked the woodlands, through which you pass, but chose to worship high up on a hill away from his house in the Torridge valley in Sheepwash. On the map you can still see some strips of common land near Sheepwash Bridge. Is this where the carpenter grew his vegetables?

Links

There is one restricted local bus service from Hatherleigh and Holsworthy. The Tarka Trail.

Question

What is the name of the carpenter from Sheepwash Bridge?

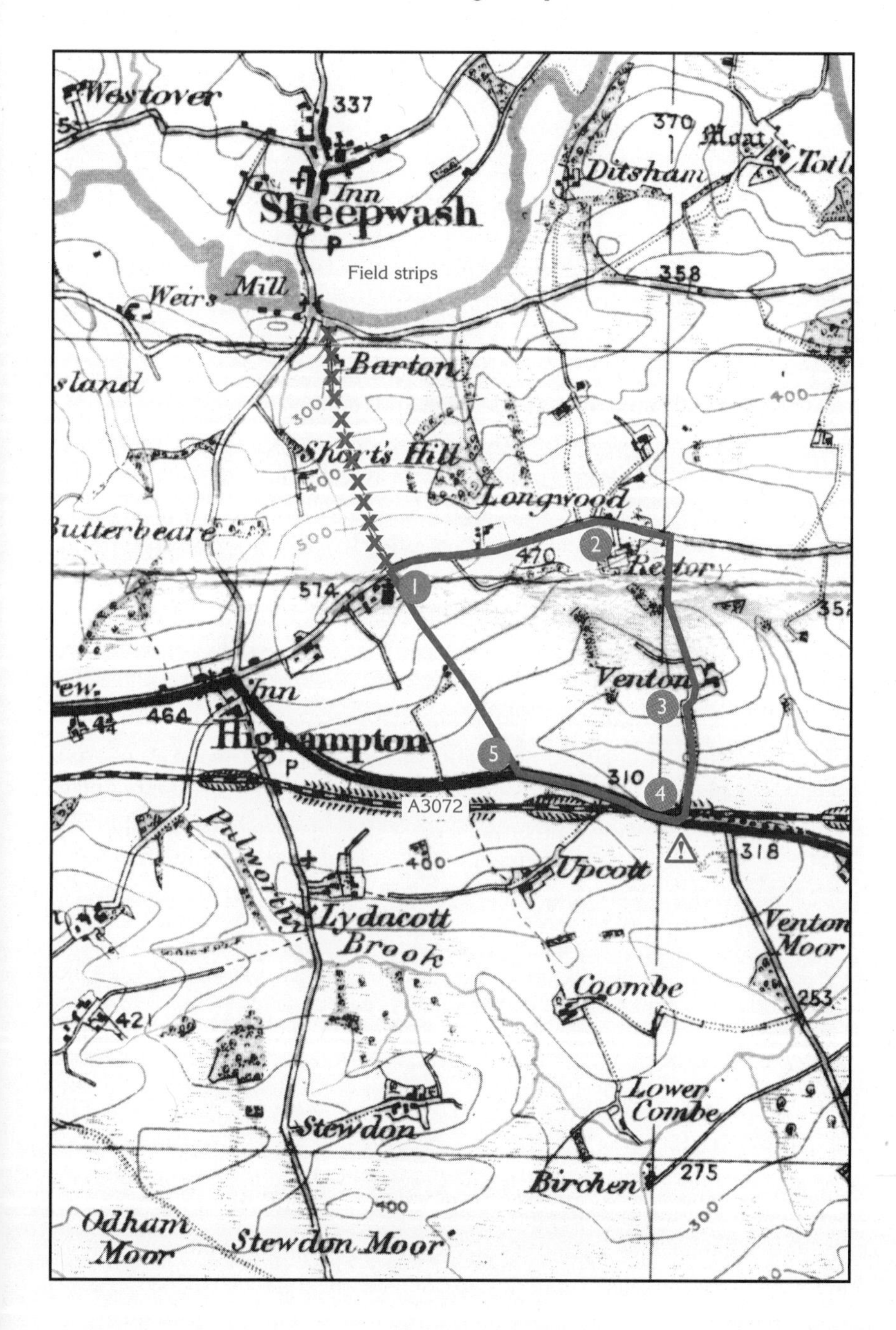
Westover
337
370
Moat
Ditsham
Inn
Sheepwash
P
Field strips
358
Weirs Mill
Barton
sland
400
300
Short's Hill
400
Longwood
Butterbeare
500
470
Rectory
574
352
Venton
Inn
464
Highampton
P
310
A3072
318
Pulworthy
400
Upcott
Lydacott
Brook
Venton Moor
Coombe
253
421
Lower Combe
Stewdon
275
Birchen
400
300
Odham Moor
Stewdon Moor

Route 41

NORTHLEW

Bringing in light from the east

OS Explorer Map 113

You may feel the presence here of some of those early itinerant preachers who came up from eastern Cornwall, speaking directly to whomever they met on the way, encouraging them to give thanks for the beauty that was all around them. It is still here.

Conditions: Patches of standing water in some lanes.

Distance: 3-4 miles short circuit, 4-6 the longer one.

Starting point: SX503993. The village square.

(1) This is a fine example of one of the many villages in west Devon which have small village squares from which lanes lead out in an Anglo-Saxon grid pattern towards the fields and farms around. This also accounts for the number of green lanes still in existence today, which led to fields farmed for centuries, for the most part without any mechanical assistance.

(2) The green lane, a public footpath, runs down over the road south opposite the town square by the village hall. It is a narrow sunken footpath with mud and cobbles; there are some oaks, and furze in the hedges. You go over a stile and footbridge into a field.

(3) Here go through a gate into Southcombe Lane. This is a wide lane, with views of Ashbury Church breaking through. There is a large standing poplar tree to the left at the top, then the lane falls away through Northlew Copse, so called because the trees in here would have been coppiced on a seven-year rotation for the long poles used in thatching, for hurdle-making and providing handles for rakes etc. There is a bit of a waterfall to negotiate at the bottom, but then you climb up, keeping to the right through a gate. Follow the field edge to the left and you will come out by a house called The Tythe.

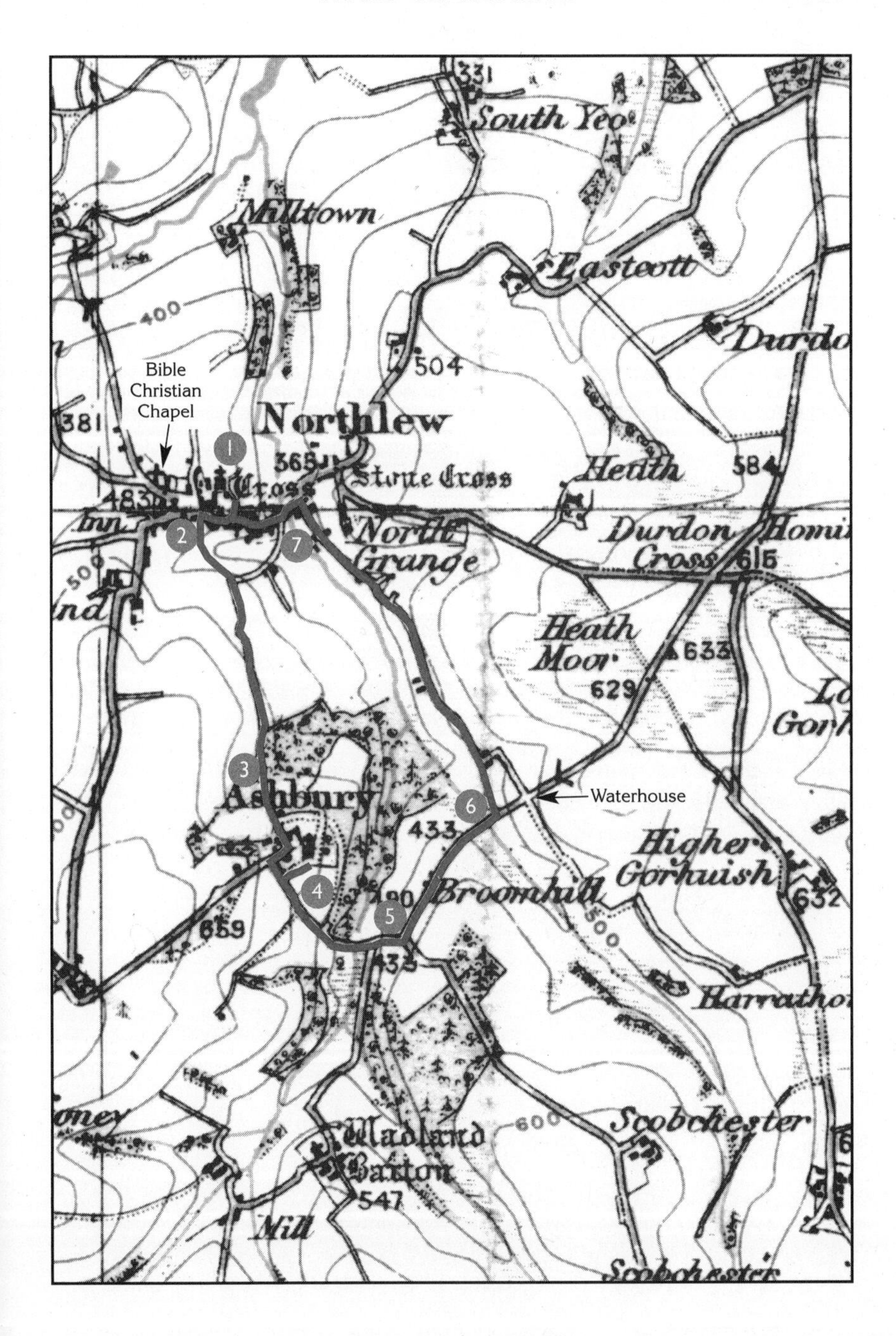
South Yeo
Milltown
Eastcott
Durdo
504
Bible
Christian
Chapel
Northlew
381
365
Stone Cross
Heath
584
483
Inn
North
Grange
Durdon
Cross
615
Heath
Moor
633
629
Waterhouse
Ashbury
433
Higher
Gorhuish
Broomhill
632
659
Harrathor
Scobchester
Madland
Barton
547
Mill
400
500
600

(4) Unfortunately it is not possible to visit the church here, but you can enjoy its stunning position looking out over Dartmoor and guarded by a magnificent stag's-headed oak tree nearby. Walk out onto the road through the granite pillars, and turn left towards **(5)** Kennel Bridge. This is where Squire John Morth Woollcombe kept his two packs of hunting hounds in the 18th century. There is a great 'engboo' (see page 120) here on the left as you descend. Another type of hanging is associated with Hanginghill Wood to your right.

(6) Just before Broomhill Cross you may feel lured on by the sight of the River Lew flowing so tranquilly through the manicured parklands below, and continue your walk round into the Gorhuishes (a gore is a triangular piece of land). If you are following this route, then turn left and you will be walking through a wide landscape broken up by standing oaks and beeches. You will come to an 'Unsuitable for Motors' sign to your left; this leads into a short section of muddy lane, which then opens out into a minor road back up to the village.

(7) There is a well on the left at Ford Cottage, which has been restored to include a cascade of water over some zigzag multi-rocked stonewalling. Turn left here. Back in the square, take time to visit the beautiful church of St Thomas à Becket, heralded by the Preaching Cross dating back to the 15th century. It is said that the devil died of cold on Sourton Moor and is buried under here; others say it was the resting-place for a white stag which proved difficult to hunt down; yet others for a fighting cock called 'the devil' which is entombed below this rough-hewn granite structure. At any rate, Billy Bray, the great Bible Christian preacher, believed that something evil was here. So finish your trip by visiting the little chapel which has been restored twice in its long life, in 1858 and 1886.

By the way

This walk is dedicated to all those itinerant Bible Christian preachers who came forth from Cornwall and who had been "directed to go into the highways and hedges – to compel them [the labouring folk] to come in" from this area, which they declared to be a moral and spiritual wilderness. One preacher said that he sensed the presence of Satan following him like a great bear on its hind legs. The preachers had descriptive names such as Hootaway, Roarwell, Plague-Chaser, and included women in their numbers.

Although we now consider them extreme, in their time they gave much comfort and hope to the ordinary working people, including those who had come back from the Napoleonic Wars hoping to take up work again in a struggling, harsh, farming community, where the established Church presented a hard distant face in league with the gentry.

Their homecoming was to prove just as hard as fighting Bonaparte, and sometimes even as dangerous; 1816, the year after Waterloo, was known as the year with no summer. There are two fine granite crosses in this area. Grundy, the map-maker, when talking of crosses on ridgeways, believed that it was a very reliable sign that the road was ancient, especially if they were found at a crossroads.

Links

There is a restricted local bus service from Okehampton.

Question

What year was the first Bible Christian chapel built here?

Route 42

BRATTON CLOVELLY

A well-ordered, wide landscape

OS Explorer Map 112

The spectacularly high, isolated position of this village, and its size, in part explain why there are so many long footpaths and green lanes reaching up towards and away from it.

Conditions: Some standing water alongside woods and in the valley.

Distance: Either 3-4 miles or 5-6, according to choice.

Starting point: SX477924.

Having explored the village and enjoyed the views from the church, walk down towards Boasley, passing two potentially longer green lane routes to your right and left, and the impressive Calehouse standing white and square above the road, as the origin of its name ('calu', meaning 'bare' or 'exposed' in Old English) implies. Its isolated position brings to mind the now forbidden verse of 'All Things Bright and Beautiful', that popular Victorian hymn containing the lines: "The rich man in his castle, the poor man at his gate."

(1) Turn right into a bridleway towards Fursdon. It has a concrete surface, which falls away by the farm into a wide deep lane. You climb up to a T-junction at **(2)**. Veer slightly left and go straight on into a grassy lane, then through a metal hunting gate.

(3) Another gate will take you into a field edge. Cross into the coppice ahead, passing a straggly furze and hawthorn hedge with some dogwood at the end.

(4) You will now have to ford the stream, and carry straight over and up into the pebbled lane ahead. There is a woodland glade to your left here, and the hedges are mainly of standing oaks.

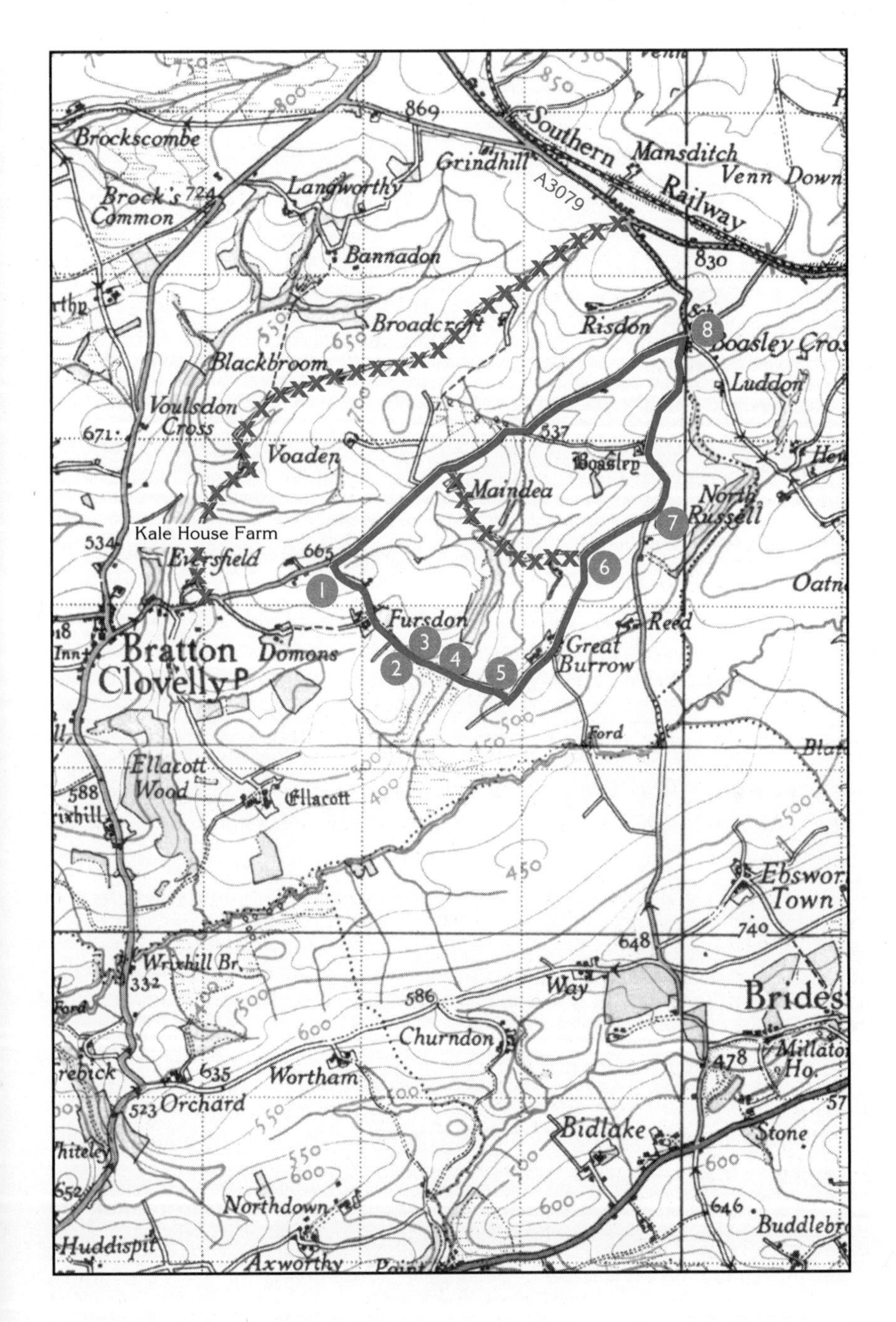
Brockscombe
869
Grindhill
Southern Railway
Mansditch
Venn Down
A3079
850
Brock's Common
724
Langworthy
Bannadon
830
Broadcroft
Risdon
8
Boasley Cross
Blackbroom
Luddon
Voulsdon Cross
671
537
Voaden
Boasley
Maindea
North Russell
7
Kale House Farm
534
Eversfield
665
6
1
Oatn
Fursdon
Reed
3
Bratton Clovelly
Domons
4
Great Burrow
2
5
500
Ford
Ellacott Wood
588
Ellacott
400
450
500
Ebsworthy Town
740
648
Wrixhill Br.
332
Way
586
Brides
Churndon
478
Millaton Ho.
635
Wortham
523 Orchard
Bidlake
Stone
600
550
Northdown
646
Buddlebr
Huddispit
Axworthy

(5) Turn left into a wide lane surfaced with original cobbling. This is still signposted as a bridleway because this is an area where many minor roads have become reclassified as such. The lane gives way to tarmac as you pass Great Burrow to your right.

(6) Here you may wish to follow the bridleway to your left to Little Burrow and Mendea (Celtic for 'little hill'), through similar scenery as the green lane between **(1)** and **(4)**, but there is a footbridge over the stream in this one. Continue to where the bridleway joins the road at **(7)**. Because the lanes you now walk which take you back to **(1)** have verges, there is a non-Devonian feeling about the route: on minor roads anywhere in Devon, you usually need to squash up against a hedge or jump into a ditch whenever cars whizz by.

Take a moment to look behind you and see how you are held in a crescent of moors; Dartmoor to your left, the distant hills of Exmoor to your right, and Bodmin Moor in front of you. Moving on, notice the plantations to your left; these are mainly conifers for the Christmas trade. You are walking through what was once scrubby moorland edge, as the name Boasley (a 'clearing in bristly furze') implies.

(8) At Boasley Cross you will pass the large Bible Christian Chapel (1904) called Salem (from the greeting 'Shalom'). Turn left, passing the Old Post Office on your left, and notice the new Boasley Community Primary School to your right. This has replaced the Bratton Clovelly School, next to the church in the village and founded in 1877. At this school by 1901 there were 140 places, but only two-thirds of these were taken up at any one time. One of the reasons for non-attendance was that children often helped out on the farm or at home; a quarter of the population at this time were children, a large free workforce.

However, one of the main reasons for low numbers was that they did not have shoes to wear in which they could walk to school. Yet there were three boot- and shoemakers in the village at the turn of the century, mainly for the benefit of the hunting fraternity. With a pair of children's shoes priced at 14 shillings, the same as the weekly wage of a farm labourer, it is no wonder that attendances in these remote areas was so low.

At this point you may want to extend your route even further and pass the school northwards towards Broadbury Cottages, where another long bridleway begins to your left. However, for this circuit carry on down the minor lane. When you reach the one large oak on the horizon at the top of the hill, look over onto the A30. To your right in the distance on the moor there is a wide old drovers' road surfaced with grass, leading up onto the moor. The tower of Brentor church can just be seen to the far right from here; below, the new A30 roars silently along. Here speed and salvation share the same landscape under the sweeping Dartmoor skyline.

By the way

There was a Church of England church with a National School attached (1835), a large County School, and a Bible Christian Centre ('Providence', 1859).

There were three blacksmiths, a wheelwright, a tailor, a shopkeeper, a saddler, a miller, and a poultry dealer with the Cornish name of Jabez. There was a post office in the village, and an inn called The Pack Horse, proving that there were plenty of travellers passing this way. A famous song collector, the Reverend Sabine Baring-Gould, lived nearby at Lewdown, where unfortunately very few green lanes are to be found. But there were many criss-crossing the moor and the Cornish border, which enabled him to collect this observation in a song taken down from James Parsons, a hedger from Lewdown and recorded in *Songs and Ballads of the West.*

The Roving Journeyman
I am a roving journeyman
And I rove from town to town
Wherever I get a job of work
I'm willing to set down.
With my kit upon my shoulder
And my stick held in my hand
It's down the country I will go
A roving journeyman.

Many people passing through could have boosted the membership of the Bible Christian congregation here.

Other green lanes in the area

Northlew and Ashbury, Route 41.
Highampton, Route 40.
Bridestowe, Route 43.

Links

There is a bus route which runs from Bude to Exeter via Holsworthy, Okehampton and Bratton, which can be accessed from a turn along this route. National Cycle Route 27.

Question

What did the inn in the village used to be called? You'll have to go in to research the answer.

Route 43

BRIDESTOWE

Cyclists, sailors and forest feasters

OS Explorer Map OL 28 Dartmoor

It is very appropriate that a National Cycle Route should run through here, as it is just one of two places in the county where a plaque to welcome cyclists in the 1920s was affixed to a pub by the Cycling Tourist Club. Its design is that of a cycle wheel with flying wings attached. These straight roads, running east to west, up and down into Cornwall, have always been favourite cycling country. They mark the beginning of the active tourist invasions to come, using lanes which although still used for agricultural purposes were soon to experience more rapid forms of transport. For the walkers, there is the glory of the lines of beeches out-whispering the sound of the A30 at most times of the year.

Conditions: Mainly good surfaces, but some standing water in places.

Distance: Anything from 2 to 6 miles, depending on how you choose to limit your circuit. There are many green lanes in this area.

Starting point: SS515895. At the Church of St Mary, formerly dedicated to another Celtic Saint, Bridget (but belonging mysteriously to the Archdeaconry of Totnes).

(1) Set off with the church to your right, passing the inn to your left and into Rectory Road, which has a fine granite well on the corner. Further along, this lane becomes Pig's Leg Lane – an unusual name, as most of the lanes displaying this feature are known as 'dog's leg' lanes. From here, good views of the moor emerge to your right.

(2) Carry on round, passing the ladder stile to your left and along to a staggered crossroads, turning right then sharp right again into a green lane.

(3) This is a narrow, secret lane where you might be lucky enough to see deer; there are plenty of slot (tracks) in the muddy surface here. These forest feasters have lived in this beech and oak fringe area for centuries.

(4) Cross the stream at the end of this lane; the footbridge, granite clapper-bridge style, is to be found near the gate to your right. The lane which follows is wide, and lined with many 150 to 200-year-old pollarded beeches towering above, full of birds and burnished or shimmering leaves. With a high wind running through them, the sound of the A30 disappears. It is along this lane, and the others to follow, that further evidence of landscape management for deer emerges. There are deep ditches on one or both sides, almost like ha-ha hedges created to prevent deer leaping across from one area to another.

(5) If you wish to make a large circuit, carry on over into the bridleway (which is part of the Dartmoor Way) at the other side of the road, and which will take you down to Fernworthy. If not, turn right into a short section of road here bordered by closely grown beeches with elephantine trunks atop the hedge-banks; a reminder of how church architecture often imitates woodland trees in height.

(6) On your left, take the footpath through into woodland with a good deal of understorey and some pines.

(7) When the woodland meets the road, turn sharp right and uphill, passing The Knole. You are on the road back to the village.

(8) At the junction, turn left. Here stands a fine cast-iron fingerpost with a ball finial indicating your route back as being half a mile. **(9)** brings you past another well on your right to Station Road and then to the Post Office. To the left is a plaque giving details of the Trafalgar Way. This was the route used to bring the good news in 1805 of Nelson's victory. It came first from Falmouth, and took 37 hours to reach London, covering 271 miles with 21 changes of horses. In the 1950s, holidaymakers from London in their Ford Poplars took pride in travelling through here on the congested A30, the most widely used route into Cornwall until the Tamar Bridge was built in 1962.

Take a moment to visit the church, and see how its population must have suffered during the plague years, when six priests were lost in succession: Annery 1377, Hertford 1377, Pratta 1409, Wykington 1413, Weston 1415, Foss 1416. This moor-edge environment is a harsh one, and the end has probably been nigh here, more than once.

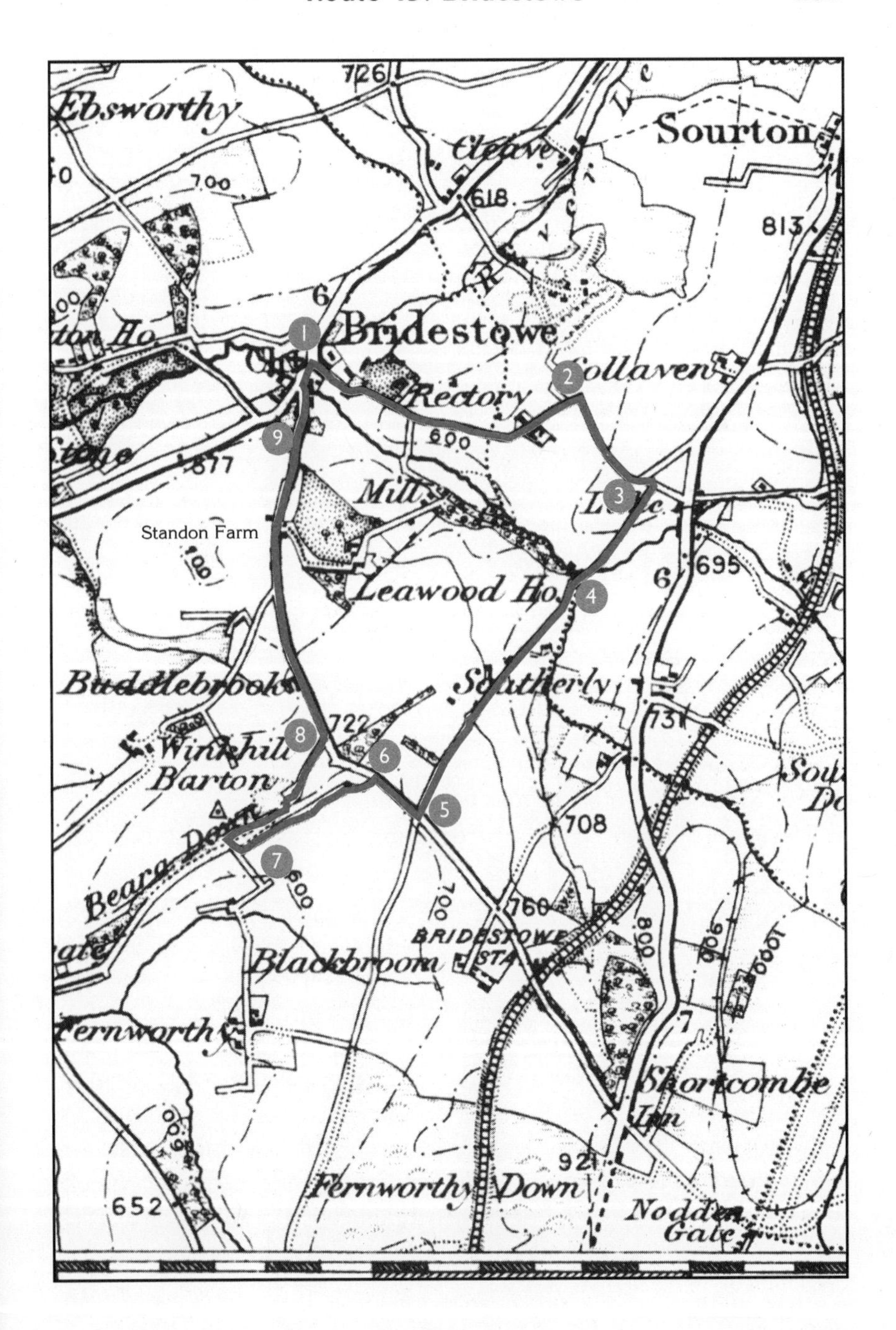
Ebsworthy
726
Sourton
Cleave
700
618
813
Bridestowe
Collaven
Rectory
690
877
Mill
Lake
Standon Farm
Leawood Ho.
695
Buddlebrook
Southerly
722
731
Winkhill
Barton
708
Beara Down
600
700
760
BRIDESTOWE STA
800
Blackbroom
Fernworthy
Shortcombe
Inn
921
652
Fernworthy Down
Nodden Gate
1
2
3
4
5
6
7
8
9

By the way

This moor-edge walk reflects the success of the old MSC Green Lanes project which first involved me in the subject. At least two principal lanes, which were then unclassified roads, have since become byways with the help of the county-wide survey which was made during the 1980s.

Other green lanes in the area

The Anglo-Saxon grid pattern lanes at Lydford.

Links

On the bus route from Plymouth to Barnstaple.
On National Cycle Network 27.
The West Devon Way.
The Two Castles Way.
The Trafalgar Way.
Also on the route of the old A30.

Question

What's the name of the pub which carries the flying wheel?

Route 44

LYDFORD

Drive, driven, drove

OS Explorer Map OL 28 Dartmoor

So much has been written about Dartmoor that I feel it almost speaks for itself now, but I have included this walk as a north-west circuit because it has stood where important routes have crossed for centuries. Alfred the Great set up one of the four Saxon burghs in this part of the south-west here to drive out the indigenous tribes. The Saxons suffered defeat here by the Vikings in AD 997 and were driven out. But the town grid pattern which they established survives here, mostly in the form of green lanes. Despite all the grisly justice dispensed in the Castle's Stannary Courts, domestic traffic continued to use the lanes in this circuit some as drove roads up to Lydford Commons.

Conditions: Some standing water.

Distance: No more than a couple of miles, but allow time for doubling back and exploring the other monuments here.

Starting point: The Castle at SX507844.

(1) By the side of the Castle Inn next to the church is the first of many short passages forming part of the Anglo-Saxon grid pattern. Follow the lane round to the right, where it soon joins a bridleway. Continue straight on to the left, where the lane widens. Here there is the site of an 'ancient spring' which issues forth from an arched stone cover in a hollow wet area full of daffodils and snowdrops in spring. Because this area is known to be Saxon, the width of the hedgerows and the presence of double banks should come as no surprise.

(2) Turn left into a narrow lane, passing Sidleys to your left. The lane widens and becomes muddy on the bend.

(3) The lane comes out onto a minor road. Turn right here back towards Lydford. The banks are still wide, and to the left by the crossroads a tumulus rises in the corner of the field. Go straight across at the War Memorial into the 'Road Unsuitable for Motor Vehicles'. You plunge into a well-walled lane which comes out **(4)** at a green lanes crossroads – always a rarity. Take the Lichway towards Prescombe.

(To your right is the end of Silver Street, and to your left a green lane which climbs up giving access to Lydford Common, an old drovers' route to summer shielings.) The Lichway is cobbled and wide, with a camber. It was used to bring coffins to be buried at the Celtic church of St Petrock in Lydford. If you lived anywhere within the Forest of Dartmoor, then this is where you had to come; Widecombe-in-the-Moor was the only other place to be legally buried. You pass under Lydford viaduct, across which from 1865 the trains from Plymouth to Okehampton ran. Mill Cottage is to your left; go down a set of granite steps to the footbridge and through a gate, keeping to your right through the edge of the wood.

(5) This is a deeply sunken way, hewn out of rock on one side and bordered by large beech trees in Ingo Brake on the other.

(6) There is a gate at the top by a big boundary beech which leads out onto a newly designated bridleway. Turn right and follow the lane which runs parallel with the railway track here before it becomes The Granite Way.

(7) You come out onto the main road on a bend – be careful. Turn right here, and take the opportunity to look down into the gorge from over the bridge; a good place for such rogues as the Gubbinses, a gang of highway robbers, to hide in. There is a pavement on the right, which will take you back up to the Castle. From here you can continue to explore the grid pattern of the town, or go back along Silver Street and up the lane which leads to the moor.

By the way

There is plenty of road history around this seemingly small settlement. Once, when I managed the Green Lanes Project in the 1980s, a group of surveyors took me along one of these Saxon streets where a 'Take Off' stone formed part of a garden gate. These stones, dating back to 1807, were placed at the top of particularly steep inclines by the turnpike companies and indicated that the extra horses you used to haul your carriage up must now be taken off and hitched to the stone. There is one still in place at nearby Beardon.

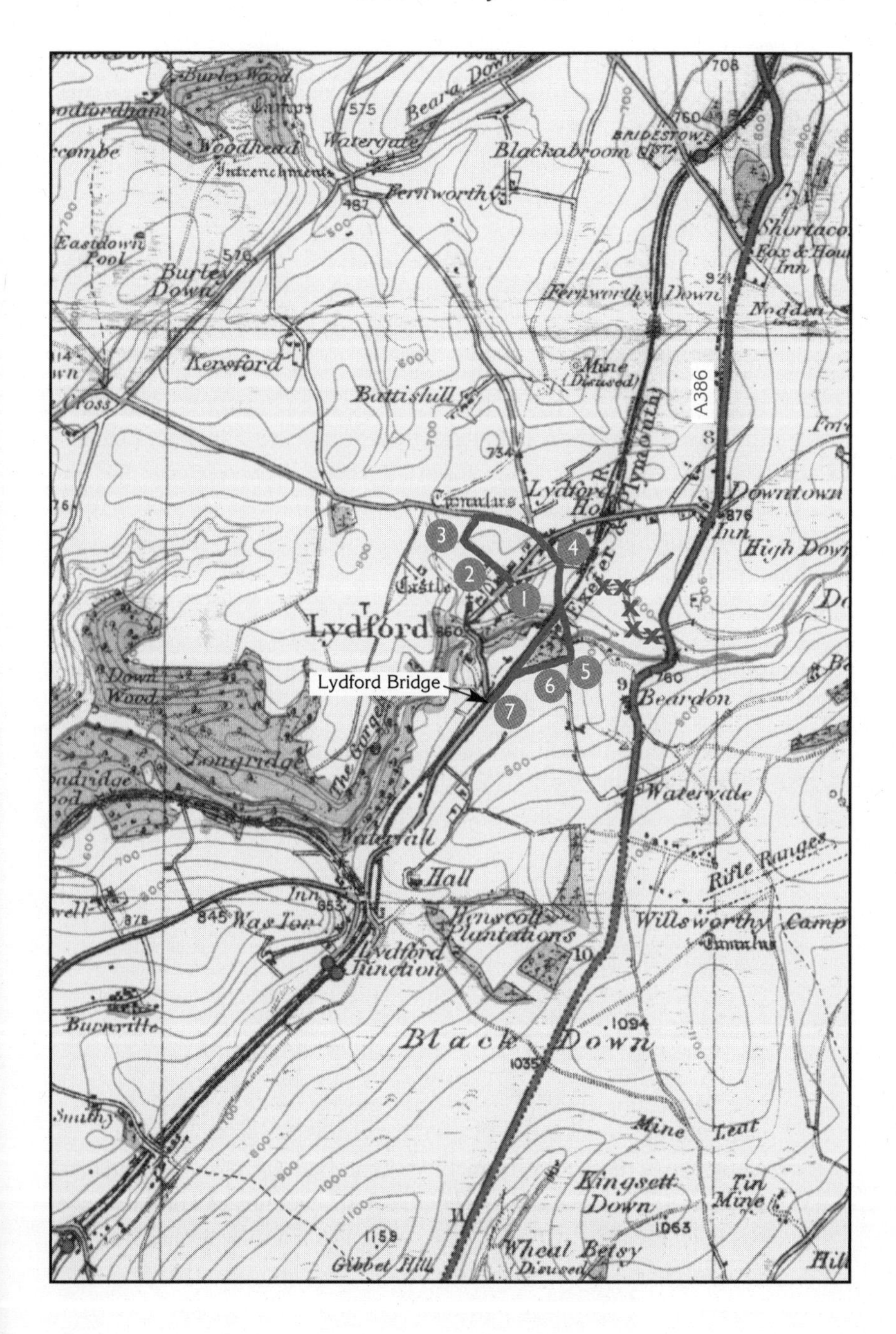
Burley Wood
Camps
Beara Down
Watergate
Woodhead
Intrenchments
Blackabroom
Fernworthy
Bridestowe Sta.
Eastdown Pool
Burley Down
Fernworthy Down
Shortacombe
Fox & Hounds Inn
Nodden Gate
Kersford
Battishill
Mine (Disused)
A386
Lydford
Castle
Lydford Ho.
Exeter & Plymouth R.
Downtown
Inn
High Down
Down Wood
Longridge
The Gorge
Lydford Bridge
Beardon
Watervale
Waterfall
Rifle Ranges
Hall
Was Tor
Inn
Henscott Plantations
Willsworthy Camp
Tumulus
Lydford Junction
Burnville
Black Down
Smithy
Mine Leat
Kingsett Down
Tin Mine
Wheal Betsy
Disused
Gibbet Hill
1
2
3
4
5
6
7

Other green lanes in the area

All well-documented access lanes to the moor, mostly footpaths and bridleways.

Links

Lydford is on the bus route which passes along the A386 from Plymouth to Barnstaple, an old, well-used way.

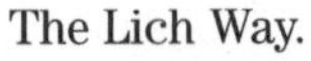

The Lich Way.
The Granite Way (a cycle path along part of the old railway line from Okehampton to Lydford).
The West Devon Way.
The Dartmoor Way.
National Cycle Route 27.
Bridestowe, Route 43.

Question

There is a stone by the wayside which you might 'C' without understanding. (See Templeton, Route 9 for the answer).

Route 45

COOKBURY

Still in the footsteps of the faithful

OS Explorer Map 112

This circuit takes you through a fairly even stretch of open countryside once dominated by the Domesday manors of Dunsland and Bradford. The recently planted conifer forests do not dominate, and the views towards the moors are uninterrupted. You can see anyone approaching for miles in the distance, as this is open ridgeway country connecting north Devon to mid-Devon.

Conditions: Patches of standing water.

Distance: 4-5 miles.

Starting point: SS405038.

This is **(1)** Dunsland Cross on the ridgeway, just up from the former London and South-West Railway station. Turn right towards Brandis Corner, so named because of the three-cornered junction which looks like a brandis iron, Devonian for a 'trivet' – a stand for pots round an open fire.

(2) Turn left here at the Bickford Arms, named after one of the prominent landowners of the area. Standing on the left at the end of the groups of new houses you will see a house with an ecclesiastical brick arch to it. This is the first of the Bible Christian chapels on the way. The road is flanked by a strip of woodland on the right and standing oaks to the left, for we are passing through a once thickly wooded area.

(3) Turning to the left towards Cookbury, you meet the entrance pillars to Dunsland, a National Trust Property now. This was an Elizabethan manor house which was accidentally burnt down during the course of its restoration. Only the grounds can be visited now. There is also an unusually designed Victorian postbox here.

(4) Keep bearing left and the road from here will take you down to a sturdily built little bridge with granite blocks as quoins, a reminder that we are in Dartmoor country. Climb up to Cookbury, its green and **(5)** its church, which were held communally. You are passing Middlecott Commons, which was given to the church by former residents of Dunsland in exchange for being able to occupy two pews in the church. There is an impressive text over the rood-screen which reads 'I am the Bread of Life'.

(6) Retrace your steps from here, and take the 'Unsuitable for Motor Vehicles' lane to your left passing Broadgates Cottages and Farm on your left. Now go down into a lane where there is a falling cob barn on one side and a wooden-gated well on the other. Immediately after, on the curve of the lane to the right, is a square drab building with a modest porch on its plain-rendered walls.

This Bible Christian chapel was built in 1840 and Pevsner describes it as "a rare survival of the contemporary vernacular style". Yet it seems to have no style at all, and will send you moving swiftly on into this long lane, which passes directly through meadow and moorlands. The lane is known locally as Alan's Lane. It must have been an important connecting back road between Cookbury and Bradford, as it is cobbled nearly all the way through. Ash and beech trees border the lane.

(7) The lane's nature changes here: silver birch are dominant and the cobbles give way to grass and yellow clay, the hedgerows grow wider and higher with tall stands of bracken. You cross over a concrete bridge, and the lane twists and turns its way up becoming a hazel tunnel before it opens out with cobblestones underfoot once again. There has been some savage-looking but essential hedge-laying done here.

(8) Turn right towards Bradford and follow the road round, passing the footpath sign on your left and descending to take a look at the plain, undedicated granite roadside cross here, very similar to the one to be found on the Northlew walk. Turn to the left here and follow the path to the church. Go through the lych gate and down into **(9)** the deeply sunken green lane here. You go over one stile and through two gates, and are flanked by larch and beech as you climb up towards the road.

(10) Turn right here away from Priestacott towards Lana Cross. Here you will see one of the few surviving black-and-white cast-iron painted fingerposts with a triangular finial inscribed 'DCC'. This crossroads isn't just a memorial for this type of fingerpost, as its place name has historic signifi-

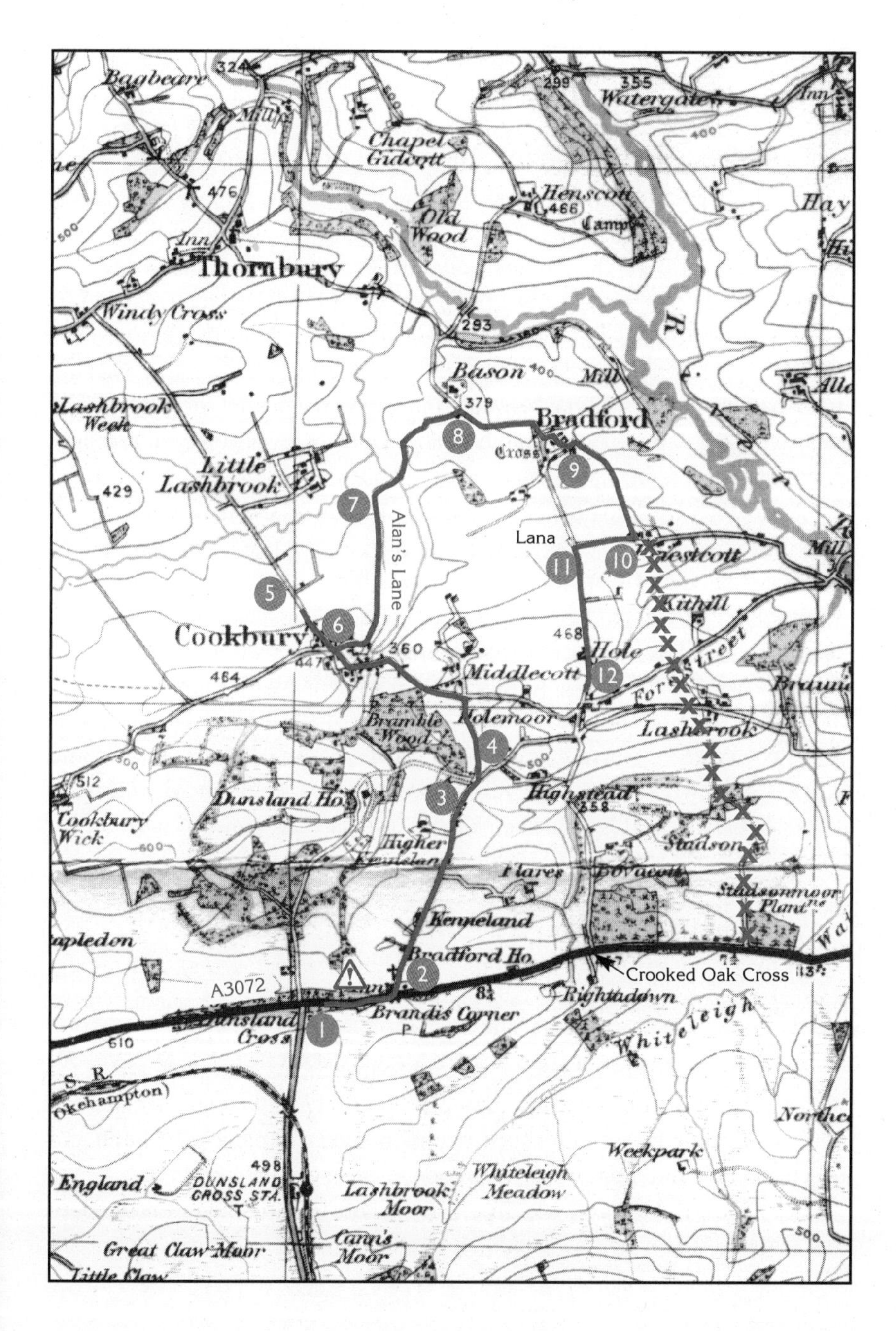
Bagbeare
Thornbury
Windy Cross
Chapel Gidcott
Henscott
Old Wood
Watergate
Bason
Bradford
Cross
Lashbrook Week
Little Lashbrook
Alan's Lane
Lana
Cookbury
Middlecott
Holemoor
Bramble Wood
Dunsland Ho.
Cookbury Wick
Highstead
Higher Kenneland
Kenneland
Bradford Ho.
A3072
Crooked Oak Cross
Brandis Corner
Dunsland Cross
Rightadown
Whiteleigh
S. R.
(Okehampton)
England
DUNSLAND CROSS STA.
Lashbrook Moor
Whiteleigh Meadow
Weekpark
Great Claw Moor
Cann's Moor
Little Claw

cance too. The Dumnonii, resisting the Anglo-Saxon invasions, used the name '-lana' to refer to a burying ground for their own tribesmen.

There is a Saxon encampment shown at Henscott SS427084 overlooking the Torridge, where it is said that the invading Saxon Hengist (without Horsa) came to defend his fellow fighters. It certainly was a long way from Kent, where they first landed, but shows how great the Viking threat and Celtic unrest were in this area.

Turn left here and down to Hole Farm on your right; this is a large dairy farm. We are in cattle-breeding country here, and nearby Halsdon Barton was once famous for this in the 1800s. The trade directory guide talks of three cow-keepers, two female and one male, living in the parish. With reports that it is likely there will be no dairy farmers in existence at all in five years' time, it is comforting to know that at least in the past it took only three such specialists to keep the milk flowing in one parish. There is hope! On the dip to your left you cannot fail to notice the grey buildings enclosed by a low cast-iron fence.

(11) These buildings form the Bible Christian Chapel of Bradford, built in 1839 and restored in 1891, with its Sunday School standing right by its side and its small burial-ground in front. Lights blazed forth from these two still-well-used buildings as I walked by. Take any of the roads here to bring you back to the A3072 and Brandis Corner. If you have time as you make your way back, there is a footpath to your left which leads via East and West Flares to a point known as Crooked Oak. It is no longer indicated on the

map. There is a record of the famous tree which stood here for over 800 years, and was a rallying place for the local hunt. It is reputed to have been haunted. It might have been one of those large hollow oaks in which families of farm labourers once lived and were 'saved' by itinerant Bible Christian preachers. Haunting indeed.

By the way

This walk is in the area of no less than three Bible Christian chapels, including the first one in Devon at Bridgend on the Cornish border, and the one at Sheepwash, where a college for the training of Bible Christian priests was founded.

Links

Off the bus route from Exeter to Bude which stops at Dunsland Cross.
National Cycle Network Route 3.
Route 40 at Highampton.

Riddle

> "Through frost and snow and sunlight
> Through rain and night and day
> I go back to where I come from
> I pass all things, yet stay."
> – Brian Patten

Route 46

NORTH TAWTON (A)

'The labyrinth of brambly burrow lanes'

OS Explorer Map 113

North Tawton is where Ted Hughes, the former poet laureate, lived for many years. He lived, wrote and farmed here, and captured the essence of 'Moor Town' as he called it.

This is a walk through the heart of mid-Devon, along ridgeways and down into wooded valleys, with stunning views of west Dartmoor at your side. There are some interesting differences between the 1907 map and the current one, which have been underlined here. Walk this shorter circuit marked with (a's) before following in the footsteps of Roman soldiers so far from home.

Conditions: Steep damp sections.

Distance: 4-5 miles.

Starting point: North Tawton, the foot of Bouchers Hill at SS664022, which can be found by taking the road signposted to Bondleigh.

(1a) There are large oak pollards in the hedges here, which give way to ashes then drifts of bracken as you make your way to Ashridge, with the winds from the north moving the tall ashes as you pass. You descend through North Tawton Wood. When I walked through here, the huge farm complex at Ashridge stood eerily empty, with old drab curtains hanging at the windows, reminiscent of the Luxtons in Route 49. Farming fortunes are changing all the time. When the railway arrived in the 1870s, farmers in this area dropped corn production and went over to dairying. The lane is steep and fairly wide. Here is just a brief guide as to where and which birds live in hedgerows: where hedges are low and compact, you will hear yellowhammers and whitethroats, and always wrens.

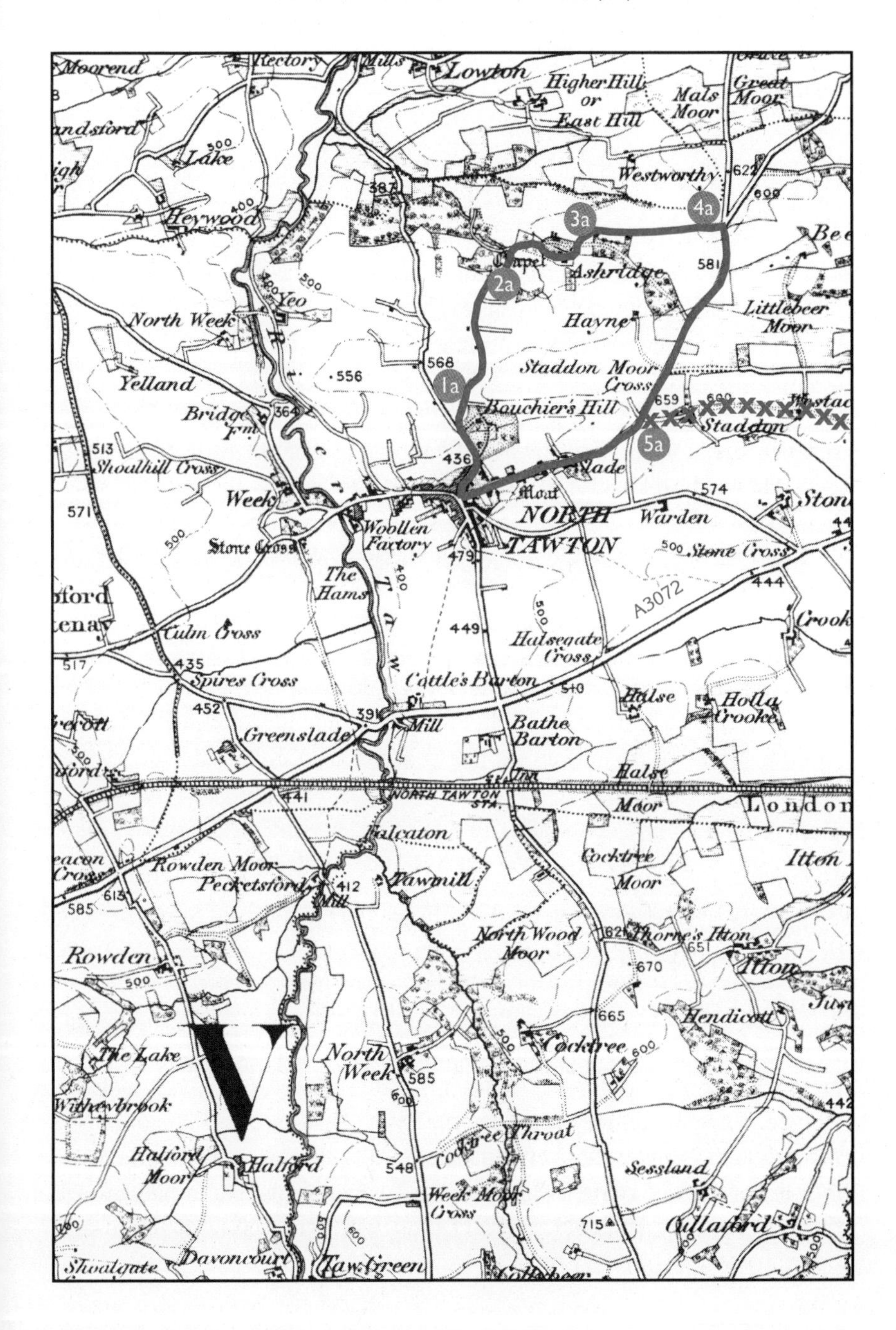
Moorend
Rectory
Mills
Lowton
Higher Hill or East Hill
Mals Moor
Great Moor
Lake
Heywood
Westworthy
622
600
387
1a
2a
3a
4a
5a
Chapel
Ashridge
581
Yeo
North Week
Hayne
Littlebeer Moor
Yelland
568
556
Staddon Moor Cross
Bridge Fm.
364
Bouchier's Hill
659
Staddon
513
Shoalhill Cross
436
Slade
Week
Moat
NORTH TAWTON
Warden
574
571
Woollen Factory
Stone Cross
479
The Hams
A3072
444
Culm Cross
449
Halsegate Cross
517
435
Spires Cross
Cattle's Barton
510
Halse
Holla Crooke
452
391
Greenslade
Mill
Bathe Barton
Inn
Halse Moor
441
NORTH TAWTON STA.
London
Falcaton
Cocktree Moor
Rowden Moor
Peckets ford
412
Tawmill
613
585
North Wood Moor
621
Thorne's Itton
651
Rowden
670
Itton
500
665
Hendicott
The Lake
North Week
585
Cocktree
600
Withybrook
Cocktree Throat
Halford Moor
Halford
548
Sessland
Week Moor Cross
715
Cullaford
Shwalgate
Davoncourt
Taw Green
V

If the hedge is taller and thicker, then birds such as chaffinches, greenfinches, goldcrests, blue tits, great tits, coal tits and long-tailed tits will be there.

A very tall hedge with mature trees is home to woodland birds such as tawny owls, great spotted woodpeckers or nuthatches.

(2a) Follow the lane to your right for a glimpse at this huge deserted farm complex made up of cob buildings, some corrugated roofs, brick-built pigsties and lap-timbered lean-tos. Return to the path and follow it round and up by the bulging walled garden which has some curious crenellations.

(3a) At the top by 'Elwyns', you turn right into a concrete road. Once you leave the wood behind, you are in high moorland country.

(4a) At Ashridge Moor Cross turn right and descend to **(5a)** Staddon Gate, passing a wild boar farm on your right. There is another green lane circuit to your left here, worth pursuing for its views eastwards. And so back into North Tawton to start the long circuit.

By the way

North Tawton at the end of the 19th century was the same size as Okehampton. It had a woollen mill and a flour mill, but both closed down with the arrival of the railway and the sharp change from arable to pasture land. Its creamery still stands as a testament to this change.

Other green lanes in the area

There are those leading over towards the east at Staddon as indicated.

Links

There are two main bus routes through here between Barnstaple and Exeter, and another to Okehampton.

Question

A common hedgerow bird beginning with 's' is known in Devon dialect as a 'spadger', What is it?

Route 47

NORTH TAWTON (B)

A walk through Ruby country

OS Explorer Map 113

This long walk takes you through Ruby Red beef-producing country, along ways which were once walked by, amongst others, Roman soldiers and 16th-century part-time militia. Unlike us now, they would have been making their way through densely wooded countryside. If you start from North Tawton, there is a footpath all the way to the station. In the spring, the road from the town down towards the De Bathe crossroads is lined with banks of daffodils. You can also begin from South Tawton. (You can walk from one bus route in North Tawton to another in South Tawton.)

Conditions: Very muddy in parts, but mainly on the level.

Distance: According to choice, 3-6 miles.

Starting point: Depending on how far you want to walk in one go, there are really two routes here. You can start them at Spreyton, or North or South Tawton, but the place the numbers in this text begin is at Langdown Cross SS677967.

(1) Notice the church-like porch of this house. It was another Bible Christian chapel and school on the Chagford circuit, built in 1865, and appears in the 1907 map as a school. Unlike Church of England priests, the Bible Christians always walked to their chapels, and only used horses when their place of worship was more than six miles away. It is likely that everyone walked to this meeting-place, from North Tawton and in the south from South Zeal and other places towards Okehampton. This is a fast road, with lots of big lorries about (but no priests on horseback), so be careful. Immediately you are over the A3124, traffic noises decrease on the road leading to Cullaford which takes you into the heart of this tranquil country.

(2) Before turning left at the road triangle into one of the longest green lanes in this area, marked 'Unmetalled Road', notice the granite-built barn in front of you, with a fine wagon entrance at its centre. This lane runs alongside the River Yeo, and in places has a marked raised camber.

(3) Turn left at Brandis Corner (to find the 'brandis' here, there is a short length of lane down to Ford). Enter a metalled road by a lone standing alder in the hedge to your left. The lanes now become curiously flat for Devon, and are bordered by what look like Roman ditches in many parts. All around you the fields are full of fine-looking cattle.

(4) At Justment Cross, go straight over into a very wide green lane and follow along to the lane end, where there is a gate and a granite pillar with a carving at its base – which is nothing to do with the old Roman road that it guards. This is an area where the Dumnonii still lived in nearby 'nýmet' land – so the Romans kept their road and fort open in this area, in case the tribes gathered against them. Running to left and right and mostly now in a flooded ditch is the course of one of the most westerly pieces of Roman road in Devon. In front of you is an area which, through subsequent road-building and the coming of the railway, has remained disconnected from roads in both north and south. It is here that nine wind turbines may be placed in the shadow of the old Roman Fort. I am sure that if the Romans had harnessed wind power as well as they did water, there would have been no objections.

Retrace your steps back to Justment Cross, so named from medieval French and referring to a piece of grazing land which is let. No doubt party to many a just wrangle in the past, it stands close to where this new wind turbine development is to be placed. Follow the road round to Itton. The lane is straight, and bordered with verges and ditches. There is a watery area with a lake to the right, which may be the Bath Pool referred to in the nearby de Bathe crossroads.

At **(5)** Itton Cross you are on the A3124 again. Turn left here, away from North Tawton and negotiate the stretch of this busy road, which will take you to **(6)** the green lane marked 'Unsuitable for Motors', which is called Cocktree Throat after an Anglo-Saxon called Caca who had a tree here. This is a wide lane, well-surfaced, with a ford and footbridge at its centre. The trees you pass by in the copse are mainly Caca's beeches, but there are some larch here too.

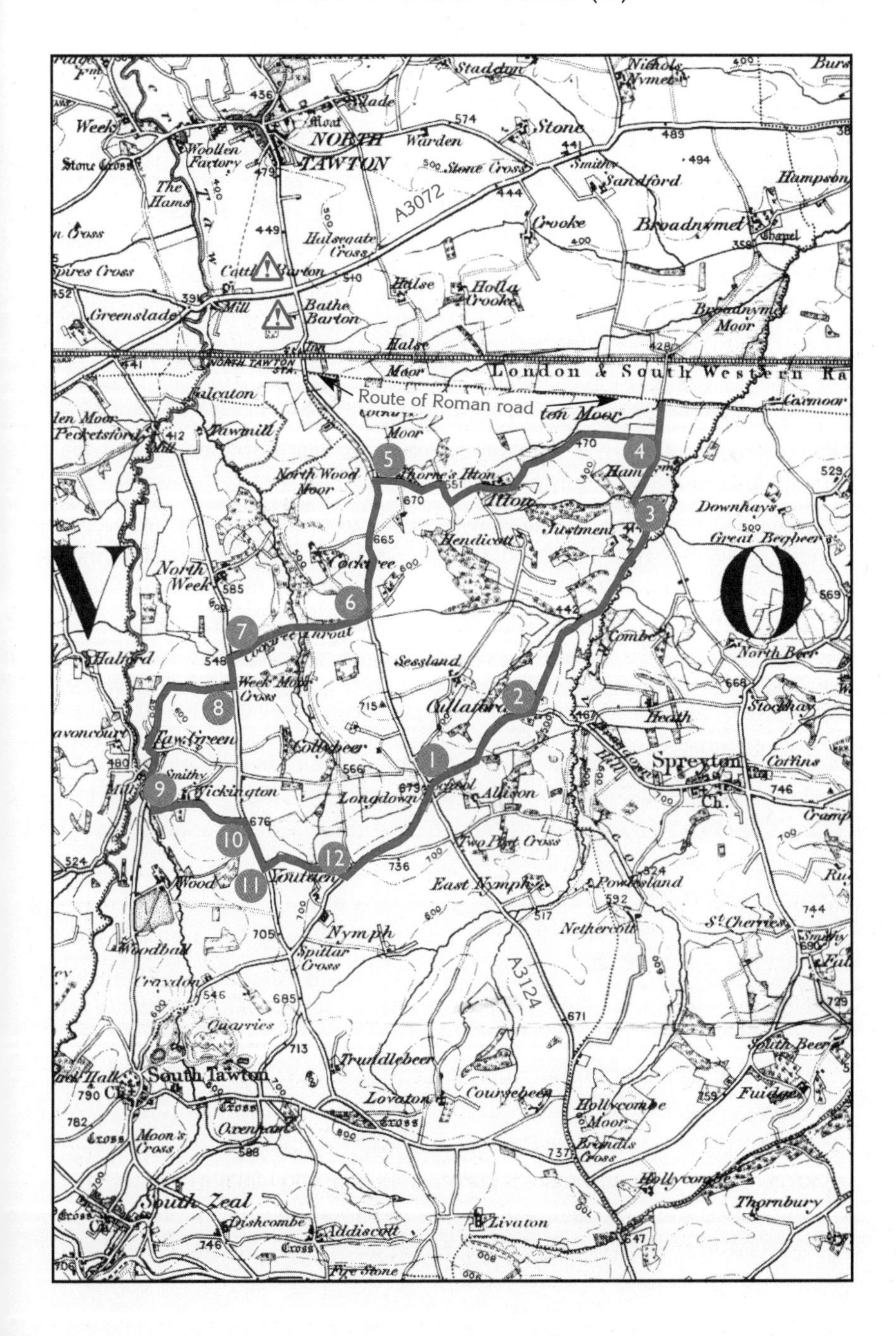
NORTH TAWTON
Woollen Factory
The Hams
Week
Stone Cross
Staddon
Nichols Nymet
Stone
Warden
Sandford
Hampson
Broadnymet
Chapel
Crooke
Halse
Holla Crooke
Halsegate Cross
Cattle Barton
Bathe Barton
Greenslade
Spires Cross
Mill
Broadnymet Moor
A3072
London & South Western Ra
North Tawton Sta.
Route of Roman road
Falcaton
Sawmill
Pecketsford
Moor
North Wood Moor
Thorne's Itton
Itton
Hendicott
Justment
Downhays
Great Begbeer
North Week
Cocktree
Cocktree Throat
Halford
Week Moor Cross
Taw Green
Collabeer
Cullaford
Combe
North Beer
Heath
Stockhay
Spreyton
Ch.
Coffins
Smithy
Wickington
Longdown
School
Allison
Two Post Cross
East Nymph
Powsland
Nethercott
St Cherries
Wood
Nymph
Spittar Cross
Woodhall
Croydon
Quarries
South Tawton
A3124
Trundlebeer
Lovaton
Coursebeer
Hollycombe Moor
Brandis Cross
South Beer
Fuidge
Oxenpark
Moon's Cross
Cross
South Zeal
Dishcombe
Addiscott
Livaton
Hollycombe
Thornbury
Fire Stone

(7) Turn right into the minor road here, and walk towards North Wyke. You will be treading in the footsteps of John Weekes (known as 'Warrior Weekes'), named as Captain and Constable of the parish of South Tawton in 1552.

Turn back to Wyke Moor Cross **(8)**, where you might wish to take a further detour along the Tarka Trail to Taw Green **(9)**. Turn left at Mill House into Wilmington Lane.

(10) Turn right into the minor road, which will take you down to another green lane on your left marked 'Unsuitable for Motors' at **(11)**. This has a camber and cobbles, and a large patch of standing water. The hedges in this area are all flat and wide, a kind of hedge known as a 'butt'. (This same word also means a small cart or sledge, a beehive, a target for archery practice, a high hedge where rabbit burrows are to be found and, in an open field, it is where the 'butt-ends' of the strips meet one another).

(12) You emerge into a minor road and turn left towards Langdown, passing on your right a beautiful stand of tall ashes and beeches, a reminder that this area was once covered in such nymets.

By the way

North Wyke is at least four miles from South Tawton, but it was to the armoury here that the 'young men' of the militia brought their weapons to be stored. Weapons were usually kept in the church or the church tower. Perhaps it was more appropriate to keep them here close to Sampford Courtenay, as it is close to the scene of the dreadful battle at Greenhill. Between 1560 and 1570 firearms gradually came into use alongside the longbow which, after 1590, they rapidly superseded.

The reference in the church to the Italian 'arquebutters' on the side of Lord Russell at Sampford Courtenay goes some way to explain their victory at the nearby Battle of Greenhill. Armour and horse harness would also have been stored here.

In 1588 (Armada year) we find Richard Drake paying extra to the Tinners who had their own, very effective militia ready to be called upon by the King during these times. They were a class apart, but a fierce one. The demise of the Wykes in this area (their name can be spelt in sixty different ways) is a tale of legal wrangling.

In the 1660s a Wyke came down from London to visit his consumptive relative, John, living here then with his mother and daughter. He took his ailing relative to Plymouth to a doctor he knew there. Because of this kindness, John agreed to have a new will made out declaring Richard his sole heir, with some provisos which he was too ill to consider and were going to be made later. On returning to Wyke, John died, and although Richard inherited initially, ceremoniously kicking out Richard's relatives, a long legal case followed over the wording of the will which drained all the riches of the estate.

Other green lanes in the area

Some at Zeal Monachorum and Down St Thomas. Many of the lanes in this circuit have recently been granted Public Right of Way status.

Links

The Tarka Trail.
On the bus routes from Exeter to Okehampton, and Exeter to Barnstaple on the A3072.

Question

What is the sign on the stone by the Roman road for? Draw this here.

Typical carrier's cart, bringing goods from Bideford.

Route 48

SAMPFORD COURTENAY

Tinker, tailor, soldier . . . goodbye!

OS Explorer Map 113

This walk is dedicated to all those who lost their lives in the Prayer Book Rebellion of 1549, and especially to Thomas Underhill, tailor, who died fighting in his home village and, like many of the combatants, could not really be considered a red-blooded man of war.

Conditions: Muddy and damp in places.

Distance: 4 to 5 miles.

Starting point: SS633015. At the Church steps on the wall of the Church House here there is a plaque which reads:

> "On Whit Monday 1549 Sampford Courtenay people killed a local farmer William Hellyons, and then joined themselves with the Cornish in the Prayer Book Rebellion which ended in defeat by the King's army outside this village."

Inside the church there is a lot of information about the Western Rebellion, as it came to be known. So start by visiting this church, which has a spacious cathedral-like feel. Above the altar are some wooden bosses depicting three hares chasing each other. This may be a grey hare-witch from Celtic times. Up there you can also see an angel with a straight-toothed, wide-mouthed grin, and the swirly woodland headgear of some old Green Men from the former Celtic wildwood. Turn right out of the church gate and pass the Barton.

(1) Here there is a green lane to your right with a cross placed on the hedge under a horse chestnut tree which overshadows it. This cross is one of four, which may have been placed here as a memorial to those who fell in the battle which finished beneath the high banks of this lane to your right. In August 1549 the rebels were beaten by Lord Russell's army, which included

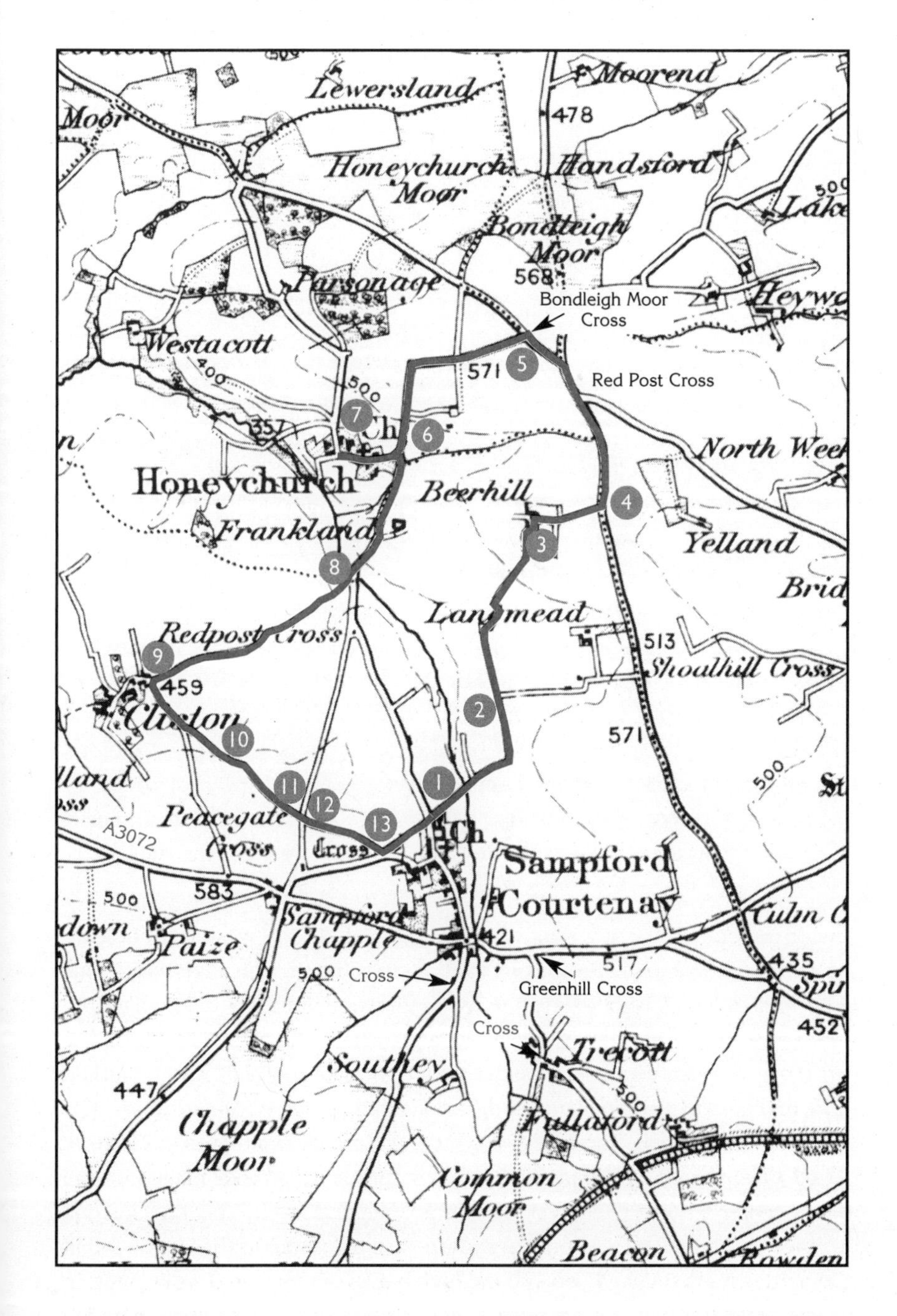
Bondleigh Moor Cross
Red Post Cross
Cross
Greenhill Cross
Cross
A3072
Lewersland
Moorend
Honeychurch Moor
Handsford
Bondleigh Moor
Parsonage
Westacott
Honeychurch
Beerhill
Frankland
North Week
Yelland
Langmead
Redpost Cross
Shoalhill Cross
Peacegate Cross
Sampford Courtenay
Sampford Chapple
Paize
Southey
Trecott
Fullaford
Chapple Moor
Common Moor
Beacon

Italian 'arquebutters' over here not to defend their faith. The rebels were routed and fled – floundering in the boggy patch at Weirford Bridge, no doubt. Today watch out for the huge leaves of the winter heliotrope which grows here. The lane, deeply rutted, plains and straightens out at the top where the hedges flatten and there is a good view of the white tower of Honeychurch ahead.

(2) There is a granite gate post in the lane here which looks as if it has served some marker purpose too. Go through the metal gate, and you will wade through this cottongrassed lane to Beer Hill Farm.

(3) Take the concrete path on the right along towards the A3124, and **(4)** turn left into it. Pass Red Post Cross, and at **(5)** take Bondleigh Moor Cross to the left. This leads to an oak tree triangle. Keep to the left here until the next junction at Rowtry Cross **(6)**. Here there is a well on the right, restored in 2000, and a boundary stone for Honeychurch and Bondle, whose initials are carved in the granite in an abbreviated form.

(7) You pass Eastdown to the church which is all that it claims to be – Honeychurch.

On leaving, notice on the lintel ends either side of the door two carvings of knightly, eastern-looking faces. After the terrible massacres at Sampford Courtenay's larger (Parish) church, this one may have seen record attendances in the 16th century, and the number of footpaths leading to it confirm the direction that the worshippers favoured.

(8) Take the one which leads down to Frankland Ford Bridge opposite the church entrance. If you go back down the lane, notice to the right of the lane buried in the hedge a granite stone which has some strange and barely decipherable marks on it. Take the footpath by the bridge over the footbridge into the field, and go straight across into a green lane entrance in the far corner. This lane will take you to the Cliston group of farms **(9)**.

Go towards them for a glimpse to your right of the fine cob-built walls here, but turn back and go into the tarmacked road following it round until, on your left a green lane marked 'Unsuitable For Motor Vehicles' appears at **(10)**. Follow this muddy lane through to **(11)** Peacegate Cross and cross over into the next **(12)** green lane.

(13) At the next crossroads you will find a granite cross set into the hedge. From here, take the green lane back towards the first granite cross you found or follow the road back to the village, passing the Village Hall, which once was the school, to your left.

By the way

There is much to tell about the Prayer Book Rebellion, when local people objected to what they saw as the King's act of imposing a popish book upon them. This is difficult for us to understand, as this 'popish' book was in fact in English and not in Latin, as it had been up until then. It was the imposition which caused the violence, and was probably linked with many other repressions in the structure of rural society at the time.

Links

A cycle route signed in brown at Honeychurch.
On the Barnstaple to Exeter bus route.

Question

The faces that guard the door inside here are like the one that is banished to the porch at Bow – friends or foe?

Route 49

WINKLEIGH

Farming to the end – the Luxton legacy

OS Explorer Map 113

Back in 1975, news items which dealt with murder cases never seemed to be as numerous or shocking as they do now. So when news came through that Frances Luxton (aged 67) and her two brothers Robert (65) and Alan (54) had been found dead in strange circumstances that looked like a suicide pact on their own farmyard near Winkleigh, the impact of such a horror in such a beautiful place made a lasting impression.

This is a linear walk, illustrating the usefulness of green lanes, which always linked farming settlements. You can curtail it at any time, as indicated on the map. One of these alternatives takes you by a water-bottling plant. I am reminded of the Luxtons and their farming methods, which involved bringing their sheep from the fields to the farm to drink twice a day. This walk is dedicated to the memory of the Luxtons of Chapple Farm.

This can be done as a long linear walk which can start at Winkleigh on the Exeter to Barnstaple bus route and end at Lapford on the Tarka Railway line; alternatively it can be done as a circular walk (see map). It is a fine day out through the heart of Devon.

Conditions: Some patches of standing water.

Distance: 4-5 miles.

Starting point: SS649082. Before setting out on this walk visit Winkleigh's All Saints Church, formerly dedicated to Thomas à Becket, and marvel at its restored state – especially the 70 angels lined up on the corbel ends of the wooden barrel roof.

The church leaflet states that: "Winkleigh Church must now rank as one of the finest specimens of a village church in its state of preservation." This is indeed true, and the pamphlet states that it is due to the financial

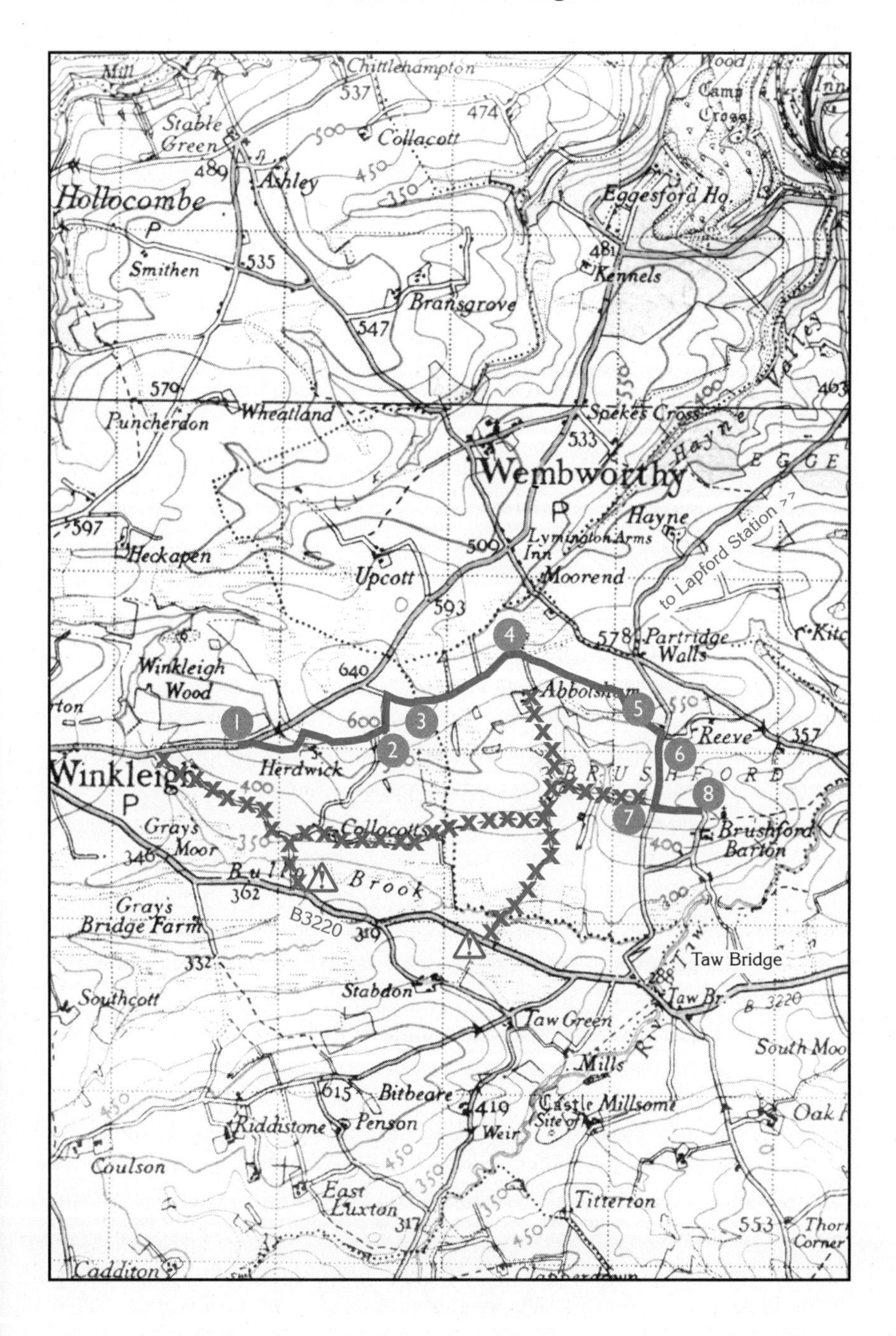
Chittlehampton
Stable Green
Ashley
Collacott
Hollocombe
Smithen
Bransgrove
Eggesford Ho.
Kennels
Camp Cross
Puncherdon
Wheatland
Spekes Cross
Wembworthy
Hayne
Lymington Arms Inn
Moorend
Heckapen
Upcott
to Lapford Station >>
Partridge Walls
Winkleigh Wood
Abbotsham
Reeve
Winkleigh
Herdwick
BRUSHFORD
Brushford Barton
Grays Moor
Collacott
Bullow Brook
Grays Bridge Farm
B3220
Taw Bridge
Taw Br.
Southcott
Stabdon
Taw Green
South Moor
Mills
Bitbeare
Riddistone
Penson
Castle Millsome
Weir
Coulson
East Luxton
Titterton
Thorn Corner
Cadditon
Eggesford Ho.
Winkleigh Wood

support of the Luxtons. Now walk out on the Eggesford road to SS648088, just opposite the eastern edge of Winkleigh Wood.

(1) To your right at the crest of the hill is the surface of a green lane, now signposted as a footpath, with wonderful views of the Okehampton face of Dartmoor in front of you. The path leads down past Herdwick, whose cob buildings are glimpsed between the trees. There is a lot of holly in these ancient hedgerows. Round by the farm take a sharp left up and into a hazel holloway which runs to **(2)**.

At Lifton Cottage, veer to the right then follow the sign to the left which runs along a field edge. Abbotsham is behind you, with glimpses of red brick through the trees. **(3)** At the corner of the meadow, follow the edge to the right where you cross over a stile into a meadow; go through another two gates through meadows, and through the gate of the last one out into a lane.

(4) Take this green lane to your right, which then turns eastwards to your left where it becomes a cutaway green lane running through a silvery sallow and furze copse where fleabane and tansy grow. The bridleway lane remains well cobbled to its end at Steer Cottage.

(5) Turn right into the minor road here and down to the next green lane on your left at **(6)**. This will take you through Higher Reeve, Middle Reeve and Lower Reeve. Medieval reeves performed the tasks of present-day land agents. The farms along this lane spill out into the road, and long may they do so: being neat and tidy is not the main attribute of a working farm. From here, retrace your steps and drop down to **(7)** at Brushford Cross and then along the lane to Brushford Barton and Farm. The small churchyard **(8)** here is the resting place of Frances Luxton (note the seat in front of the church), who wanted to be buried close to the Barton where her relatives once ran one of the most important farming enterprises in the valley.

From here you can go back into the churchyard and follow the footpath through towards Westacott Wood and over to Nymet Rowland. You can then take the train at Lapford, or at Brushford Cross follow the alternative route back to **(4)** at Abbotsham, or follow the other green lanes as indicated which will bring you back closer to Winkleigh.

By the way

The presence of farming Luxtons in this area goes back 700 years, when they were known as the Luggesdons. The reasons why these remaining farming Luxtons decided to stop farming forever are compellingly laid out in the book

Earth to Earth (See bibliography). Whilst in this area, a word about "the savages of north Devon". These were reported in a Victorian publication of 1874 as residing in Nymet Rowland. In fact they were the numerous legitimate and illegitimate members of the Cheriton family, first recorded in the 18th century, who lived as best they could in little more than an almost underground hovel on their 30-acre farm. (See Route 45 at Cookbury, where labourers were said to have lived in the Crooked Oak). The Cheritons were often caught poaching and stealing other farmers' crops and, in one case, wood from the vicar, for which crime two weeks' imprisonment with hard labour was handed out. They were famous for abusing the clergy and churchgoers, as they lived right in front of the rectory. One of their number was known as a white witch. She had the gift of healing scrofula, also known as 'the King's Evil'.

The truth is that although the Cheritons were troublesome, they were also expensive for the parish. As the number of farms decreased and the labourers went elsewhere for work, the Cheritons remained. Their continued presence pushed up the parish poor rates paid by those farmers, now made richer by absorbing smaller failed ones. It is said that one of their number went on to become a constable and a rich man, and in place of the Cheritons' former hovel built Nymet House.

Other bands of wandering, homeless, feral Devonians were written about by the Victorians: the Gubbinses of Lydford, the Greggs of Clovelly and the Doones of Exmoor. Colourful, but tragic.

Other green lanes in the area

There are many, the main three being those leading down from Brushford to Taw Bridge and those in the Coldridge area. These lanes run through what was once parkland owned by the Duke of Dorset, and form part of a short circular route round Lapford (published in a pamphlet Devon County Council).

Links

There is a bus which passes through Winkleigh from Exeter to Barnstaple.

Question

What kind of spring water is bottled here?

Route 50

BOW

A dispossessed church

OS Explorer Map 113

This walk contains just two short sections of green lane, but the history surrounding them is turbulent. They have survived despite all the clashes between early Romans, Christians and Celts in the area. The main direction of communications is in an east-west direction. To trace a further Roman road connection, go back to the chapel at the junction, and search for the strange street name of 'Iter' (see map), meaning a day's journey or march.

Conditions: Some muddy and rocky patches.

Distance: 3-4 miles.

Starting point: Bow Crossroads SS723017.

Follow Station Road south and a sign to Nymet Tracey until you come to **(1)** a cross. Its haft looks ancient, but its cross is new. Follow this footpath, which soon becomes a lane sinking towards Den Brook. Here you will find water pepper, rosebay willowherb, meadowsweet and a hop hedge.

The strangest watery site is provided by a group of willow stumps from which grow tufts of pedunculate grass **(2)**. Cross a field and turn left into the minor road which leads round to the church standing next to a huge tithe barn at **(3)**. If the church is locked, the important thing to notice here is in the porch. Continue on the road, turning left out of the gate.

(4) Back on the minor road, seek out the holy well of Puddock, named after Bishop Putta of Devon who was murdered at Copplestone in 974. You will find it at the foot of a gnarled ash tree at SS731006. A Roman garrison was kept in the fort in this district to keep an eye on the insurgent tribes of Dumnonia living in their sacred 'nymets' and guarding their holy wells.

(5) Follow the road round, passing Walson Barton and Walson Cross.

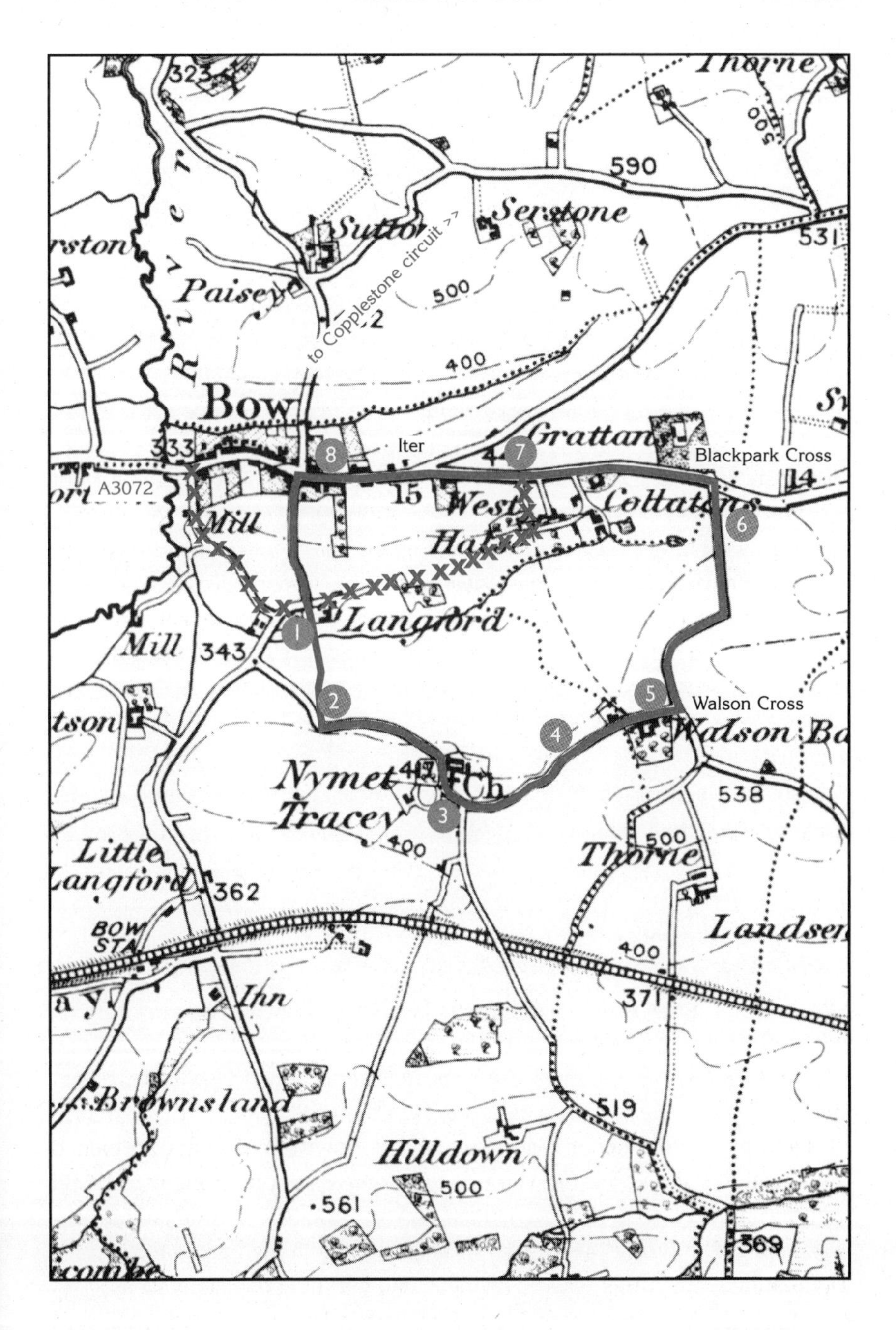
to Copplestone circuit >>
Bow
Iter
Blackpark Cross
A3072
Walson Cross
Langford
Nymet Tracey
West Hatch
Coltatons
Grattan
Serstone
Sutton
Paisey
River
Thorne
Landsend
Hilldown
Brownsland
Little Langford
Inn
BOW STA
590
531
500
400
333
343
362
538
371
519
561
369
323
15
14

The 'wal' element in these place names gives us another clue as to the Celtic nature of the country here, as 'wal' meant stranger – in this case the Dumnonii still holding their own settlements from the Saxons.

(6) At Blackpark Cross, turn left along the road to West Halse.

(7) On the left here there is another short section of green lane which will take you back over the meads to the ever-watchful wayside cross at **(1)**.

By the way

Take any map of rural England and you will notice how the churches appear at crossroads and junctions in the centre of a village or hamlet. A study of where people worshipped in a rural community can help us find out where they were coming from in order to get there. So why has the church of St Bartholomew been placed so far back from Bow, although records show that the main settlement was here originally too? Does it have something to do with the fact that Sir William de Tracey was one of the knights who took part in the murder of St Thomas à Becket in 1170? For as a penance he built some other churches in north Devon: at Newton Tracey, and another, in truly penitential fashion, as far away as possible from human habitation, at Mortehoe.

Bow stands on a very straight section of road, which is Roman in origin. Its Silver Street is a favourite venue for time-trial cyclists. To trace connections with the Romans, go back to the hidden chapel and search for the unusual street name of 'Iter', as mentioned above **(8)**.

Other green lanes in the area

Continue through to the Copple Stone connection by lanes marked with crosses on the map. Westwards towards North Tawton.

Links

Bow is on the bus route from Exeter to Okehampton and from Exeter to Barnstaple.

Question

Whose face looks out at you under the porch?

Route 51

TEDBURN ST MARY

Walking back to the beginning to avoid 'The End'!

OS Explorer Map 114

You are about to walk back towards the place and historical period where Route 1 begins. When you reach point **(11)**, you may choose to go straight on to Boniface's Crediton, or there is the option of returning to Tedburn and then by bus to Exeter from the strangely deserted old A30. In 1939 there were two million cars in the UK; by 2000 there were 26 million. Many of these millions must have travelled along here towards the West on holiday before the new A30 was built in the 1980s. However, this number of motorised travellers would be dwarfed if we were to count all the travellers who have ridden or walked along this ancient way over time.

Once known as the longest lane in England, the old A30 is, like an old Morris Traveller, finding its way back into rural tranquillity once more. However, in an ironic reversal, the villagers are now protesting because they feel they have been cut off by the new road layout.

Conditions: Steep and muddy in places.

Distance: 3-4 miles and more depending on how you finish the circuit.

Starting point: **(1)** The crossroads at Tedburn SX816943 on the B3220.

There is a plaque announcing this route as part of the Trafalgar Way (see Route 43, Bridestowe). If you have time, there is an old green lane footpath which runs round the back of The Old Forge, close to the pub, and gives you an opportunity to get really close to an old cob-built wall. It emerges into Blackacre Lane, with views of the church looking strangely close because of the perspective lent by the deep valleys all around. Follow the road downhill with views of Dartmoor ahead.

(2) Turn right at this old crossroads, and notice the footpath on the other side of the road, which once gave it its crossroads status. This is how people would have reached the original settlement and the impressive Colley House from the south. There were snowdrops in the hedgerow here in late January.

(3) The green lane footpath to the left runs parallel towards the church here and would have provided an alternative (less muddy) way to the church.

(4) The church is an historic one, and so not always open. On leaving the lychgate go straight ahead, passing the huge farm to your left, and then go straight down into a green lane on your left by Bonfield House. There are two holly trees at the end here, and many more down the lane ahead.

(5) Turn sharply to your right here, passing Cummins Cross and Church Lane until **(6)**, where a footpath on the left at a house entrance runs across a field to lead you back to the Crediton road at **(7)**. Turn left and climb up to Frankford Lane on your right at **(8)**. This wide lane takes you down to the Great Fairwood Farm, where there is a fine cob barn, then narrows to the left down a damp lane through a gate and into a wide, straight lane bordered by multi-armed, pollarded oaks. Where the ploughing turn bend begins in the lane, watch out on your left for a venerable pollarded oak, long-living because of such management. There is also a small plantation of alders to the left in this section – more about these trees later.

As you descend towards East Frankford farm, where there are more cob buildings, follow the footpath sign to your left which will take you over a footbridge by a ford and out into another lane which borders the woodlands to your right. Oldridge Wood is a mixture of conifers and broadleaved trees, with some patches of furze on the slopes. Go straight over a break in the path through a muddy meadow, and you are alongside Blackalder Wood.

The woodland here is mainly understorey holly bushes and tall beeches and oaks now. But when the alders were growing here, and planted up from the stream on your left to the rise of the hill, they were considered a valuable source for making gunpowder. Alder charcoal, because of its mixture of carbon sulphur and potassium nitrate, was used from the 17th century onwards for this purpose.

There is further place-name evidence to corroborate this, at nearby Gunstone Mill. Handily this mill is on the south side of Crediton's green lane system where Cromwell's troops mustered in the Cut, a deeply sunken lane – renamed Cromwell's Cut after the Civil War. (Lord's Meadow, where the

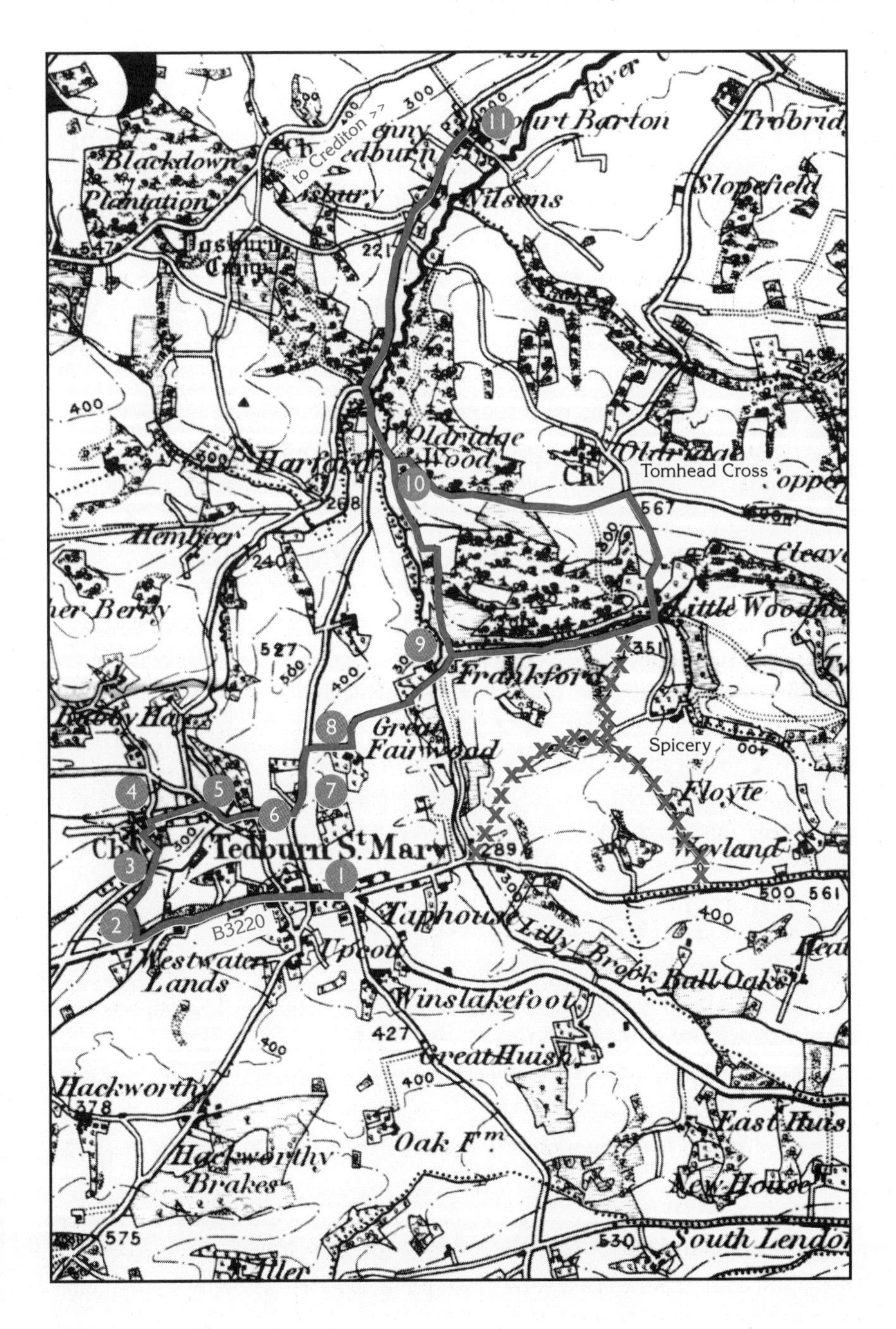
to Crediton >>
Tomhead Cross
Spicery
B3220
1
2
3
4
5
6
7
8
9
10
11
Blackdown Plantation
Oldridge Wood
Frankford
Great Fairwood
Tedburn St. Mary
Taphouse
Winslakefoot
Oak Fm.
Hackworthy
Hackworthy Brakes
Floyte
Ball Oaks
South Lendon

Royalists gathered, has been given a more permanent memory in place-name terms).

(10) Go straight on at the end of the lane, having crossed the high foot-bridge over the Lilly Brook which you have followed all the way. This streamside is bordered by broken oak pollards, giving way to the meadows where Mr Crocker grew teazles up to the end of the 19th century. These were used in the more peaceful occupation of napping cloth.

Turn right at the end into the road, and over the bridge to Meetford Cross. Here the wood to the left is of beech, ash and overgrown chestnut stands. By walking up the valley you will reach point **(11)**, passing point (3) on Route 2. The pull towards Crediton is great, and you may want to go and take another look at Posbury Camp, bravely defended by the Celts against the Saxons in 661 and which you first saw on Route 2.

Were the Celts driven northwards from here, or did they just disappear into the woods which covered all of this area then?

The clumps of beech and oak which remain by the camp now hang picturesquely and peacefully on the hillside overlooking a valley which is a model of pastoral tranquillity.

Did these remaining Celts, these Dumnonii, with their worship of fire, keep up their beliefs centuries later by producing gunpowder?

A veteran farmer who was out fencing by the hill on a stormy November day told me that below is where the volcanoes lie. He said they were quiet now, but they will blast out again soon – a farmer's prophecy of global warming. With this in mind, perhaps now is the time to abandon exploring green lanes in the north and north-west, and take the Oldridge Road towards the east and the south. See you there!

By the way

Tedburn St Mary Church stands at the centre of the original settlement, as do all the churches on these circuits. It dates back to the 12th century, and is well placed for the Saxon farmers who first ploughed here, as it sits between two water supplies. But this didn't make it so good for travellers from the east and west, so gradually the settlement moved to the line of the old A30 around the crossroads where The King's Arms stands today.

There is a lot of highway history to be seen here. Here stands Fry's Garage on the site of one of the earliest petrol stations in the county, first listed as Wyatt's Garage in 1935. There was a refreshment room here too, at The White House. Although this would have served motorists, it was probably visited by cyclists and those walking out from Pathfinder village. Take a look at the milestone and the well, known as Taphouse and placed at the head of the long drag up Five Mile Hill from Exeter.

Carriers came this way from Exeter, Okehampton, Chagford, South Zeal and Drewsteignton. In Devon at the beginning of the 20th century, 55,000 people were employed in the domestic services and 22,000 in transport. But only 12 of these worked with motorised transport.

In the 1950s it was said that the traffic flow was so great at the Crediton turn here that every Saturday in the summer months a policeman was here on duty just to let the traffic out and in towards Crediton. You will have no need of his services today.

Other green lanes in the area

Those which lead from **(11)** back down to Welwyn.

Links

Route 1.
The Tarka Line.
Bus routes from Exeter to Crediton.
Bus routes from Exeter, along the A30, to Okehampton.
Both Crediton and Tedburn St Mary are on bus routes from Exeter to Okehampton.

Question

You end high up on this type of road, upon which you have often travelled over the past 50 circuits.

ACKNOWLEDGEMENTS

Photographs

The Stone Breakers, Totnes Image Bank, p.119.
George Belsey pp.72, 82, 138, 143, 229 and front cover photo.

The Tunnicliffe illustrations are from the 1921 edition of Henry Williamson's *The Lone Swallows:* pp.26, 39, 52 and 54.

The Staff of Harberton Art Workshop, Totnes.
David Archer Maps.

I would like to thank the staff of the North Devon Record Office, and the friendly and helpful bus drivers on the various routes taken on these journeys.

A big thank you to the staff of Green Books for their friendly encouragement, and in particular Stephen Prior for his good humour and expertise.

BIBLIOGRAPHY

Belsey, Valerie: *Devon Roads – Past and Present.* Past and Present Publications, 1993.

Belsey, Valerie: *The Green Lanes of England.* Green Books, 1998.

Belsey, Valerie: *Discovering Green Lanes.* Green Books, 2001.

Belsey, Valerie: *Exploring Green Lanes in the South Hams.* Green Books, 2003.

Cornwell, John: *Earth to Earth – A true story of the lives and violent deaths of a Devon farming family.* Penguin, 1982.

Duffy, Eamon: *The Voices of Morebath: Reformation and Rebellion in an English Village.* Yale, 2001.

Francis, T. J.: *The Industrial Heritage of Bampton, Devon.* Fort Press, 2006.

Godfrey, Alan: Reprints of OS one inch to a mile series of maps from the 1880s to 1907.

Gray, Todd: *Blackshirts in Devon.* The Mint Press, 2006.

Grigson, Geoffrey: 'Packhorse Days in the South West'. *The Countryman Magazine,* Autumn 1951.

Grundy, G. B.: 'Ancient Highways of Devon'. *The Archaeological Journal.*

Hoskins, W.G.: *Fieldwork in Local History.* Faber and Faber, 1967.

Hoskins, W.G.: *Devon, its People.* Wheaton, 1956.

Jackson, R. Leonard: *Roads and Bridges of the Torridge Valley.* 2003.

Lovett, Jones Gareth: *English Country Lanes – a celebration of travelling slowly.* Wildwood House, 1988.

Noon, Charles: *Percy John Russell, the Hunting Legend*. Halsgrove, 2006.

Palmer, Roy: *The Painful Plough – a portrait of the agricultural labourer in the nineteenth century from folk songs and ballads and contemporary accounts*. Cambridge University Press, 1972.

Pincombe, L.C.L.: *The Call of Chambercombe*. The Chronicle Press (Ilfracombe), 1959.

Rackham, Oliver: *Woodlands*. Collins New Naturalist series, 2006.

Reay, Barry: *Rural Englands*. Palgrave Macmillan, 2004.

Shakespeare, Liz: *Fever, a Story from a Devon Churchyard*. Letterbox Books, 2005.

Stanes, Robin: *A History of Devon*. Phillimore, 1986.

Stanes, Robin: *Farming in Devon and Cornwall*. Halsgrove.

Stephens, Mark: *Ernest Bevin, Unskilled Labourer and World Statesman*. SPA Books, 1981.

Van Emden, Richard and Steve Humphries: *All Quiet on the Home Front*. Headline, 2004.

Williamson, Henry: *On Foot in Devon*. Maclehose, 1933.

Williamson, Henry: *Life in a Devon Village*. The Right Book Club, 1944.

Williamson, Henry: *Spring Days in Devon and other broadcasts*. Introduction by Valerie Belsey. The Henry Williamson Society, 1992. (See particularly the essay entitled 'First Day of Spring'.)

Other sources

Baring-Gould, Rev. Sabine: Two volumes held in Plymouth Local Studies Library c.1890s, entitled: *Songs and Ballads of the West as taken down* and *Words and Melodies from the Mouths of the People*.

Christie, Peter: 'The True Story of the North Devon Savages'. Transactions of the Devonshire Association, 1992.

There are many carefully researched and well-written leaflets available in nearly all the parish churches in the area. The people I met on these ramblings were also invaluable as sources of local knowledge.

TIME LINE

To help you identify the various periods through which the lanes you are walking have survived (adapted from Oliver's Rackham's *Woodlands*).

4,600 million	Origin of the Earth
500 million	Land plants
340 million	Big plants
140 million	Broadleaved trees
70 million	Present genera of trees
2 million	Beginning of Pleistocene glacial cycles (glaciations and interglacials)
200,000	Present human species
3800–2000 BC	Neolithic in Britain; beginning of cultivation and woodmanship
2000–750 BC	Bronze Age in Britain
750–40 AD	Iron Age in Britain
40–400AD	The Romans in Britain
400–1066 AD	Anglo-Saxon England
1066–1536 AD	Middle Ages in England
1348–1349	The Black Death (one-third of the population perished)
1536–39	Dissolution of Monasteries by Henry VIII (redistribution of property and land)
1642–1645	The Civil War

1751	First turnpike road in Devon (at Stonehouse, Plymouth)
1801	First General Enclosure Act (common land no longer available)
1815	Corn Law passed, allowing foreign corn to be imported cheaply. English corn prices dropped significantly. Repealed in 1836.
1819	Reform of Penal Code. You were less likely to be transported for minor offences.
1824	Average wage for labourers 9s 4d a week (50p approx)
1834	Tolpuddle Martyrs (a group of farm labourers uniting for better wages. They were deported.)
1834	New Poor Law Act (Workhouses established)
1844	First railway comes to Devon (Bristol to Exeter)
1870	Average wage for labourers 12s a week
1900	Average wage for labourers 15s
1914–1918	First World War
1920	Tarmacking of roads begins
1939–1945	Second World War
1977	First section of motorway opens in Devon

ANSWERS TO QUESTIONS

at the end of each numbered route

Route 1: COPPLESTONE

Question What colour is the sandstone here?
Answer Red.

Route 2: CREDITON

Question Why didn't St Boniface like oak trees?
Answer He saw them as being part of the Celtic tradition of faith. It was said that when he cut one down, a fir tree sprang up in its place, hence our Christmas tree tradition.

Route 3: CHULMLEIGH

Question Where can you see a decorated kicking-stone?
Answer Outside the George.

Route 4: KING'S NYMPTON

Question We are not on Exmoor country yet, so what kind of deer might you see?
Answer Roe deer.

Route 5: UMBERLEIGH & NEWTON TRACEY

Question Umberleigh is a poetic sounding name but has nothing to do with umbered meaning a shade of brown. What is this place named after?
Answer The river Umborne a small tributary of the Taw.

Route 6: MARIANSLEIGH AND ROMANSLEIGH

Question You have found the well and there is more evidence of the Celts nearby.
Answer The broken Celtic cross in the churchyard.

Route 7: ROSE ASH

Question As you look towards Exmoor what is the name of the group of trees isolated towards the north-west?
Answer Bampfylde Clump.

Route 8: KNOWSTONE

Question There is a lot of this fern, which has an alliterative sounding name, growing on the trees.
Answer Polypody.

Route 9: TEMPLETON

Question What saint is represented by the Red Cross on the shields in the church?
Answer St John.

Route 10: WASHFIELD

Question The plant on the green, the orange hawkweed, has another name. There's still plenty of this modified activity in the area.
Answer Fox and hounds, nickname of this plant.

Route 11: TIVERTON

Question What is the name of the big coaching inn which stands at the northerly approach to Tiverton?
Answer Hartnoll.

Route 12: BAMPTON

Question What is the lane at (10) called? A bridleway, and look to your left for another of its names.
Answer Packhorse Way on house gate in 10.

Route 13: MOREBATH (A)

Question Whose cow cake is suitable for all stock?
Answer Thorleys as advertised on the enamel sign on a farm building at Bonny Cross.

Route 14: MOREBATH (B)

Question Part of the church hedge to the left of the main entrance was maintained by Richard Rumbelow in 1531. This is what Trickey's records tell us, but how can we tell that this was so today?
Answer By using the hedge-dating theory. Count the number of hardwood species in a thirty-yard stretch of hedgerow. This stretch contains elm, elder, ash, beech, hazel and yew = the hedge is at least 600 years old.

Route 15: NORTH MOLTON

Question What is energy produced from plants called?
Answer Biofuel.

Route 16: FLITTON OAK

Question What's the name of the science which tells you how old a tree is by counting its growth rings?
Answer Dendrology.

Route 17: PARRACOMBE

Question The hedges leading up to the Moor have been cut in a special way. Sometimes a chainsaw must have been used, but what hand tool has sliced its way through here?
Answer A billhook.

Route 18: COMBE MARTIN

Question You didn't want to be caught doing this when you should have been doing the equivalent in the mines with your eyes open.
Answer Knapping.

Route 19: ILFRACOMBE

Question What kind of locomotive might you once have found here?
Answer Steam.

Route 20: SOUTH MOLTON

Question What is the name of a certain breed of small dog once associated with this village?
Answer Jack Russell terriers.

Route 21: BISHOP'S TAWTON

Question Where does the nearby railway run to and from?
Answer Exeter-Barnstaple.

Route 22: MARWOOD

Question Towards the end of the lane is a feature which tells us that this is a parish boundary bank. What is it?
Answer A double hedge-bank and ditch.

Route 23: BRATTON FLEMING

Question Under the bridge by Station House you will find just what kind of railway ran from Lynton to Barnstaple.
Answer Single track narrow gauge.

Route 24: CROYDE

Question This writer's talisman does not appear by day.
Answer The owl carved on his headstone.

Route 25: BRAUNTON

Question St Brannock came from across the water. From where?
Answer Wales.

Route 26: SAUNTON

Question Which two parishes are marked by the boundary stone?
Answer Georgeham and Braunton.

Route 27: BARNSTAPLE

Question What is the structure on the beach at 12 on the map?
Answer A lime kiln – lime was used for enriching agricultural land.

Route 28: GREAT TORRINGTON

Question The sanctuary ring: where can you find a ring of protection on this walk?
Answer On the church door at Frithelstock.

Route 29: PETERS MARLAND & BEAFORD

Question What colour are the bricks which are made from Peters Marland clay?
Answer Light yellow.

Route 30: OFF THE TARKA TRAIL – LITTLEHAM

Question Which of the two rivers of Tarka country are you passing by here?
Answer The Torridge.

Route 31: BIDEFORD

Question There was something burning here by the river before it was carted off inland.
Answer Lime.

Route 32: ABBOTSHAM

Question Is the pine tree growing at the entrance to Abbotsham Court a Scots or a Monterey Pine?
Answer Monterey.

Route 33: BUCKLAND BREWER

Question What is the original meaning of the word tithe?
Answer A tenth.

Route 34: PARKHAM TO PEPPERCOMBE

Question What year was the Goldsworthy Chapel built?
Answer 1885.

Route 35: HARTLAND (A)

Question Search for the answer to this clue after walk number 35. It depends when you decide to visit Stoke church. You've found the saints outside the church. Now look for the penguins inside.
Answer On the wall there is a commemorative stone to Allen Lane, the founder of Penguin Books. It was on Exeter station in 1935 that Allen Lane, when looking (unsuccessfully) for something reasonably priced to read on the journey, had the idea of producing paperback books.

Route 36: HARTLAND (B)

Question Just where is the helicopter going from here?
Answer Lundy Island.

Route 37: HARTLAND (C)

Question Apart from the sudden flying upwards of birds here you might be frightened by something larger in the skies. Where are they coming from?
Answer Jets whizzing over from RAF Chivenor.

Route 38: WELCOMBE

Question To which Saint is the well at (2) dedicated?
Answer St Nectan.

Route 39: HOLSWORTHY

Question When was the viaduct built?
Answer Plaque dated 1898.

Route 40: HIGHAMPTON

Question What is the name of the carpenter from Sheepwash Bridge?
Answer Christopher Ayre.

Route 41: NORTHLEW

Question What year was the first Bible Christian Chapel built here?
Answer 1815.

Route 42: BRATTON CLOVELLY

Question What did the inn in the village used to be called? You'll have to go in to research the answer.
Answer The Packhorse Inn.

Route 43: BRIDESTOWE

Question What's the name of the pub which carries the flying wheel?
Answer The Royal Oak.

Route 44: LYDFORD

Question There is a stone by the wayside which you might 'C' without understanding.
Answer These stones were set up in 1531 to denote that the bridge was to be maintained by authorities, other than the church. The bridge and the road 100 feet either side of it had to be kept in good repair.

Route 45: COOKBURY

Question

"Through frost and snow and sunlight
Through rain and night and day
I go back to where I come from
I pass all things, yet stay."
– Brian Patten

Answer A signpost.

Route 46: NORTH TAWTON (A)

The Clue A common hedgerow bird beginning with 's' is known in Devon dialect as a 'spadger', What is it?
Answer Sparrow.

Route 47: NORTH TAWTON (B)

Question What is the sign on the stone by the Roman road for? Draw this here.
Answer It is an OS trig mark indicating how high above sea level this point is.

Route 48: SAMPFORD COURTENAY

Question The faces that guard the door inside here are like the one that is banished to the porch at Bow – friends or foe?
Answer Knights from the Crusades, like de Tracey's face (to be found at nearby Bow).

Route 49: WINKLEIGH

Question What kind of spring water is bottled here?
Answer Devon Spring Water.

Route 50: BOW

Question Whose face looks out at you under the porch?
Answer Sir William de Tracey.

Route 51: TEDBURN ST MARY

Question You end high up on this type of road, upon which you have often travelled over the past 50 circuits.
Answer Ridges or ridgeways (Oldridge here).

INDEX

Entries mostly refer to people and events

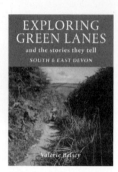

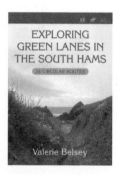

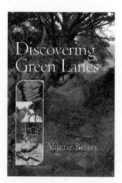